ANCIENT INDIAN RITUALS
AND
THEIR SOCIAL CONTENTS

ANCIENT INDIAN RITUALS

AND

THEIR SOCIAL CONTENTS

NARENDRA NATH BHATTACHARYYA

CURZON PRESS : LONDON
ROWMAN AND LITTLEFIELD : TOTOWA

Published by
Curzon Press Ltd. London and Dublin
and
Rowman and Littlefield, Totowa, U. S. A.

1975

by arrangement with
Manohar Book Service
2, Ansari Road, Darya Ganj
Delhi-110006

ISBN
UK 0 7007 0083 8
US 0 87471 735 3

Printed in India
Prem Printing Press, 257-Golaganj, Lucknow

To
Prof. R. S. SHARMA

PREFACE

The beliefs and ideals of different civilizations are often formulated in their rituals more explicitly than in any other cultural trait, and this gives to the study of ritualism a deeper historical significance. That is why the study of rituals should not only be restricted to that of classifying their contents, with a view to making out their distribution in geography and history, but the motives as well, by which they are characterised, are to be detected, and this is expected to reveal the actual social set-up in which they were evolved originally. Such studies in the case of Greek rituals have yielded tangible results, but so far as the Indian conditions are concerned, the scope is indeed very limited owing to the fragmentary and fabricated nature of the evidences, one has to handle. The ritualistic contents of the ancient and medieval religious texts are so much saturated with the elements of mechanical sacerdotalism of the priestly class that in many cases it often becomes absolutely impossible to derive any significance or meaning from a given set of data. It is due to the fact that the rites of the simplest level of life were transformed later into the esoteric art of the ruling or privileged class, surviving as a part of religion in their changed and distorted forms. The 'illusory technique complementary to the deficiencies of the real technique', by which the significance of a rite is to be understood in the background of pre-class societies, yielded quite an opposite result in class societies. The primitive notion that by creating illusion you can control the reality, you actually control it, which is the basis of all rites, came to convey at a later period a different meaning: illusion not to control reality, but to evade it.

The first three chapters of this book deal, strictly on the basis of the analysis of rituals, with the entire history of a stupendous socio-political transformation, showing the process leading to detribalisation and growth of state power, the transition from pre-class to class society. The analysis of the three principal rituals of royal inauguration, as we have them in their fabricated forms, clearly exhibits how with the social changes caused by the production of surplus and the accumulation of wealth in the hands of a few by raids and wars, the ancient democratic institutions were destroyed, how the tribal chiefs, the pastoral war-lords, came to acquire, step by step, more and more power which led to the institution of kingship and its aggressive imposition upon the masses who were unwilling to accept it owing to their strict adherence to the democratic values and how this rise of state power on the ruins of tribal equality, symbolised by the annihilation of Ṛta, ruthlessly exterminated the traditional social relations and introduced a qualitative change in the course of historical development. While dealing with this socio-political transformation, which appears to have taken place in different parts of India roughly between the eighth and the sixth centuries B.C., I have vigorously asserted, probably against the views of all eminent Indologists, that the institution of kingship, in the modern sense of the term, was absolutely unknown in the age of the *Ṛgveda*. The word *rājā* which has misled even the serious and critical scholars, originally meant nothing but tribal heads who used to meet together in open assemblies and settle the affairs of the tribes and clans by mutual discussions in a perfectly democratic way. The truth of this formulation was felt by eminent Vedic scholars like Keith or Macdonell, but they could not express it in the right way owing to the influence of the ideas and values of their contemporary society. The vision of the historians, despite their professed objectivity, is often circumscribed by the dominant class outlook, both of their own age and the age they study.

In this work I have argued that the precise nature of the social institutions of the ancient Indians is a question which the internal evidence is in itself too fragmentary to solve, and hence the internal evidence should be studied in the light of what is known of the surviving tribal institutions in general. For example, the role of the tribal chiefs (*rājās*) in Ṛgvedic democracy, as suggested on the basis of textual evidence, (see Ch. II), to which reference has been made above, can only be understood in its real historical perspective if we take into account the facts of contemporary tribal life. Till recently, the most remarkable feature about the tribal life of the north-eastern hill area was the fundamentally democratic basis of their social and administrative organisations. "With minor exceptions the land belongs to the community and not to any individual. Although in the Garo Hills the *Nokma* (the head of a clan or a village), in the Khasi and Jaintia Hills the *Siem* or the *Doloi* or the *Rājā*, and in the Lushai Hills, till recently, the Chief was the nominal proprietor of all lands within his jurisdiction, every villager could cultivate his plot of land anywhere as a matter of right. In society there is no distinction between high and low. Wealth and income do not confer social privileges. The once powerful Lushai Chief and the Khasi Siem who were regarded by the neighbouring peoples as *Rājā* or King were as much commoners as the humblest of the humble.... This democratic spirit was strongly reflected in the indigenous tribal administrative organisations. The Khasi Siems were constitutional monarchs. They could hardly ever give any decision independently.... Disputes are heard in open courts where all the male members of the village take part. In some areas even the women are allowed to be present at the trial of cases. The judgement passed on an offender is regarded as the judgement of the whole village and not merely of the Chief and his advisers. This system of administration suited the genius of the people and they were happy under it. The British, with their experience of administration over half the world, were wise enough not to interfere with the indigenous administrative machineries." (S. Barkataki, *Tribes of Assam,* New Delhi 1969, pp. 12-13).

Where textual evidence is fragmentary and not self-explanatory, such facts of the surviving tribal life are essential to make things transparent. They are conspicuously present in the Grand Sacrifices, and their very presence helps us to distinguish between the original and fabricated forms of these ceremonials. Accordingly, it has been shown how the simple agricultural rites, originally based upon the primitive conception of the identity of earth and woman, became step by step class oriented, how their original kernel was gradually thrown aside leading to the development of the accretions which ultimately came to take the lead and how the primitive productive techniques, by which the agricultural rites were characterised originally, having assumed sophisticated tone and colour, became decorative features of royal ceremonies. The growth of these accretions has also been studied as a result of which we have been able to make a distinction between the original and sophisticated forms of the Vedic sacrifices or *Yajñas,* their genesis in primitive magical beliefs and practices, their getting ensnared by the logic of pure illusion required for justifying the existence of class society, and their final culmination into a meaningless but profitable affair of the priests, kept shrouded in deep mystery and jealously guarded.

The adoption of the ritual of a particular group of people by another group is essentially connected with the social changes caused by the 'shifting tensions' in the primitive mode of food production.

The pastoral tribes must have borrowed or inherited many of their rituals from the hunting tribes, since hunting led to the domestication of cattle. In the second pastoral grade, as the case was with the Vedic tribes, when stock raising was supplemented by agriculture, some agricultural features were also incorporated into the pastoral rituals. In the later Samhitas and Brahmanas, for example, we have references to agricultural rituals, mainly sexual in character, while they are conspicuously absent in the earlier portions of the *Rgveda*. The same process held good in the case of agricultural tribes. The uncertainties and risks involved in the work of agricultural production, however, compelled them to have greater dependence on magical beliefs and practices, and this accounts for the growth not only of numerous fertility rituals, but also of a philosophy of life, a world-view, based on such beliefs.

Indeed, among the primitive agricultural communities, the relation between the processes of birth and generation and those of fertility in general appeared to be so intimate that the two aspects of the same mystery found very similar modes of ritual expression. The primitive notion of the supposed identical relation between the fruit-bearing earth and the child-bearing woman, which lay even at the substratum of the rites of royal inauguration practically worked out in the case of all major rituals. The peculiar tenacity with which the elements of fertility beliefs and practices have survived in the lives of the Indian people is quite striking. Probably it is due to the fact that the vast majority of them have remained the tillers of the soil even to this day. Such beliefs and practices are found abundantly in the puberty rites which have been the subject matter of the fourth and fifth chapters of this work. The decay and regeneration in nature have called forth the series of *rites de passage* at the junctions of individual existence to obtain a fresh outpouring of life and power. The transition from one grade of lift to another is effected among the tribal communities by the rites of initiation at puberty, marking separation from childhood and entrance into manhood or womanhood. The qualification for admission into the adult group is not birth, but rebirth. The idea of rebirth, which also characterises the death rites certainly owed its origin to the observation of plant life, its death and revival, and was definitely linked up with the aforesaid primitive beliefs connected with natural and human fertility to which the origin of the menstrual and sexual rites and other kindred features, associated with agricultural life, should be traced. The idea of death and rebirth in every turning point of an individual's life evidently contributed to the concepts of *Karma,* transmigration of soul, metempsychosis and so on. How thoroughly the fertility beliefs, and the cults originating from them, worked out in the lives of the Indian masses and how immense was their contribution to the development and shaping of the aforesaid ideas, a full view of all these may be found in the sixth chapter which deals mainly with rituals connected with the Female Principle, the Mother Goddess of the simpler peoples.

The connection between death rites and fertility beliefs has also been discussed in the seventh and eighth chapters, the former dealing with the popular festivals of Dewali and Holi and the latter with some proletarian rituals and festivals like Caḍaka and Gājana which are not mentioned in the religious and ritualistic texts of Brahmanical Hinduism. Long ago, Crooke pointed out that the Holi festival had derived its main impulses from fertility beliefs and rituals. To this I add that the Holi and Dewali festivals originally belonged to the same ritual complex and that they were designed to represent the beliefs and practices clustering round the primitive conception of death. Many of the surviving elements of these two festivals are marked by the colour of funeral rites. So far as the proletarian rituals are concerned, the literary sources, by themselves, do not help us to understand them fully. Still, on the basis of the apparent suggestivity of these rituals, I have tried my best to construct a fuller picture of the entire social complex responsible for their development and survival.

In all my works, which are mainly concerned with the religious history of India, I have always tried to assert that the study of any ritual or cult in itself is of no value unless it is used as a means to understand the vast and enormously complicated problems of Indian social history. How far this purpose has been served by this book, it is up to the readers to decide. The views expressed in this book are mine and so are all its errors.

NARENDRA NATH BHATTACHARYYA

Department of Ancient
Indian History and Culture,
Calcutta University,
51/2 Hazra Road,
Calcutta 700019.

ACKNOWLEDGEMENTS

The first two chapters of this work appeared in the *Journal of the Oriental Institute,* Vols. XXI and XXIII, which I should mention at the outset. I am grateful to my friends, Sri Santosh Kumar Biswas and Sri Satinath Mukherjee, who have helped me by supplying some valuable data which have been utilised in this work, and also to Prof. Debiprasad Chattopadhyaya whose contribution to the shaping of my ideas I always acknowledge with respect. My thanks are also due to Sri Ramesh C. Jain of Manohar Book Service for the sincere interest he has taken in publishing this work.

CONTENTS

PREFACE vii

CHAPTER ONE
THE PRIEST AND THE QUEEN
A Study in the Rituals of the Aśvamedha

1. Prologue: The Political Veneer 1
2. The Original Purpose Forgotten 1
3. Aśvamedha in the Śrautasūtras: The Queen's Part .. 3
4. The Earlier Sources 5
5. The Original Form 6
6. The Priest's Union with the Queen 7
7. Sexual Union Identified with Sacrifice (Yajña) .. 9
8. Vedic Sacrifices: Their Primitive and Sophisticated Forms 10
9. Why Sexual Union? 12
10. From Tribe to State 14
11. Growth of Non-Violent Religions 15
12. Kingship in Agricultural Societies 16
13. The Queen's Sexual Cycle 17
14. The Dying God 18
15. Epilogue: Birth of Literature 22

CHAPTER TWO
THE KING AND THE DICE
A Study in the Rituals of the Rājasūya

1. Prologue: Purpose of the Study 25
2. Some Important Features of Rājasūya 25
3. The Mimic Cow Raid 27
4. The Word Rājā: Its Original and Changed Meaning .. 29
5. The Election of the 'Kings': The Popular Pressure .. 31
6. The Tribal Councils 33
7. Akṣa and Ṛta 36
8. Ṛta and Varuṇa 38
9. Relics of Ancient Equality 41

10. Distribution: Casting the Lot 42
11. The Sabhāsthānu 44
12. Annihilation of Ṛta: The Śunaḥśepa Legend . 45

CHAPTER THREE
FOOD AND DRINK
A Study in the Rituals of the Vājapeya

1. Prologue 48
2. The Vājapeya and the Rājasūya 49
3. The Essentials of the Vājapeya 50
4. Keith on the Popular Character of Vājapeya .. 53
5. The Ritual of Collective Drinking 53
6. The Chariot Race 55
7. Food and Drink 57
8. The Sāmans 58
9. Yajña As the Productive Technique 60
10. Yajña and Magic: The Collective Approach .. 62
11. Metamorphosis of the Yajamāna 65
12. Conclusion 68

CHAPTER FOUR
THE TWICE-BORN
A Study in the Rituals of Tribal Initiation

1. Prologue: Birth and Rebirth 70
2. The Ritual of Upanayana 72
3. The Problem of its Original Contents 73
4. Upanayana and Puberty 75
5. Buddhist and Jain Initiation 76
6. Tribal Character of Buddhist Initiation 79
7. Primitive Rituals Connected with Upanayana .. 80
8. Conclusion 84

CHAPTER FIVE
SACRED AND ACCURSED
A Study in the Menstrual Rites of Ancient India

1. Prologue: Initiation into Womanhood 85
2. The Universal Dread 85

3. The Sanctifying Significance 87
4. The Life-giving Power 88
5. Menstrual Rites 89
6. The Indian Context 91
7. The Ceremonial Defloration 93
8. Remarks 96

CHAPTER SIX
EARTH AND WOMAN
A Study in the Cults and Rituals of Fertility

1. Prologue 97
2. A Sculpture from Nagarjunikonda 98
3. Liṅga and Yoni 99
4. Sacred Prostitution 100
5. Ritual and Myth 101
6. An Indian Cult of the Prostitutes 102
7. The Gardens of Adonis 106
8. Sītā and Persephone 108
9. Earth Goddess of Harappa Culture 110
10. Earth and Woman 111

CHAPTER SEVEN
DEATH AND RESURRECTION
A Study in the Rituals of Dewali and Holi

1. Prologue 114
2. The Cult of the Dead among the Buddhists .. 115
3. The Pīr Cult 117
4. The Maṭhas 118
5. The Miming of Burning the Dead 119
6. The Symbolism of Red 121
7. The Original Form of Holi 122
8. The Full and New Moon 122
9. The Fire Festivals of Europe 125
10. Dewali and Death 126

CHAPTER EIGHT
HOOK SWINGING
A Study in the Proletarian Cults and Rituals of Bengal

1. Prologue 130

2. The Rituals of Year-Ending 130
3. The Focus of Attention 132
4. Buddhism versus Śaivism 133
5. Buddhism and Vaiṣṇavism 135
6. The Nātha Cult 137
7. The Proletarian Elements 138
8. The Dharma Cult 141
9. The Dharma Cult and Buddhism 142
10. Dharma and the Brahmanical Deities 144
11. Dharma and Sun 145
12. The Proletarian Substratum of the Dharma Cult .. 146
13. The Gājana of Dharma and Śiva 148
14. Gājana and Caḍaka: The Participating Deities .. 150
15. The Death and Resurrection Theme in Gājana Rituals 152
16. The Caḍaka of Dharma 155
17. Kālārkarudra: The Brāhmanised Form of Dharma .. 157
18. Nīlacaṇḍikā and others 158
19. The Rituals of Caḍaka 159
20. Conclusion 163

BIBLIOGRAPHY 165

INDEX 177

I

THE PRIEST AND THE QUEEN

A Study in the Rituals of the Aśvamedha

1. Prologue: The Political Veneer

The ceremonial called the Aśvamedha or horse-sacrifice has come down to us in a political veneer. We are told that all the kings who were actually consecrated with the *Aindra Mahābhiṣeka* (Indra's great function consisting of five important ceremonies)[1] were entitled to perform the Aśvamedha. In other words a paramount king (*Sārvabhauma Rājā*) could perform it.[2] A list of such kings and princes who performed this famous rite is given in the *Śatapatha Brāhmaṇa.*[3] In the epico-puranic literature we have numerous references to kings performing the Aśvamedha sacrifice. In the historical age we find that, after the victorious wars with Vidarbha and the Yavanas, Puṣyamitra, the Śūṅga king, completed the performance of two horse-sacrifices. We have the coins of Samudragupta bearing the legend *aśvamedhaparākrama* which were apparently issued immediately after the performance of the horse-sacrifice by that great king. The Aśvamedha was also celebrated by several kings during the interval which elapsed from the time of Puṣyamitra to that of Samudragupta.[4] Even as late as the time of Bhavabhūti (eighth century A.D.) the Aśvamedha was looked upon as the only touch-stone to test the might of the kings.[5]

2. The Original Purpose Forgotten

In all probability, the aforesaid kings who performed the horse-sacrifice took it as a chivalrous achievement. Its original purpose

1. *Aitareya Brāhmaṇa,* VIII, 12-23.
2. Cf. *Āpastamba Śrautasūtra,* XX. 1.
3. XIII. 5. 4. 1-23.
4. H. C. Raychaudhuri, *Political History of Ancient India,* Calcutta, 1953, p. 548.
5. Act IV.

was definitely forgotten. Even in ancient times this sacrifice must have been rare. The *Taittirīya Śaṃhitā*[6] and the *Śatpatha Brāhmaṇa*[7] state that the Aśvamedha sacrifice was then *Utsanna,* i.e., gone out of vogue. The *Atharvaveda*[8] also appears to regard the Rājasūya, Vājapeya, Aśvamedha, the Sattras and several other sacrifices as *Utsanna.* The epico-puranic descriptions of the Aśvamedha certainly prove that many of its major rites were cancelled because their significance could not be understood. As a result of this, it so happened that the Aśvamedha sacrifice got entirely a different form, both in theory and in practice.

We may refer in this connection to the description of the horse-sacrifice as given in the Āśvamedhika Parvan of the *Mahābhārata* in which much greater stress is laid on the festive and chivalrous aspect of this royal observance. Though the general outline of the 'internals' of the Aśvamedha, as given in the *Mahābhārata,* corresponds in some cases to the prescriptions of the Brāhmaṇa literature, many items of the ceremonial are altogether ignored, e.g., the *aśva-upasaṃveśanam* of Draupadī. The ritual is mentioned, but not described. The practice of a Brāhmaṇa and a Kṣatriya lute-player singing stanzas composed by themselves in honour of the king and the so-called 'revolving legend' related by the Hotṛ in a ten day's cycle all the year round are omitted. So we shall not be wrong in assuming that, in its earlier stages, the performance of the horse-sacrifice must have had connected with it a number of rituals of a purely different character.

The *aśva-upasaṃveśanam* of Draupadī was evidently ignored considering it to be an obscene ritual inconsistent with the ethical principles reflected in the great epic. In one of the Cārvāka polemics against Brahmanism and Brahmanical rituals, quoted from the so-called *sūtras* of Bṛhaspati by Mādhava in his *Sarvadarśana-saṃgraha,* it is stated that 'all the obscene rites for the queen commanded in the Aśvamedha were invented by buffoons.[9] Here we have quoted from Cowell's free translation, but the real *sūtra* is *aśvasyātra hi śiśnaṃ tu patnīgrāhyaṃ prakīrtitam* which implies that the wife, evidently the queen, had to take the *phallus* of the horse. Certainly it is not a case of fabrication invented by the Cārvākas who were

6. V. 4. 12. 3.
7. XIII. 3. 3. 6.
8. XI. 7. 7-8.
9. Cowell's tr., London, 1914, pp. 10-11.

definitely hostile to Brahmanism. The details of the Aśvamedha referred to in ancient literature, sufficiently prove that its central ritual was the *union* of the queen with the horse.[10]

3. Aśvamedha in the Śrautasūtras: The Queen's Part

Before coming to our point, let us have a full view of the major rituals of the Aśvamedha sacrifice as given in the *Śrautasūtras*. The first rite is the cooking of rice taken from four different vessels. The cooked rice is to be smeared with *ghee* and given to the four principal priests. They will get one thousand cows each along with a certain quantity of gold.[11] Then two *iṣṭi*-s are performed, the first for Agni Mūrdhaṇvan and the second for Pūṣan.[12] Then the horse is anointed. The king cuts off his hair, cleans his nails, brushes his teeth, bathes in a tank or river, puts on new garments and wears a golden ornament. He has also to observe a vow of silence while doing all these. Then his four queens, well-dressed and wearing ornaments, come to him. The Mahiṣī (chief queen, being the first one married by the king) comes with the princesses, the Vāvātā (the favourite queen) with the daughters of the Kṣatriyas, the Parivṛkti (the queen who had not yet conceived) with the daughters of the Sūtas and village headmen, and the Pālāgalī (the queen who was the daughter of a court official) with the daughters of the court officials. The king enters the fire-hall and sits to the west of the *gārhapatya* facing the north.[13] The horse is then sprinkled with holy water by the four principal priests[14] and brought near the fire, and offerings are made near it.[15] A girdle made by *Muñja* grass or of the *Darbhas* is taken and tied around the horse's neck, and verses from the *Taittirīya* (IV. 1. 2. 1) and the *Vājasaneyi* (XXII. 2.) *Saṃhitās* are recited. Into its right ear *Vājasaneyi* XXII. 19 and *Taittirīya* VII. 1. 12. 1 are uttered. Then it is let off to roam over the countries.

Everyday during the year that the horse is absent, three *iṣṭi*-s are to be offered to the god Savitṛ.[16] A Brāhmaṇa with a *Vīnā*

10. A. B. Keith: *Religion and Philosophy of the Veda* (HOS), Part II, p. 345.
11. *Kāt*, XX. 1. 4-6; *Lāt.*, IX. 9. 8.
12. *Āśv.*, X. 6. 2-5; *Kāt.*, XX. 1. 25.
13. *Āpas.*, XX. 4. 9-14.
14. *Āpas.*, XX. 4.
15. *Kāt.*, XX. 2. 3-5.
16. *Āśv.*, X. 6. 8; *Lāt.*, IX. 9. 10; *Kāt.*, XX. 2. 6.

chants three laudatory *gāthās* in honour of the king composed by himself.[17] The features of the rite also include panegyrics of the sacrifice along with righteous kings of yore by a Kṣatriya lute-player who sings to the lute three songs composed by himself, 'such war he waged, such battle he won' etc.[18] The Hotṛ narrates a 'circle of tales', *Pāripalva Ākhyāna* which lasts by series of ten days for the whole year.[19] Every day for a year four oblations are also to be made, called *Dhṛti*.[20]

On the horse's return to the sacrificial ground it is anointed with clarified butter by the queens. They also tie 101 golden beads on the body of the horse and give the remnants of the previous night's offerings to eat uttering a *mantra* from the *Vājasaneyi Saṃhitā* (XXIII. 8). If the horse does not eat, the remnants are thrown into the water. Near the sacrificial altar a dialogue takes place between the Hotṛ and the Brahmā. The former asks by quoting the 9th and 11th verses of the 23rd Chapter of the *Vājasaneyi Saṃhitā* and the latter answers by quoting the 10th and 12th verses of the same chapter. The horse is praised by uttering the *Ṛgveda* I. 163. Then a piece of cloth is spread out over the grass. Thereon a mantle is spread out and a gold piece placed on it. The horse is taken on the mantle and killed. The four wives of the king go round the dead body of the horse thrice from left to right and thrice from right to left uttering the *Vājasaneyi Saṃhitā* XXIII. 19. They fan the dead horse with their garments and pretend a ceremonial mourning.[21]

Then commence the concluding rituals. The crowned queen lies down by the side of the dead horse. The Adhvaryu covers them with the mantle on which the horse lies, and the queen unites with it. The Hotṛ abuses the crowned queen in 'obscene' language and she returns the 'obscene' along with her attendant princesses. The Brahmā (second priest) and the favourite queen along with her attendants enter into a similar 'obscene' abuse. The same holds good in the case of two other queens and two other priests. All the priests and the queens with their attendants enter into the 'obscene

17. *Āpas.*, XX. 6. 5; *Kāt.*, XX. 2. 7.
18. *Āpas.*, XX. 6. 14.
19. *Śāṅkhyāyana*, XVI. 2; *Āśv.* X. 6. 10-13.
20. *Kāt.*, XX. 3. 4.
21. *Āśv.*, X. 8. 1ff.; *Āpas.*, XX. 9. 6-8; XX. 14. 2ff.; XXII. 17. 13; *Lāt.*, IX. 9. 17; *Kāt.*, XX. 4. 16-20; XX. 5. 11-14; etc. Here we have omitted a few items like the erection of the *Yūpas*, slaughter of numerous animals, etc.

abusive dialogue' by quoting the *Vājasaneyi Saṃhitā*, XXIII. 22-31. Finally the queens take out the fat of the dead horse in place of the omentum taken from the goat in other sacrifices.[22]

4. The Earlier Sources

From the accounts given in the *Śrautasūtras*, at least two significant features of the Aśvamedha may be derived at a glance. (1) Women in general, and queens in particular, had a very important part to play in the function. It was compulsory for the queens to stay in the sacrificial hall. Their attendants represented women of different classes coming from different strata of society. On the horse's return to the sacrificial ground, the queens had to conduct everything. When the horse was killed they had to go round it and make ceremonial mournings. Finally, the chief queen had to unite with the dead horse. They had to enter, along with their young female attendants, into an 'obscene abusive dialogue' with the priests. (II) The *Mantras* recited in connexion with the Aśvamedha are all quoted from the *Ṛgveda*, the *Taittirīya Saṃhitā* and the *Vājasaneyi Saṃhitā*.

Verses from the *Ṛgveda* (I. 162; 1. 163) were recited only in connexion with the killing of the horse. The *Ṛgveda* knows nothing of the ritual horse sacrifice which is called *Aśvamedha Yajña* in later texts. The two Ṛgvedic hymns, referred to above, reflect an eating-ritual, a relic of the previous hunting age, surviving among the higher pastorals. They describe why and how a horse should be killed. The horse, to be killed, is identified in usual Ṛgvedic style with Āditya, Trita and Yama and a belief is expressed that the horse when eaten will go straight to heaven. It is anointed with *Svaru* and fire is carried round it thrice. Then the horse is cut to pieces on a cloth and its 34 or 26 ribs are separated. Its flesh is then cooked on a pot called *ukhā* and a lump is offered to fire. Then all begin to eat uttering *āghu*, *Yājyā* and *Vaṣaṭkāra*.

All other *Mantras* are taken from the *Taittirīya* and the *Vājasaneyi Saṃhitās*, especially from the 22nd and 23rd chapters of the latter. In fact, verses from the *Vājasaneyi Saṃhitā* dominate over all the essential rituals of the Aśvamedha. In describing the ceremonials of the Aśvamedha the *Śrautasūtras* have followed the Brāhmaṇa literature

22. *Āpas.*, XXII. *Kāt.*, XX. 6. 25ff.; XX. 8. 8; *Āśv.*, X. 8. 10-13; etc.

closely. The *Brāhmaṇa*-s enumerate several ancient monarchs who performed the Aśvamedha. The sacrifice itself is identified with the kingdom.[23] Special importance is laid upon the personal rites of the king,[24] the initiation of the horse before its journey by the four principal priests,[25] the practice of a Brāhmaṇa and a Kṣatriya lute player singing, morning and night, stanzas composed by themselves[26] and the *Pāriplava Ākhyāna* related by the Hotṛ.[27] The *Mantra*-s used in connexion of all these are quoted in the Brāhmaṇa literature from the *Vājasaneyi Saṃhitā* XXII-XXIII.

5. The Original Form

The Mantras of the *Vājasaneyi Saṃhitā* may therefore enable us to reconstruct the earliest and the original form of the Aśvamedha sacrifice. Even in the days of the Brāhmaṇa literature the original form of the Aśvamedha was distorted and its real purpose was changed into a merely royal custom. We have seen that at least two features of the Aśvamedha sacrifice, *viz.* the recital of the ancient legends and the queen's union with the horse, which were introduced in the age of the Brāhmaṇa literature, had their survivals in the age of the Sūtras, but ultimately they declined and sank into oblivion in subsequent ages. From the evidence furnished by the *Vājasaneyi Saṃhitā* it appears that the union of the principal queen with the dead horse, the earliest elaborate description of which is found in the Brāhmaṇa literature, is a relic, or rather a transformation, of an older ritual in which A MAN, EVIDENTLY A PRIEST, HAD TO PLAY THE PART OF THE HORSE AND, AFTER HIS CEREMONIAL INTERCOURSE WITH THE QUEEN, HE WAS PUT TO DEATH.

Before coming to any hasty conclusion we should examine once again the data relating to the Aśvamedha furnished by the Brāhmaṇa literature. We are reproducing below the relevant portions of the *Śatapatha Brāhmaṇa* from Eggeling's translation.[28] "When the

23. *Taittirīya,* III. 8. 9.
24. *Ibid.* III. 8. 1.
25. *Śatapatha,* XIV. 1. 30-34.
26. *Taitt.*, III. 9. 14; *Śat.*, XIII 1. 5. 1ff.; 4. 2. 8ff.
27. *Śat.*, XIII. 4. 3. 1ff.
28. *Sacred Books of the East,* Vol. XLIV, pp. 316ff.

victims have been bound (to the stakes), the Adhvaryu takes the sprinkling water in order to sprinkle the horse. Whilst the Sacrificer holds on to him behind, he (in sprinkling the horse) runs rapidly through the formula used at the Soma-sacrifice and then commences the one for the Aśvamedha[29] . . . . A cloth, an upper cloth, and gold, this is what they spread out for the horse. . . . He leads up the four wives; he thereby has called upon them (to come) and, indeed, also renders them sacrificially pure. . . . "I will urge the seed-layer (the queen says), let us stretch our feet" (thus in order to secure union). 'In heaven(the Adhvaryu says) Ye envelop yourselves'. 'May the vigorous male, the layer of seed, lay seed' (she says in order to secure union[30]). . . . The Udgātṛ says (concerning the king's favourite wife),

> Raise her upwards. . . .
> Even as one taking a burden up a mountain. . . .
> And may the centre of her body prosper. . . .
> As one winnowing in cool breeze. . . ."[31]

6. The Priest's Union with the Queen

The above is what the Udgātṛ says, but what the Vāvātā ('the favourite queen') says in reply is mentioned only in the *Vājasaneyi Saṃhitā* which also relates the dialogues of the three other priests and queens.[32] These *Vājasaneyi* verses have been described above as 'obscene abusive dialogues'. However, in connexion with the aforementioned speech of the Udgātṛ, quoted from the *Śatapatha Brāhmaṇa*, we like to quote the original from the *Vājasaneyi*. My esteemed friend Sri Debiprasad Chattopadhyaya, to whom goes the credit of pointing out the ritual significance of these verses[33], has made the following free translation of the *Vājasaneyi*, XXIII. 26-27. The Udgātṛ says:

> Raise her up
> As you carry a load on the mountains;

29. XIII. 2. 7. 1ff.
30. XIII. 2. 8. 1ff.
31. XIII. 2. 9. 1ff.
32. XXIII. 22-31.
33. *Lokāyata*, Delhi 1959, pp. 318-19.

Then let her middle portion be expanded,
As (the grain) is dried in cold wind.[34]

The Vāvātā says in reply:

Raise him up
As you carry a load on the mount.
Then let his middle region begin to function,
As (the grain) is dried in cold wind[35] . . .

The *Śatapatha Brāhmaṇa* offers an artificial political explanation of the speech of the Udgātṛ, and we are quoting it from Eggeling's translation[36]: "RAISE HER UPWARDS, the Aśvamedha doubtless, is that glory, royal power: that glory, royal power, he thus raises for him (the sacrificer upward). EVEN AS ONE TAKING A BURDEN UP A MOUNTAIN, glory (pomp), doubtless is the burden of royal power: that glory, royal power, he thus fastens on him (as a burden): but he also endows him with that glory, royal power. AND MAY THE CENTRE OF HER BODY PROSPER, the centre of royal power, doubtless, is glory: glory (prosperity) food, he thus lays into the very centre of royal power (or the kingdom). AS ONE WINNOWING IN COOL BREEZE, the cool or royal power, doubtless, is security of possession: security of possession he procures for him."

But its real interpretation is found in Uvaṭa's and Mahīdhara's commentary on the *Vājasaneyi Saṃhitā*. Here we are quoting Chattopadhyaya's translation of the relevant portions of Uvaṭa's commentary:

"The Udgātā unites with the Vāvātā. He asks some one, 'Raise this woman. Raise up this Vāvātā high'. How? As a load is carried up clasping it at the middle, fix her high up. As in the place, i.e. so raise her that the waist and the genital region of this

34. Ūrdhvamenamucchrāpaya
girau bhāraṃ haranniva/
Athāsyai madhyamedhatāṃ
śīte vāte punanniva//

35. Ūrdhvamenamucchrāyatād
girau bhāraṃ haranniva/
Athāsya madhyamejatu śīte vāte punanniva//

36. *Sacred Books of the East*, Vol. XLIV, p. 324.

Vāvātā may be extended. So hold her as it may expand. As a peasant, drying the paddy (seeds) quickens the sowing by taking these and releasing."[37]

"In reply, Vāvātā told the Udgātā: "Thou, too, should be made to act in a similar way." Here the female is playing the role of the male. As a load is carried uphill. Then let his middle region begin to function, i.e. be engaged in the reproductive function. Then press him down. As a peasant, drying the barley (seeds) in cool air quickens the sowing by taking these and releasing.[38]

7. Sexual Union Identified with Sacrifice (Yajña)

If we try to reconstruct the ritual from the verses of the *Vājasaneyi Saṃhitā*, the following scene flashes before our eyes: the queen is raised up high by a few men, and so is the priest. And in that condition they make sexual intercourse, as the ritual demands. This ritual was later transformed into the Aśvamedha sacrifice. But the question is: Why sexual intercourse?

In the *Śatapatha Brāhmaṇa* we come across numerous passages in which sexual union is identified with sacrifice.[39] In the *Chāndogya Upaniṣad* we have the following passage: "One summons; that is a *hiṃkāra.* He makes request; that is a *prastāva.* Together with the woman he lies down; that is an *udgītha.* He lies upon the woman; that is a *pratihāra.* He comes to an end; that is a *nidhāna.* He comes to a finish; that is a *nidhāna.* This is the *Vāmadevya Sāman* as woven upon copulation. He who knows thus this *Vāmadevya Sāman* as woven upon copulation, comes to copulation, procreates himself from every copulation, reaches a full length of life, lives long, becomes great in offspring and cattle, great in fame. One should never abstain from any woman. That is his

37. Udgātā vāvātāmabhimethayati. Ūrdhvamenāṃ kaṃcitpuruṣamāha Ūrdhvamenāṃ vāvātāṃ ucchritāṃ kuru. Kathamiva. Girau bhāraṃ madhye nigṛhya haret evamenāṃ madhye nigṛhya ūrdhvamucchrāpaya yathā asyā vāvātāyā madhyaṃ yonipradeśaḥ edhatāṃ. 'Edh Vṛddhau'. Vṛddhiṃ yāyāt athaināṃ gṛhniyāḥ. Śīte vāte punanniva. Yathā krṣivāalaḥ dhnyaṃ vāte śuddhaṃ kurvan grahaṇamokṣau jhaṭiti karoti.
38. Vāvātā pratyāhodgātārāṃ. Bhavatopyetadevam. Ūrdhvamenaṃ udgātā ramucchrāyatām ucchrāpaya. Atha striḥ puruśāyate; girau bhāraṃ haranniva. Athaiva kriyamāṇasyāsya madhyaṃ prajananaṃ ejatu calatu. Athainam nigrahiṣva śite vāte punanniva yavān.
39. 1. 9. 2. 7; 1. 9. 2. 11; VI. 4. 3. 7; VI. 6. 2. 8.; VI. 6. 1. 11; etc.

rule,"[40] In many scattered passages of the Upaniṣads, the woman is conceived as the sacrificial fire, her lower portion as the sacrificial wood, the genitalia as the flames, the penetration as the carbon, and the copulation as the spark.[41] The *Bṛhadāraṇyaka Upaniṣad*[42] says that the lower portion of a woman (*upastha*) is to be conceived as the sacrificial altar (*vedī*), the pubic hairs (*lomāni*) as the sacrificial grass, the outerskin (*bahiścarman*) as the floor for the pressing of the soma plants (*adhiṣavana*), and the two labia of the vulva (*muṣkau*) as the inmost fire. He who remembers this during copulation gets the reward of the Vājapeya sacrifice. The same text goes on so far as to state that, if a woman refuses sexual union, she must be forced to do so.[43]

8. Vedic Sacrifices: Their Primitive and Sophisticated Forms

It is to be remembered in this connexion that there is a gulf of difference between the original and later forms of the sacrifices. Originally the sacrifices were simple rituals, magical rather than propitiatory. "The majority of the sacrificial ceremonies", says Winternitz, "as also the Yajus formula, do not aim at 'worshipping' the gods, but at influencing them, at compelling them to fulfil the wishes of the sacrificer."[44] Keith has also to admit in connexion with the sacrifices as described in the Brāhmaṇa literature that "in the vast majority of these cases the nature of the ritual can be solved at once by the application of the concept of sympathetic magic, and this is one of the most obvious and undeniable facts in the whole of the Vedic sacrifice: it is from beginning to end full of magic elements."[45] Similar views are held by Bergaigne, Geldner, Weber and others. Macdonell writes: "It is thus impossible to suppose that the sacrificial priests of the *Ṛgveda*, the composers of the old hymns, should have occupied an isolated position, untouched by magical practices derived from a much earlier age and afterwards continued throughout the priestly literature of later times. In

40. II. 1. 3. Hume's tr.
41. Cf. *Chāndogya*, V. 8. 1-2; *Bṛhadāraṇyaka*, VI. 2.13.
42. VI. 4. 3.
43. VI. 4. 6-7.
44. *History of Indian Literature*, Calcutta, 1922, Vol. I, p. 181.
45. *Religion and Philosophy of the Veda*, pp. 258-9.

fact, a close examination of the hymns of the *Ṛgveda* actually affords the evidence that even in them the belief in magical powers independently of the gods is to be found. . . . Every page of the Brāhmaṇas and the Sūtras shows that the whole sacrificial ceremonial was overgrown with the notion that the sacrifice exercised power over gods and, going beyond them, could directly influence things and events without their intervention. An incipient form of this notion already appears in the *Ṛgveda*, where exaggerated sacrificial powers are attributed to ancient priests."[46]

"Primitive magic is founded on the notion that, by creating the illusion that you control reality, you can actually control it. It is an illusory technique complementary to the deficiencies of the real technique. Owing to the low level of production the subject is as yet imperfectly conscious of the objectivity of the external world, and consequently the performance of the preliminary rite appears as the cause of the success in the real task; but at the same time as a guide to action magic embodies the valuable truth that the external world can in fact be changed by man's subjective attitude towards it."[47] Referring to the potato-dance of the Maori, George Thomson observes: It is not possible that the potatoes will be influenced by the dance, but the dance may influence the dancers themselves. At least they believe that their dance has something to do with the growth of the plants, and when they tend the plants with this belief, their capacity and self reliance obviously increase.[48] The means of production were meagre and insufficient in the earliest stages of human history. The impetus derived from collective magical performances was thus valuable. It was also a means of production, probably the most valuable instrument.

The original purpose of magic was thus economic. It was directly connected with food-gathering or food-production, though so great a scholar like Sir Frazer did not care to understand this. The original purpose of the Vedic sacrifices was also the same. Reference has already been made to the *Sattra-yāga* which may be regarded as one of the earliest forms of the Vedic sacrifices. One of the significant rituals of this *Sattra* was called *Mahāvrata*.[49] Since

46. *Encyclopaedia of Religion and Ethics,* Vol. VIII, p. 312.
47. G. Thomson: *Aeschylus and Athens,* London, 1941, pp. 13-14.
48. *Studies in Ancient Greek Society,* Vol. I, London 1949, p. 440.
49. A. B. Keith: *The Veda of the Black Yajus School,* HOS 1914, p. CXXX.

Mahāvrata means *anna* or food,[50] it may be assumed that the purpose of the *Sattrayāga* was originally connected with food. Another ancient Vedics acrifice was called *Vājapeya*[51] which means 'food and drink.' Though in subsequent ages its purpose was changed, it was originally an agricultural ritual, as Keith has pointed out rightly.[52] So it appears that the original purpose of sacrifice does not differ fundamentally from that of magic. Though with the change in the technique of production the pre-class tribal societies disintegrate, magical practices do not die entirely. But their purpose begins to change. Thus in class societies primitive magic transforms itself into the esoteric art of the ruling or privileged class. It survives as a part of religion in its changed and distorted form.[53]

9. Why Sexual Union?

In a preceding section we have quoted a passage from the *Bṛhadāraṇyaka Upaniṣad* which states that by copulation, according to the rules prescribed, one gets the results of the Vājapeya sacrifice. Since *Vājapeya* means 'food and drink' there is no difficulty in thinking that by sexual union, as the said Upaniṣad suggests, one is entitled to get food and drink. In other words, sexual union is regarded as a means, or rather a technique, of food-production. Reference must be made in this connexion to the passages of the *Vājasaneyi Saṃhitā* describing the priest's ritual intercourse with the queen which we have already quoted along with the commentary of Uvaṭa. The ritual intercourse between the priest and the queen is brought there significantly in relation to the act of sowing in the field: *yathā kṛṣivalaḥ dhānyaṃ vāte śuddhaṃ kurvan grahaṇamokṣau jhaṭiti karoti*.

The magical or religious rites intended to secure the fertility of the fields were thought as belonging to the special competence of the women who were the first cultivators of the soil and whose power of child bearing was believed to have a sympathetic effect on the growth of the plant.[54] The association of sexual union with agri-

50. *Śatapatha Brāhmaṇa*, IV. 6. 4. 2; *Tāṇḍyamahābrāhmaṇa*, IV. 10. 2; Cf. Kane: *History of Dharmaśāstra*, Vol. II. p. 1243.
51. For details see *Sacred Books of the East*, Vol. XLI, pp. XXIIIff. cf. *infra*, pp. 48-69.
52. *The Veda of the Black Yajus School*, pp. CX-CXI.
53. G. Thomson: *Religion*, London 1950, p. 9. See *infra*, pp. 60-68.
54. R. Briffault, *The Mothers*, London 1952, Vol. II pp. 251-52.

culture is thus universal. The aborigines of Central America employ some persons for the purpose of sexual union on the eve of sowing. The Musquakis select a man and a woman to make sexual intercourse in the field. Similar customs are in vogue in Peru, Chile, New Mexico, Nikaragua and other Latin American countries. Referring to these customs Briffault observes that "the belief that sexual act assists the promotion of abundant harvest of the earth's fruits and is indeed indispensable to secure it, is universal in the lower phases of culture."[55] Frazer also cites similar examples from Central America, Java, New Guniea and many other countries.[56] Among the Hos of Chotanagpur, during the harvest festival, complete sexual liberty is given to the girls. The Kotas of the Nilgiri hills have a similar festival of sexual freedom. In Orissa, among the Bhuiyas sexual freedom is given to the girls during their harvest festival called *Māgh Porāi*. In Assam, woman are allowed during spring festivals complete freedom 'without any stain, blemish or loss of reputation'. The same holds good in the harvest festivals of many other tribes of India.[57] (See Chs. V-VI).

"The relation of the queen and the horse, according to Oldenberg, is clearly a fertility spell, while the 'obscene' language, he thinks, might be explained in the same sense."[58] We have seen that the 'obscene dialogue' used in the Aśvamedha sacrifice during the queen's union with the horse is found in an earlier text called the *Vājasaneyi Saṃhitā* and that from the said 'obscene dialogue' is found the relic of an older ritual in which the queen, instead of lying with the horse, had to make sexual intercourse with the priest. We have also suggested that the AŚVAMEDHA WAS THE GRADUAL TRANSFORMATION OF THIS OLDER RITUAL IN WHICH, IN ALL PROBABILITY, THE PRIEST HAD TO DIE AFTER HIS CEREMONIAL INTERCOURSE WITH THE QUEEN. Eggeling held that the Puruṣamedha or human sacrifice developed out of the Aśvamedha,[59] but the fact was reverse: the horse became a substitute for the man.

But still we are to answer a number of questions: If it was originally a fertility magic, why was the queen specially selected

55. *Ibid.*, Vol. III, pp. 207ff.
56. *The Golden Bough*, pp. 135-36.
57. For these and other examples see my *Indian Puberty Rites*, pp. 45ff.
58. Keith: *Religion and Philosophy of the Veda*, p. 345.
59. *Sacred Books of the East*, Vol. XLIV p. XXXIII.

for sexual union with the priest? What are the grounds for supposing that the priest was killed after his sexual intercourse with the queen? Why and how a collective agricultural ritual became in later times the affair of a king and began to be looked upon as the symbol of royal greatness?

10. From Tribe to State

The pre-class tribal societies disintegrated owing to the revolutionary changes in the technique of production. In the higher pastoral grade when stock-raising was supplemented by agriculture or in the higher agricultural grade when agriculture was supplemented by stock-raising, there was a 'revolutionary' change in the field of production, since surplus began to be produced. This change in the mode of production also changed the existing social values and relations. Conflict arose regarding the ownership of the surplus and thus developed class division and the growth of a privileged class. In order to look after the interest of the privileged class, laws were enacted, police or military system was introduced. In other words, characteristics of modern state revealed their ugly appearances over the pre-class undifferentiated tribal societies.

The process of the rise of kingship in pastoral societies can be traced even to the *Ṛgveda*. In every chapter of the *Rgveda*, desire for cattle is reflected[60] and there is every ground to believe that the Ṛgvedic people did not depend on agriculture. They despised it as the occupation of the conquered people. References to agriculture are very few in the *Ṛgveda*.[61] Out of its 10,462 verses, only 25 refer to agriculture, most of which belong to the later portions of the text. Cattle-lifting was a usual practice of the Ṛgvedic tribes. The term *gaviṣṭi* used for cattle-lifting was also a term for war. Stories of cattle-lifting are found in the *Ṛgveda*; the Paṇis were renowned cattle-lifters.[62] Even in the days of the *Mahābhārata*, cattle-lifting was regarded as token of heroism. The great Kurus did not feel ashamed to rob the cattle of king Virāṭa. In the *Ṛgveda*, intertribal warfare, a characteristic of pastoral society, is frequently mentioned.

Still in the *Ṛgveda*, we come across passages bearing relics of

60. Winternitz, *History of Indian Literature*, Vol. I, p. 64.
61. E. W. Hopkins in *Journal of the American Oriental Society*, Vol. XVII, pp. 84-85.
62. See Ch. II Sec. 3. pp. 27-29.

their pre-class or undifferentiated state. Originally there was a type of communism among the Ṛgvedic gods,[63] said Max-Müller, and he coined a term Henotheism to denote that state, but subsequently with the growth of class division among human beings its reflection was seen even in the Vedic pantheon. There are so many passages in the *Ṛgveda* which refer to wealth and cattle as common property and to their equal distribution.[64] In the concluding verses of the *Ṛgveda* unity of mind and determination is desired and in that connexion the following statement is significant: *devā bhāgaḥ yathāpūrve saṃjānānā upāsate.*[65] This implies that there was once a time when the gods used to sit together and take their respective shares collectively and consciously, and in all probability refers to a lost age when men used to do the same, the age when society was undifferentiated.

11. Growth of Non-Violent Religions

The general character of the *Ṛgveda*, therefore, reflects a society based upon class division, though here and there in the same text are found relics of an undifferentiated society through which the Vedic tribes passed their pre-pastoral hunting stage. The Ṛgvedic religion was mainly connected with sky, in which astral and nature myths predominated. The deities of the *Ṛgveda* were in most of the cases personifications of different natural phenomena under which the herders had to live. This was a new religion gradually adopted by hunting tribes coming into pastoral stage. But they could not give up the religious practices of their pre-pastoral life. Deities of the pastoral religion were propitiated with pre-pastoral rituals. Of these rituals, animal sacrifice was obviously the most important. With the growth of organised priesthood in the post-Ṛgvedic age, the sacrifice of cattle became a senseless source of the destruction of cattle wealth.

In higher pastoral societies, cattle are used principally for milk and wealth, not for meat, and therefore the flesh of domestic animals—especially female—is commonly tabooed.[66] This alone explains the taboo of beef-eating which is one of the main characteristics of present day Hindu society. The higher pastoral attitude

63. Cf. RV. 1. 25. 6; I. 111. 2; IV. 59. 2; V. 87. 4; VII. 73. 2; etc.
64. 1. 24. 3; 1. 27. 6; 1. 102. 4; I. 141. 1; II. 14. 12; III. 2. 12; VI. 66. 1; VII. 52. 21; VII. 76. 45; etc.
65. X. 191. 2. See Ch. II Sec. 9-10. pp. 41-44.
66. W. Robertson Smith, *Religion of the Semites,* London 1927, p. 406.

towards the pre-pastoral tribal habit of meat-eating is reflected in a verse of the *Ṛgveda* which denounces the Kīkaṭas, a tribe of Magadha, for their misuse of cattle.[67] Higher pastorals, and also higher agriculturists, led to the production of surplus and prepared the ground for the rise of urban settlements. Trade was facilitated in which cattle served as the best medium of exchange. The Brahmanical religious practices did not suit this new condition. The Brahmanical attitude towards trade was not helpful.

The Buddhist and Jain emphasis on non-injury to animals thus assumes a new significance in this context. The *Suttanipāta* states that cattle should be protected because they are the givers of food, beauty and happiness.[68] This was certainly a teaching based upon the growing demands of the traders. In fact, this was the crying demand of the age; even the Kṣatriya rulers desired to depend more upon the wealth of the traders than upon the magical powers of the Brāhmaṇa priests. The Brahmavidyā (knowledge of *Brahman*, the absolute, the universal soul) of the Upaniṣads was sponsored not by the Brāhmaṇas but by the Kṣatriyas who held that the Brahmanical sacrificial religion was useless.[69] In fact, Buddhism was not a sudden rise. It gave moral support to all the demands of the trading class. Money-lending, usury and slave-keeping are not condemned in the Buddhist texts.[70]

12. Kingship in Agricultural Societies

The Ṛgvedic tribes were pastoral and it was quite possible that they learnt agriculture from their neighbouring tribes. Only a few verses dealing with agriculture are found in the *Ṛgveda* and the majority of them are found in the first and tenth *maṇḍalas*. This implies that the Vedic tribes were acquainted with agriculture when the later portions of the *Ṛgveda* were being composed. In the later *Saṃhitās* as well as in the *Brāhmaṇa* literature we come across numerous agricultural rituals. These were evidently adopted from the agricultural peoples who lived side by side with the pastorals. One should not fail to recall in this connexion that the economic basis of

67. III. 53. 14.
68. VV. 296-97, 309.
69. See my paper 'On the Kṣatriya Authorship of Brahmavidyā' in *The Modern Review*, Feb. 1961.
70. R. S. Sharma in *Das Kapital Centenary Volume*, New Delhi, 1968, p. 63.

the pre-Vedic Harappa culture was agriculture.[71]

Kingship in agricultural societies did not develop in the same way as it did in the pastoral societies. "The development of agricultural civilization without any intervening pastoral phase enhanced the matriarchal position of women not only as owners and heiresses of the arable land, but also through their traditional association with magic or religion."[72] There is every reason to believe that the earliest magicians were women and that it was their duty to take an important part in the performance of the rites so that the land might yield a good harvest. Here the concept of ruling originated from the magical functions which archaic queens or priestesses were expected to discharge on behalf of the community. In societies, where father-right elements were not aggressively imposed, we have the superiority of the priestess over the priest, or the queen over the king, based on a corresponding superiority of the goddess or divine ancestress over the god or the divine ancestor. Accordingly not only the royal office was filled by a woman, but the queen was in every stage of development of that office considerably more than merely the wife of the king.

13. The Queen's Sexual Cycle

The combination of the priestly with kingly office in the 'divine kingships' widely reported from many parts of the world, led Frazer to suggest that the institution of divine kingship was derived from the belief that the well-being of the social and natural orders depended upon the vitality of the priest-king, who must therefore be slain when his powers began to fail him and be replaced by a vigourous successor. The priest's or king's tenure of office was limited in early times to a prescribed period at the end of which he was put to death. In a series of ritual acts he had to make intercourse with the priestess or goddess-queen, mark out the soil for distribution among the clans, turn the first sod with his sacred hoe, cut the first ear of corn with his sacred sickle and, finally, at harvest he was put to death, to be replaced at the new year by a successor of unimpaired vitality.[73]

71. V. Gordon Childe: *What Happened in History,* London 1957, p. 125; *New Light on the Most Ancient East,* London 1954, p. 176.
72. Briffault, *The Mothers,* Vol. II p. 251.
73. See Frazer's *Dying God* (G. B. III); Cf. S. H. Hooke, *Myth and Ritual,* Oxford 1933.

The killing of the king or the priest was thus originally nothing but an incident in the women's ritual cycle. Thomson writes: "It was necessary for the queens to conceive in order that the earth might bear fruit. Their sexual life was a cycle of mimetic magic. Accordingly, the procreation was imagined as a god in the first instance, no doubt, the god of the moon, which in primitive thought is the cause of pregnancy in woman and fertility in the soil and after serving their purpose the men in whom this god was embodied were put to death. They had to die in order that the crops might live. This ritual, which inspired the myths of Ishtar and Tammuj, Isis and Osiris, Venus and Adonis, is the precursor of the Greek sacred marriage, in which it was adopted to the conditions of monogamy".[74]

14. The Dying God

Now, we are in a position to answer why the queen was especially selected for sexual union with the priest and why the latter was killed after the performance of such a ritual.

Of course, it will be foolish to expect that, in the historical period when the class division became fully established and a feudal system developed out of it, kings or priests would dedicate their physical bodies in this way. Beasts were supplied as substitutes for men in such rituals, as we find even now-a-days articles like the pumpkin becoming substitutes for beasts in non-violent religions. However, in the matriarchal zones of India, as is reasonable to expect on the basis of what we have stated above, we come across the existence of certain customs reflecting the rituals of the 'dying god'. Duart Barbosa who travelled in the Malabar region in the sixteenth century stated that in some places of that region the king could hold his office only for twelve years and then he was put to death.[75] The kings of Calicut were also god-kings who had to commit ceremonial suicide after twelve years of kingship. Towards the end of the seventeenth century this system was slightly changed. Twelve years over, there was a big ceremony at the end of which the king was killed. He was kept surrounded by his bodyguards. He who could break the barricade of the bodyguards and kill the king was assigned

74. *Studies in Ancient Greek Society*, Vol. I, pp. 158-59. cf. *infra*, pp. 122-25.
75. *Description of the Coasts of East Africa and Malabar*, Tr. H. E., Stanley, London 1866, pp, 172ff.

to a fresh liege of kingship for twelve years.[76] Gopal Panikkar informs us that not only the king but the high officials as well had to undergo the same sort of ceremonial slaughter. This held good also in the case of the village headmen. For five years they had absolute power, but after that they were put to death.[77]

But such examples are very few in the historical period, and so we should return once again to the mythical traditions. D. D. Kosambi after a penetrating analysis of the Urvaśī-Purūravas myths came to the conclusion that Purūravas was killed at a sacrifice after having begotten a son and successor upon Urvaśī; he pleaded in vain against her determination.[78] Kosambi's interpretation of RV, X. 95 clearly substantiates the dying-god theme. Urvaśī is addressed by Purūravas as *ghore*, which means the 'grim' or 'dreaded' one, hardly a lover's term. Urvaśī apparently tells her lover to get back to his home, *punar astam parehi*. The term *punar astam ehi* is really connected with death, as we find it in the funerary hymn (X. 14. 18) where the dead man is sent back to the ancestors and Yama with these words. Purūravas himself says that he is to die, in X. 95. 14 where going to a far distance, lying down in the lap of Nirṛti and so on are familar idiomatic circumlocutions for death. Urvaśī seems to console him in the next verse by assuring him that he is not to die. The assurance 'thou dost not die' is given in almost identical terms to the horse going to be sacrificed in RV. I. 162. 21: *na vai ṯu etan mriyase*. Purūravas is, however, assured that he is not to die a common profane death, not to be eaten by wolves like any untended corpse; he is to be sacrificed to or by the gods; that is his destiny; so he is called *mṛtyubandhuḥ* (X. 95. 18), not an ordinary mortal, but one literally bound to death at the sacrifice. This explains why Urvaśī has the heart of hyena (X. 95.15), why Purūravas's son can never know his father, but must console himself with thinking of his mother's sacred office (X. 95. 12-13). In the concluding verse of the dialogue Urvaśī says: 'Thus speak these gods to thee, son of Ilā: inasmuch as thou art now doomed to death, thy offspring will offer sacrifice to the gods, but thou thyself rejoice in heaven.[79]

Clearly Purūravas was killed at a sacrifice, also according to the tradition preserved in the Brāhmaṇa literature. The *Śatapatha*

76. Pinkerton's *Voyages and Travels*, Vol. VII, p. 374.
77. *Malabar and Its Folk*, Madras. 1909, pp. 120ff.
78. *Myth and Reality*, Bombay 1962, pp. 42ff.
79. *Ibid.*, p. 56.

Brāhmaṇa account[80] which is a commentary on the Ṛgvedic hymn, though not explaining the most obscure feature of the latter, states that Purūravas became a *gandharva* after making himself the upper and lower *araṇi*-s of Aśvattha wood from which fire results. Elsewhere in the same text,[81] the working of two portions of fire-drill or fireplough is conceived in terms of human procreation symbolised by Urvaśī and Purūravas. The association of the working of fire-drill with sexual intercourse is met with in the *Bṛhadāraṇyaka Upaniṣad*[82] and in other places. Moreover, the *Śatapatha Brāhmaṇa* states that Purūravas became a *gandharva* after transforming himself into the *araṇi*-s. He could become that only after his physical death. Though the *gandharvas* possess a separate heaven of their own, a human being can attain it only as a spirit. This is also supported by the evidence furnished in the *Bṛhadāraṇyaka Upaniṣad*.[83]

In the pages of the Brāhamṇa literature we come across passages which indicate that Prajāpati was killed at a sacrifice after a ceremonial sexual union. The name Prajāpati is significant because it means 'a lord of men or subjects'. The legend which we find in the Brāhmaṇa literature is already sophisticated. In the *Śatapatha Brāhmaṇa*,[84] the legend is stated thus: "Prajāpati conceived a passion for his own daughter—either the Sky or the Dawn. 'May I pair with her', thus (thinking) he united with her. This assuredly was a sin in the eyes of the gods. 'He who acts thus towards his own daughter, our sister, (commits a sin), they thought. The gods then said to this god who rules over the beasts (Rudra): 'This one surely commits a sin who acts thus towards his own daughter, our sister. Pierce Him'. Rudra, taking it, pierced him. Half of the seed fell on the ground. And thus it came to pass. Accordingly it has been said by the Ṛṣi with reference to that (incident): 'When the father embraced his daughter, uniting with her, he dropped his seed on the earth'. This (became) the chant (*uktha*) called *Agnimaruta*; in (connexion with) this it is set forth how the gods caused the seed to spring. When the anger of the gods subsided, they cured Prajāpati and cut out that dart of this (Rudra); for Prajāpati doubtless is this sacrifice"[85] According to the version of the legend given

80. XI. 5. 1ff.
81. III. 4. 1. 22.
82. VI. 4. 22.
83. III. 4.; III. 7.
84. 1. 7. 4. 1.8; Cf. II. 1. 2. 9 (Madh); II. 7. 2. 1-8; I. 1. 2. 5-6 (Kan.).
85. *Sacred Books of the East*, Vol. XII, pp. 208-10.

in the *Aitareya Brāhmaṇa*,[86] Prajāpati transformed himself into a roe-buck (*ṛṣya*) and approached his own daughter who assumed the shape of a dow (*rohit*). Out of their most fearful forms the gods then fashioned a divine being called Bhūtavat (i.e. Rudra) in order to punish Prajāpati for his incestuous deed. The latter was accordingly pierced by Bhūtavat's arrow and bounded up to the sky, where he became the constellation called *Mṛga*, while his daughter became the star *Rohiṇī*. The legend is found also in the *Pañcaviṃśa Brāhmaṇa*.[87]

From the two versions of the same legend, we find that the woman with whom Prajāpati had sexual union was his own daughter. Then he was simply killed and just as Purūravas became a *gandharva* only after his physical death so also Prajāpati became the star *mṛga*. The whole thing is regarded as an affair of incest of the father with his daughter and the killing of Prajāpati was interpreted as an act of punishment. Up to this the traditional interpretation may be regarded as consistent, and there is no doubt that this interpretation gave rise to the Puranic legend of Brahmā and Śatarūpā. But the subsequent stages of the legend show that this traditional interpretation is over-simplified. It is stated that, disgusted at the vile act of Prajāpati, Rudra discharged an arrow at him, whereupon Prajāpati was pierced and his semen (*retas*) fell upon the ground. Why is there reference to the semen of Prajāpati? Then it is stated that the semen was seen by Bhaga and at once he became blind. Why was it seen by him and why did he become blind? Again it is stated that the semen was tasted by Puṣan as a result of which he lost his teeth. Why did such things happen? Had it been a simple case of incest the matter could be ended with the punishment of Prajāpati. Why then Bhaga and Puṣan had to suffer? According to the *Aitareya* version of the story, the daughter, before her union with Prajāpati, assumed the shape of a *rohita* (*rohitaṃ bhūtam*). The word *rohita* has been translated as doe, but according to Sāyana it means *menstruous*: *rohitaṃ lohitaḥ bhūtā prāptā ṛtumatī jātetyarthaḥ*. This reminds us of the menstrual rites, (See Ch. V) associated with vegetation and fertility, current in different parts of the world.[88] So it appears that the legend with which we are dealing refers to a very old ritual, the significance of which could not be understood even in

86. III. 33-34.
87. VIII. 2. 10.
88. See my *Indian Puberty Rites*, Calcutta 1968, pp. 5ff.

the age of the Brāhmaṇa literature. The same legend is found in the *Ṛgveda* in which Rudra is described as playing the part of Prajāpati[89]. There it is stated that Rudra had sexual union with his daughter Uṣā but this was not regarded as incestuous. "The semen, capable of producing heroic children, increased and was about to overflow. He, then, for the welfare of beings, discharged that. He infused that semen into the body of his own beautiful daughter. When the father conceived such passion for his own youthful daughter, he united with her and she extracted much semen from the copulation. That semen was infused into a lofty frame, the container of good deeds. When the father made sexual intercourse with his own daughter, *he did that with the earth* and infused semen therein. The intelligent gods made the Brahman out of it and created Vāstoṣpati, the protector of rites." So we find that the attitude of the *Ṛgveda* towards the father's union with his daughter is basically different from that of the Brāhmaṇa literature.

The story of Prajāpati's union with his own daughter has come down to us in an extremely mutilated form and in the Brāhmaṇa literature it has been much fabricated with theological speculations and sacrificial technicalities. However, in spite of everything, the fact remains that Prajāpati was killed after a ritual intercourse with a woman, supposed to be his own daughter. In the same way, Purūravas was also sacrificed after his union with Urvaśī. Reference may be made in this connexion to the Puranic episode of king Veṇa who was slain on account of his wickedness according to the traditional interpretations.[90] But the most interesting feature of the Veṇa episode is that when his body was given to the sacrifice, he was reborn in a new form. The rise of Pṛthu from the body of Veṇa obviously implies that the god-king was put to death to be replaced by a successor of unimpaired vitality. Interestingly enough, Veṇa is described as a god in the *Ṛgveda*[91] who was sacrificed and thus became a *gandharva* after his ritual intercourse with a celestial nymph.

15. Epilogue: Birth of Literature

Referring to the Puruṣamedha sacrifice,[92] Eggeling remarks:

89. X. 61. 5-7.
90. Cf. *Mbh.*, Śānti, LIX.
91. X. 123. 4-7.
92. *Śat Br,* XIII. 6. 1. 2; *Sān. S. S,* XVI. 10. 1-21; *Vaitāna Sūtras,* XXXVII. 10-26.

"In fact it is nothing more than what Śāṅkhāyana appears to claim for it, *viz.* an adaptation, and that a comparative modern adaptation of existing Aśvamedha ritual".[93] Though the form in which it is reproduced in the Brāhmaṇa and the Sūtra literature does not appear to be so archaic, yet there are grounds to believe that the Aśvamedha was originally the Puruṣamedha in which a man was sacrificed instead of the horse after his ceremonial intercourse with the queen. The very fact that the whole ritual of Aśvamedha was included in the Puruṣamedha[94] proves that both were identical in the beginning but later branched off in two directions, the former being taken by the royal class. Puruṣamedha could be performed by any wealthy individual. The list of different classes of human victims to be offered in the Puruṣamedha sacrifices, as we find in the Brāhmaṇa literature, proves that such victims could be bought or managed from the conquered and exploited peoples.

A few other points should be explained here in connexion with the Aśvamedha sacrifice. In the earlier stage of the Aśvamedha sacrifice, a Brāhmaṇa and a Kṣatriya lute-player used to sing stanzas composed by themselves in honour of the king and the Hotṛ used to relate a 'revolving legend' in a ten days' cycle all the year round. Winternitz points out that germs of later literature can be traced to these recitals.[95] But why such things formed part of the ritual? An oversimplified answer may be given at once. These were recited or sung in the honour of the king for his performance of such a big affair as the Aśvamedha. But things are not really what they seem.

I have a book in Bengali on the early history of world literature. The most interesting fact that had come to my notice while I was writing the book was that all the ancient great literary works were tragedies and that they were all composed in verses with the purpose of singing or reciting before an audience. The relation was not between individual writer and reader, but a collective relation in which the speaker and the audience used to feel the same emotion. The same tradition is not completely lost even today, at least in places where literature has not become entirely sophisticated, individualised and urbanised. Poetry, music and dance were originally undifferentiated, and at that time it was not an art of

93. *Sacred Books of the East*, Vol. XLIV, p. XLIV.
94. *Śān. S. S.*, XVI-10. 2. 3.
95. *History of Indian Literature*, Vol. I, p. 272.

leisure; it was a guide to action 'designed to effect some change in the external world to impose illusion on reality'.[96] "The melodies of the *Sāmaveda* were looked upon as possessing magic power even as late as in the Brahmanical times. There is a ritual book belonging to the *Sāmaveda* called *Sāmavidhāna Brāhmaṇa* the second part of which is a regular handbook of magic, in which the employment of various *Sāmans* for various purposes is taught."[97] Singing is still a technique of work, as we find in reaping the harvest, in sailing the boats, in patting the roofs, in sinking the tubewells, in carrying the logs. Dance was the first to secede from the undifferentiated trio and the next to do the same was melody.

The earliest form of literature was thus quite different in purpose. It was a guide to action. The Aśvamedha, as we have seen, was a composite ritual connected with the increase of production. The undifferentiated poetry, music and dance was thus an essential feature of the original ritual, though in subsequent ages its purpose was changed. Besides the stanzas of the lute-players or the legends of the Hotṛ, there were other literary items connected with the Aśvamedha. Reference should be made in this connexion to the dialogues between the priests and the queens. These were the earliest form of drama, the dialogues being designed to imitate certain original performances. Already in the *Ṛgveda* we have references to the dialogue-hymns which were clearly meant to be acted. Mention should be made in this connexion of RV. I. 165 (Agastya, Indra, and the Maruts), I. 179 (sexual dialogue of Agastya and Lopāmudrā), III. 33 (Viśvāmitra and the rivers), IV. 18 (Indra, Aditi and Vāmadeva), X. 10 (Yama and Yamī), X. 14 (funeral rite), X. 95 (Urvaśī and Purūravas), X. 108 (Saramā and the Paṇis), X. 135 (Yama and Kumāra, the nucleus of the later legend of Yama and Naciketas). Most of the Ṛgvedic hymns are meant to be chanted by one or more priests, but these dialogue-hymns are of more importance since they are meant to be performed or mimed before a group of persons assembled for a certain purpose. The dialogue of the priest and the queen, as is found in the *Vājasaneyi Saṃhitā* in connexion with the Aśvamedha, is likewise meant to be part of a ritual act performed by two characters representing the principles and is thus a substitution for an earlier, actual sacrifice of the male.

96. See Thomson, *Studies in Ancient Greek Society*, Vol. I, pp, 439-40.
97. Winternitz, *op.cit.* Vol. I, p. 167.

II

THE KING AND THE DICE

A Study in the Rituals of the Rājasūya

1. Prologue: Purpose of the Study

In our study in the rituals of the Aśvamedha we have seen that there developed a gulf of difference between the basic and sophisticated forms of the Vedic Yajñas or sacrifices, that the original principles of sacrifice did not differ essentially from those of magic and that, with the change in the technique of production resulting in the rise of class society and state power on the ruins of tribal equality, primitive magic transformed itself into the esoteric art of the ruling or privileged class. We have also seen that the general character of the Vedic texts reflects a society based upon class division, although here and there in the same texts are found relics of an undifferentiated pre-class society through which the Vedic tribes had to pass their earlier stages, and in view of this we have tried to explain how a collective agricultural ritual like the Aśvamedha became in later times the sole affair of a king and began to be looked upon as a symbol of royal greatness. The purpose of the present chapter is also same, to unlock the closed door of ancient Indian social history with the essentials of the Rājasūya as the key, since we believe that the study of any cult or ritual *in itself* is of no value unless it is used as a means to understand the vast and enormously complicated problems of Indian social history.

2. Some Important Features of Rājasūya

As is known to all students of ancient Indian history, the Rājasūya was one of the principal ceremonies of royal inauguration. It consisted of a long succession of sacrificial performances which began on the first day of *phālguṇa* (February-March, the spring time of India) and spread over a period covering at least two years. The details of the Rājasūya are found in the *Śatapatha*

Brāhmaṇa.[1] Its main features, as summed up by Prof. H. C. Raychaudhuri, are as follows:[2]

(1) *Ratnināṃ haviṃṣi* or presents to the divinities of the *Ratnins* (the bejewelled ones or those possessed of the jewel offering or the aristocratic class). The *Ratnins* consisted of the *Senānī* (the Commander of the Army), the *Purohita* (Royal Chaplain), the *Mahiṣī* (Chief Queen), the *Sūta* (Charioteer and Bard), the *Grāmaṇī* (Leader of the Host or Village Headman), the *Saṃgrahitṛ* (Treasurer), the *Kṣatṛ* (Chamberlain), the *Bhāgadugha* (Collector of the Royal Share, i.e. Taxes), the *Akṣāvāpa* (Keeper of the Dice), the *Go-Vikartana* (lit. Cutter-up of Cattle, i.e., the King's Companion in the Chase) and the *Pālāgala* (Courier).

(2) *Abhiṣecanīya* or besprinkling ceremony which began with offering to Savitṛ, Agni, Soma, Bṛhaspati, Indra, Rudra, Mitra and Varuṇa. The consecration water (*abhiṣecanīya āpaḥ*) was made up of seventeen kinds of liquid including the water from the river Sarasvatī, sea-water, and water from a whirlpool, a pond, a well and dew. The sprinkling was performed by a Brāhmaṇa priest, a kinsman or brother of the king-elect, a friendly Rājanya and a Vaiśya.

(3) *Dig-Vyāsthāpana* or the king's symbolical walking towards the various quarters as an indication of his universal rule.

(4) Treading upon a tiger's skin, thus gaining the strength and the pre-eminence of the tiger.

(5) Enthronement.

(6) A mimic cow raid against a relative or a sham fight with a member of the ruling aristocracy.

(7) Narration by the *hotṛ* priest of the story of Śunaḥśepa of the *Aitareya Brhāmaṇa*. VII. 13 ff.

(8) A game of dice in which the king takes part.

Of the aforesaid eight items, the first five, *viz.* offerings to the household deities of the privileged persons, besprinkling ceremony, king's symbolical walk, treading upon the tiger's skin and enthronement, belong evidently to the sophisticated stage of the Rājasūya, and they are quite in accordance with the principles of royal inauguration of the later Vedic age. These were rituals through which the king was consecrated after his election.[3] These rituals reflect

1. V. 2. 3. 9ff; *Sacred Books of the East*, XLI, pp, 42-113.
2. *Political History of Ancient India*, Calcutta 1953, pp, 165ff.
3. Cf. *Śatapatha Br.* V. 3. 3, ff.; *Pañcaviṃśa Br.*, XVIII. 8 ff.; *Taittirīya Br.*, I. 7. 5; *Aitareya Br.* VIII. 5. ff.

the ideal of monarchy and that of a class society. The rise of class society and state power on the ruins of pre-class tribal life is a significant historical process and one of our main aims in these pages is to throw light on this subject. Very frequently many of our historians use such terms as 'tribe', 'tribal-king', 'tribal-coin', etc. without caring to understand the real nature of tribal society and the process of its disintegration yielding to the rise of the state. The three other rituals of the Rājasūya—the mimic cow raid, narration of the story of Śunaḥśepa and the game of dice—are likely to supply us valuable data relating to the growth of class society and the establishment of kingship in ancient India.

3. The Mimic Cow Raid

In our study in the ritual of the Aśvamedha we have argued that the early Ṛgvedic tribes were purely pastoral, and this point is indeed significant. "The growth of private ownership", writes George Thomson,[4] "derived a powerful impetus from the domestication of cattle. Game is perishable and land is immovable, but wealth in the form of cattle is durable and easy to steal or to exchange. Being necessarily nomadic, pastoral tribes are quick to increase their wealth by cattle raids and war; and since warfare, which had grown out of hunting, was waged by the men, it reinforced the tendency already inherent in pastoral society, for wealth to accumulate in their hands. Constantly on the move, these turbulent tribes plunder one district after another. The male captives are killed, the women are carried off as chattels, their skill at the loom being measured in terms of cattle. But warfare requires unity of leadership, and consequently these tribes develop a type of kingship not magical, but military. In reward for their successful leadership, the kings receive the lion's share of the spoils, and the wealth thus amassed promotes social inequalities which shake the whole fabric of tribal society, beginning at the top."

The importance attached to the possession of cattle is shown by numerous passages of the *Ṛgveda*. The word *go* denoting the cow is used as one of the synonyms for *pṛthivī*, the earth. According to the *Nighaṇṭu*,[5] nine other terms were also used to denote the cow.

4. *Aeschylus and Athens*, London, 1950, p, 32. Cf. *Supra*, Ch. I. Sec. 12. pp. 14-15.
5. II. 11.

Even in the *Ṛgveda*[6] the gods are invoked as offsprings of the cows and the poets do not hesitate to compare their songs with the lowing of the cows[7] or to designate the starry heaven after the term *gāvaḥ*.[8] We have many passages in the *Ṛgveda* referring to forays for cattle. So common were such raids that the word *gaviṣṭi* indicating 'battle for cattle' came to denote any 'conflict' or 'battle'. The Bhāratas are frequently described as a host desirous of cows.[9] The *Ṛgveda* is in fact burdened with the events of cattle raids and, as Dr. D. R. Das has shown,[10] such events were common even in historical times, at least the ancient tradition of *go-grahaṇa* was maintained by Indian kings as one of the features of their royal duties.

The character of Indra, as depicted in the *Ṛgveda,* is that of an unscrupulous war-leader of the pastoral peoples—an ideal king of later times—plundering one district after another for the sake of cattle-wealth. He manifests his character not so much as the protector, but as the lifter of cattle.[11] His help is sought for seizing the cattle of the enemies[12] like the Kīkaṭas.[13] He is invoked as the discoverer of concealed cows.[14] He seizes the cattle of the Dasyus and releases them from the *goṣṭha*.[15] There is reason to believe that the Ṛgvedic episode, in which Indra forcibly released the cows kept by the Paṇis in mountain forts, has a factual basis.[16] In one episode Indra is seen releasing the cows after having killed Vṛtra.[17] He boasts of killing Vṛtra, giving all his cows to Trita, plundering the wealth of the Dasyus and driving all the cows to Dadhīca and Mātariśvan.[18] In another place, it is stated that Trita, being sent by Indra, fought and killed Triśiras with the weapons of his father and obtained all the cows of Tvaṣṭṛ's son Viśvarūpa who was be-

6. VI. 50. 11. etc.
7. VII. 32. 22; VII. 106. 1; IX. 22. 2; etc.
8. I. 156. 6; VII. 36. 1.
9. Cf. III. 31. 10; See Ch. I. Sec. 10. p. 14.
10. *Go-grahaṇa, in Social Life in Ancient India* (ed. D. C. Sircar, Calcutta 1971) pp. 30-38.
11. III. 44. 5; IV. 17. 11; VI. 17. 1; VI. 26. 2; X. 38. 1; X. 48. 4.
12. IV. 31. 13; VI. 35. 2; VI. 42. 2; VIII. 21. 11; X. 24. 14; etc.
13. III. 54. 14.
14. IV. 28. 5.
15. IV. 19. 7; VI. 45.4.
16. III. 31. 6; VI. 39. 2; VI. 44. 22; VI. 73. 1-3; VII. 9. 2; IX. 22. 7; IX. 111. 2; X. 62. 2; X. 67. 3-8; X. 68. 2-11; X. 108.
17. I. 32. 12; V. 86. 3; VIII. 3. 19; X. 89. 7.
18. X. 48. 2.

headed by Indra.[19]

Such examples of Indra's exploits can be multiplied. Since cattle was the form of wealth, to be increased by raids and wars, successful leadership in cattle-raids was regarded as one of the essential qualifications for the candidature of 'kingship' in the early Vedic age. There is reason to believe, as we shall see in a subsequent section, that kingship in that age was in most of the cases elective, although the conception of hereditary kingship was gaining ground. The Vedic tribes were getting detribalized, owing to the changes in the mode of production caused by the introduction of Higher Pastoralism. In the *Ṛgveda*, however, the term for war-chief was *rājā* which later on came to mean 'king'. The comparatively modern meaning of the word had led some of our scholars to discover *kings* and *monarchs* in the *Ṛgveda*. But this conclusion, as we shall see later, is based upon a wrong understanding. Nevertheless, it must be remembered in this connection that it took several centuries to get the whole of the *Ṛgveda* composed and that this long period must have witnessed a great social transformation, a qualitative transition from the pre-class to class-divided society.

In view of what we have stated above, we are now in a position to understand why a mimic cow raid was an essential ritual of the Rājasūya. All rituals are symbols of earlier social realities. The mimic cow raid is therefore an *illusory technique,* founded on the primitive magical notion that by creating the *illusion* one can actually control the *reality*.[20] Accordingly, the sacrificer, who has been elected 'king' for his successful leadership in the war or is holding his office as the descendant of such a 'king' previously elected, places a hundred or more than a hundred cows of one of his relatives to the north of the *āhavanyīa* and takes part in a sham fight. He stops his chariot in the midst of cows guarded by a Rājanya with a bow in hand. The king then shoots his arrow at him and having thus, as it were, overpowered the enemy, he wheels round. Then he touches the cow with the end of his bow saying. 'Together with energy, I overpower them. I seize them'.[21]

4. The Word Rājā: Its Original and Changed Meaning

The mimic cow raid is therefore an imitation of the actual cow

19. X. 8. 8-9.
20. Cf. *Supra,* Ch. I, Sec. 8. p. 11.
21. *Śat. Br.,* V. 4. 3. 1-2; *SBE,* XLI, pp. 98-101.

raids of the earlier pastoral tribes. Our main line of approach is that successful leadership in such raids was once regarded as an essential qualification for the ruler and that in a later period when the institution of kingship in the modern sense was established, the kings in the time of royal inauguration used to mime those feats which they or their predecessors once performed in reality. But this conclusion will be of no value unless it is brought in relation to the bigger problem of the growth of the institution of kingship in the Vedic age.

Many scholars have spoken of the 'Vedic tribes' and described their social and political institutions *without trying to understand what the tribal society really is.* A few words should therefore be spoken in this connection. The tribe is composed of a number of clans, and its affairs are conducted by a tribal council composed of the elected chiefs from different clans. Likewise the affairs of a clan are conducted by the clan-assembly composed of all the adult members of the clan. In a word, the tribal administration is maintained at all levels by democratic institutions, like the tribal-council, the clan-assembly, and so on.[22] If the Vedic peoples were originally organised in tribes, it is logical to assume that they also must have once passed through a stage of similar democratic organisation. And this should be the basis of the study of the social and political institutions of the Vedic peoples, a point which has been clearly ignored. True, the terms *Sabhā, Samiti* and *Vidatha* indicating 'popular assemblies' according to the modern interpretation, are widely discussed subjects, but what has not been discussed in connection with the said institutions is their real social and political role during the period under review.

Owing to this gross misunderstanding of the tribal institutions, the historian has no hesitation in stating that "the tribes of the *Ṛgveda* were certainly under kingly rule: there is no passage in the *Ṛgveda* which suggests any other form of government, while the king under the style *rājan* is a frequent figure".[23] As Chattopadhyaya has rightly observed: "Evidently, the scholars who have discovered 'monarchy' among the Vedic tribes are misled by the word *rājan.* This is clear from the way *The Vedic Age* (*History and Culture of the Indian People*, Vol. I, ed. R. C. Majumdar) has echoed the *Cambridge History*: 'as

22. L. H. Morgan, *Ancient Society,* pp. 71. ff.
23. *Cambridge History of India,* I, p. 94.

a general rule, monarchy was the system of government prevailing in this age. The term *rājan*, king or chieftain, is of frequent occurrence in the *Ṛgveda*.' The premise is true but the conclusion untenable: the word *rājan* is there in the *Ṛgveda* but it does not prove the existence of a monarchical form of government. We shall mention here two decisive evidences. Even in the latest stratum of the *Ṛgveda* we come across the epithet *rājā vrātasya,* and this is a synonym for *gaṇasya senānīḥ*. This means nothing but the tribal chief. Secondly, one of the famous battles was referred by the *Ṛgveda* as *dāśarājña*; under the set idea that *rājā* could mean nothing but the king, this is taken to mean the *battle of the ten kings*. But who were the ten *kings*? In preparing the list of these so-called *kings* even the contributor of the *Cambridge History* was frankly obliged to use the word 'tribe' instead: 'Of the ten tribes five are of little note, the Alinas...the Pakthas...the Bhalānases...the Śivas...and the Viṣāṇins. Better known in the *Ṛgveda* are the other five, the Anus... the Druhyus..the Turvaśas and Yadus..and the Purus'. If those were tribes, then the battle amongst them *could not be* a battle of the 'ten kings'. And if this were so, the use of the word *rājan* in the *Ṛgveda* is far from being a sure proof of hereditary monarchy".[24]

5. The Election of the 'Kings': The Popular Pressure

"The ceremony of the Rājasūya or royal consecration," says Keith,[25] "hints at recollections of an elective kingship by the consent of the people". What we are trying to suggest on the basis of the available data is that the *rājās* of the *Ṛgveda* could not have been kings of the later times. They were, like the chiefs of tribal society, definitely elected by the people. The clearest reference to the *rājā* being elected by the people is found in the *Atharvaveda*.[26] "The hyperboles of the Vedic poets", says Chattopadhyaya,[27] "appear to be all the more exaggerated by modern translator's preoccupations with the later ideas. Beneath all these overgrowths, however, the tribal custom of the people electing the chief and the chief in turn sharing out the wealth among the people are evident enough." The evidence of the clan council and tribal assemblies in the *Ṛgveda*

24. D. Chhattopadhyaya, *Lokāyata*, Delhi 1968, pp. 593-94.
25. *Religion and Philosophy of the Veda*, Cambridge 1925, p. 481.
26. III. 4. 2.
27. *op cit.*, p. 591.

shows that the Vedic people were largely at the tribal stage in which there was no place for hereditary kingship. Of course, with the disintegration of the tribal organisation, it became customary to elect chiefs from the same family which ultimately resulted in hereditary succession and finally kingship in the modern sense of the term.

Many passages of the *Aitareya Brāhmaṇa* speak of the election and consecration of rulers.[28] The expression *rāja-kartṛ* (king-maker)[29] points to the important part played by officials including headmen of villages in the choice of the ruler. In the *Śatapatha-Brāhmaṇa*[30] the persons specified as *rāja-kartṛ* or *rājakṛt* are the Sūta and the Grāmaṇi. Prof. R. K. Mookerji observes: "It is apparent from the lists of persons aiding in the royal coronation that both official and non-official or popular elements were represented in the function".[31] In the *Aitareya Brāhmaṇa*[32] emphasis is laid on the possession of moral qualities. The leader on whom the choice falls is *ojiṣṭha, baliṣṭha, sahiṣṭa, sattamaḥ, pārayiṣṇutama* and *dharmajña*. We have evidence that the peoples sometimes expelled and even executed their rulers together with unpopular officials. The *Aitareya Brāhmaṇa*[33] refers to rulers who were expelled from their states. The *Śatapatha Brāhmaṇa*[34] says that the Sṛjñayas expelled their hereditary ruler together with the *sthapati*. In later Jātaka literature there are numerous references to the power of the people to depose a king and elect another.[35]

That the real power was with the people is proved by the testimony of the *Atharvaveda*[36] where it is stated that concord between king and assembly was essential. In the *Jaiminīya Upaniṣad Brāhmaṇa*[37] we find references to the *Pariṣad*, the *Sabhā* and the *Saṃsad* where people used to meet. It refers to the disputations (*Saṃvāda*) and witnesses (*Upadraṣṭṛ*) in connection with the popular assemblies.

These organisations were same as the *Samiti* or the *Pariṣad* of the Upaniṣads and served as the general body of the people (*Janāḥ*),

28. U. N. Ghosal, *A History of Hindu Political Theories*, 1927, p. 26.
29. *Ait Br.*, VIII. 17; *Śat. Br.*, III. 4. 1. 7.
30. III. 4. 1. 7; XIII. 2. 18.
31. *The Fundamental Unity of India*, p. 83.
32. VIII. 12.
33. VIII. 10.
34. XII. 9. 3. 1 ff.
35. Nos. 73, 247, 378, 401, 462, 529. etc.
36. VI. 88. 3.
37. II. 11. 4; III. 7. 6.

an assembly of the whole people.[38] The *Chāndogya Upaniṣad*[39] mentions the *Samiti* of the Pañcālas, while the *Bṛhadāraṇyaka*[40] uses the term *Pariṣad* instead of *Samiti.* The analogy of the Licchavi *Pariṣā* and of similar assemblies mentioned in Buddhist works shows that the functions and powers of the *Pariṣads* were by no means insignificant.

6. The Tribal Councils

The examples, mentioned above, are carefully selected from the post-Ṛgvedic literature belonging to the period when the institution of kingship was spreading its root in the class-divided soil of India. Even then the ancient democratic institutions, the popular assemblies did not cease to function, although their importance was going to be minimised, as is natural to expect. The decay of the old tribal, and hence democratic, assemblies was complete in the period represented by the Great Epic. Hopkins[41] says: "The earliest assembly for adjusting political affairs in Aryan India was the clan-assembly, called *sabhā* (cf. the German *sippe*)....Where the people met 'in assemblies' to discuss political matters, we may perhaps see a trace of the original function of the people's assembly, though such a meeting had, of course, long ceased to be what the *sabhā* had been—a village assembly for counsel—and corresponds neither to the regular *sabhā* of the old nor the antique state council in which the king took part (*samiti*), the latter having now become a meeting place of the nobles and king....The assembly of the people had become an assembly of nobles. The military power of the people had quite become the possession of the king. In all public matters appertaining to the story itself, the priests are as good as silent, and the people are suppressed".

But the picture was different in the age of the *Ṛgveda.* The *Ṛgveda* as a whole is a literature of a long transitional period retaining on the one hand memories and relics of the pre-class society and on the other foreshadowing the realities of class society. In any case, as it is natural to expect, the democratic institutions with their original tribal character must have survived with greater vigour

38. Raychaudhuri, *op. cit.*, p. 174.
39. V. 3. 1.
40. VI. 2. 1.
41. *JAOS*, XIII, pp. 148-51.

and vitality in the age reflected by the *Ṛgveda.* The terms for such institutions, as found in the *Ṛgveda,* are *sabhā, samiti* and *vidatha.* As regards the specific character of these institutions, the Vedic scholars are not unanimous. Therefore it will be more justified if we take into account the functional aspects: the institutions as they functioned in the Vedic society.

Macdonell and Keith rightly observed that the kings had to attend the *Sabhā* and the *Samiti.*[42] But since they understood the term *rājan* in the modern sense of 'king' they found it difficult to explain precisely the position of the king in the tribal democratic assemblies. Keith, who had to admit the *democratic* and *tribal* character of these institutions, therefore observed that "the power of the king cannot have been in normal circumstances arbitrary or probably very great. There stood beside him as the mode of expression of the will of the people, the assembly, which is denoted by the terms *Samiti* and *Sabhā* in the Saṃhitās".[43] In the same page he writes: "If indeed the king was ever elected by the cantons, the election took place in the *Samiti*".[44] So great a scholar like Keith has thus made confusing statements, and this is due to a simple misunderstanding of the real significance of the term *rājan.* If he could assert that originally, at least in the earlier phase of the Ṛgvedic society, when class division was not as yet sharp, the word *rājan* denoted tribal leaders and that in a later period it came to denote king, there would be no difficulty in explaining the relation between the so-called 'king' and the assembly. Here we like to refer to a significant verse of the *Ṛgveda*[45] which contains *rājānaḥ samitau iva* (as 'kings' assemble in the *samiti*). Note that the use of the word *rājā* is made in plural. This plurality of the so called 'kings', the presence of a number of kings in the *samiti,* proves that these *rājās* were no other than tribal leaders. They could not be monarchs because a plurality of them gathering in assembly makes hardly any sense.

One should not fail to recall in this connection what Morgan wrote about the European misunderstanding of the tribal organisation of the Americas: "(American) Indian Chiefs are described as Lords by Spanish writers ....It is a misconception to style an

42. *Vedic Index,* II, p. 427 n.
43. *Cambridge History of India,* I. p. 96.
44. *ibid.*
45. X. 97. 6.

(American) Indian chief in the European sense, because it implies a condition of society that did not exist. One belongs to political society and represents an aggression of the few upon the many; while the other belongs to gentile (tribal) society and is founded upon the common interests of the members of the gens (clan)".[46] Even while dealing with European history many of the modern scholars were not conscious about the real distinction between the tribal and political societies. "The trouble with this school of historians," says Thomson,[47] "is that they are trying to explain the tribal institutions of early Rome without raising the question of what tribal society is."

Now about the functional aspects. If the *samiti* were crowded by the so-called 'kings', we have argued that they were not really kings in the modern sense of the term. They were tribal leaders, war-chiefs. This is supported by the evidence furnished by the *Nighaṇṭu*[48] according to which the word *samiti* is a *saṅgrāma-nāma* (a name for war). To conduct the tribal wars was evidently one of the important functions of the tribal assemblies, but they had other functions too, of which the most important was the distribution of wealth. This has been shown by Prof. Debiprasad Chhattopadhyaya[49] who has collected numerous passages dealing with the distribution of wealth in the popular assemblies from which we are quoting a few: "Ah let the happiness of the assembly come to us; we offer praise to the speedy ones; because today Savitṛ, the custodian of wealth, is in the act of sharing out this wealth. . . .[50] Suparṇa gives the share of water continuously in the assembly. . .[51] O god (Agni), for proper enjoyment you disbursed your wealth in shares in the assembly. . .[52] O Agni, this assembly of ours shines among the gods, you, the custodian of food, divide wealth among us here and give us shares full of wealth."[53]

Thus the assembly is often referred to as the place of the division of wealth. But how this division took place? What have the

46. Morgan, *op. cit.*, p. 208.
47. *Studies in Ancient Greek Society*, London 1949, I, p. 97.
48. II. 17.
49. *op. cit.*, pp. 578 ff.; Cf. his *Bhāratīya Darśan* (Beng.). I. pp. 138 ff.
50. RV. VII. 40. 1.
51. I. 164. 21.
52. II. 1. 4.
53. X. 11. 8.

Vedic texts to say on this point? What were the forms of division in the pre-class society and what were those in the earlier phases of class society? Does the *Ṛgveda* help us in understanding these problems? How was the custom of equal division abolished with the further growth and consolidation of class society? Do the functions of royal consecration, as found in later literature, contain relics of such vanished customs? Is there in the Rājasūya any act or miming of any act which presents an illusion of such a lost reality?

7. Akṣa and Ṛta

We should not fail to recall in this connection that *sabhā* was the place for the distribution of wealth, as we have seen above, and that one of the names of the dice and the dicer was *sabhāsthānu*. Sabhā and Sabhāsthānu therefore may not be unconnected, and in view of this we can reasonably raise the question whether dicing or casting the lot had anything to do with the primitive distribution of wealth: whether the king's taking part in the ritual dicing was an *illusory* survival of the lost *reality* of equal distribution of wealth through *casting the lot*.

The following is what the king had to do with the dice in the Rājasūya: "He then throws the five dice into his hand with (*Vājasaneyi Saṃhitā* X. 28) 'Dominant thou art: may these five regions of thine prosper'; now that one, the *Kali*, is indeed dominant over the (other) dice, for that one dominates over all the dice: therefore he says, 'Dominant thou art: may these five regions of thine prosper'; for there are indeed five regions, he thereby causes to prosper for him".[54] Descriptions of the ritual use of dice at the Agnyādheya and the Rājasūya ceremonies are also found in other works.[55]

It appears that although in later times dicing was reduced to gambling, its original purpose was different. The *Akṣa-sūkta* (X. 34) belongs to the later portion of the *Ṛgveda* and it has very little to do with ritual-dicing. But there are certain indications in this *sūkta* which we should not overlook. The entire hymn is a combination of two different themes, one of which is ecstatic praise of *Akṣa* in connection with *agriculture* while the other is designed to denounce

54. *Śat. Br.*, V. 4. 4. 6; *Sacred Books of the East*, XLI, p. 106.
55. *Maitrāyaṇī Saṃhitā*, IV. 4. 6; *Taittirīya Br.*, I. 7. 10. 5; *Kātyāyana Śrauta Sutra*, XV. 7. 5. ff.; *Āpastamba Śrauta Sūtra*, XVIII. 18. 16 ff.; *Bhudhāyana Śrauta Sūtra*, II. 8. 9; etc.

Akṣa in connection with *gambling.* According to Sāyana, the deity of this *sūkta* is *akṣa-kṛsipraśaṃsā akṣa-kitava-nindā ca,* i.e., 'the praise of the lot as (related to) agriculture (*kṛsi*) and also the denunciation of the lot as (related to) gambling (*kitava*)'. The praise of agriculture shows that the hymn was composed at a later period. The pastoral Vedic peoples resorted to agriculture at a considerably late period. However, we shall presently see that the lot or *akṣa* was *not designed by the early Vedic people for the exclusive purpose of gambling.*

In several passages of the later Saṃhitās and Brāhmaṇas, lists are given of expressions connected with dicing.[56] Of such names Kṛta, Tretā, Dvāpara and Kali (=Abhibhū and Akṣarāja)[57] are significant. These are well known names of the mythical ages of India, from which it may be presumed that in each of the 'supposed ages' dicing underwent some changes in purpose and form. The change took place from time to time in accordance with the corresponding social changes. Lüders shows that in a considerable number of passages in the *Ṛgveda*, Kṛta means a 'throw' (not 'a stake' or 'what is won') and this sense is clearly found in the *Atharvaveda.*[58]

It is interesting to note that in the *Atharvaveda* the *Akṣa* is connected with Varuṇa and Ṛta. "King Varuṇa sees through all that is between the heaven and the earth, and all that is beyond. He has counted the winkings of men's eyes. As a (winning) gamester puts down his dice, thus does he establish these (laws)."[59] Thus the establishment of Varuṇa's laws is conceived in terms of dicing. The relation between Akṣa and Ṛta is also anticipated in the Akṣa-sūkta of the *Ṛgveda*[60]: *Yo vaḥ senānīrmahato gaṇasya rājā vrātasya prathamo vabhūva tasmai kṛṇomi na dhanā ruṇadhmi daśāhaṃ prācīstadṛtaṃ vadāmi.* Here the Akṣa is conceived as the leader of *gaṇa* and the first chief (*rājā*) of the *vrāta.* The poet having addressed the Akṣa in such terms declares that he is not withholding wealth. With his ten fingers stretched he is speaking the *Ṛta.*

The promise of *not withholding the wealth in the name of Ṛta* indicates something other than gambling. As Macdonell and Keith[61] have

56. *Taittirīya Saṃ.*, IV. 3. 3. 1-2; *Vāj. Saṃ.*, XXX. 18; *Taitt. Br.*, III. 4. 1. 16.
57. Cf. *Śat. Br.*, V. 4. 4. 6; Macdonell and Keith, *Vedic Index,* I, p. 3.
58. Macdonell and Keith, *op. cit.*, p. 3.
59. *AV.* IV., 16. 5; *Sacred Books of the East,* XLII. p. 88.
60. X. 34. 12.
61. *Vedic Index,* I. p. 3.

pointed out, the Vedic gods were compared to the throws of dice as giving or destorying wealth, and such conceptions, as we shall see later, were not without any social basis. However, the most interesting point in the Ṛgvedic passage is the conception of the *Akṣa* as the leader of *gaṇa* and *vrāta*, the tribal collective. That the term *gaṇa* evidently denoted 'tribe' has been proved by numerous references to it in the same sense in ancient literature, and since scholars are more or less unanimous in this interpretation, there is no need of any further discussion on this point. Kātyāyana[62] said that the words *śerṇi, pūga, gaṇa, vrāta* and *saṃgha* meant *samūha* or *varga*, i.e. 'group'. Interestingly, Sāyana in his commentary on the said Akṣa-sūkta of the *Ṛgveda* has equated *gaṇa* with *vrāta*.

Thus the Akṣa-sūkta itself points at the tribal character of the original dicing. It also contains the relics of the very old social characteristic that wealth should not be withheld, because that would go against the principles of *Ṛta*. Evidently these were the social values prior to the development of the conflict between social wealth and individual appropriation. In the earlier stages of class society, when the tribal organisations disintegrated, the king, although he had by this time established his individual right on the large portion of social wealth, paid lip-loyalty to the ancient tribal customs. This explains why in the Rājasūya the king took the dice in his own hand. The dice were the symbol of ancient social justice, the ideals of which the king was expected to uphold.

8. Ṛta and Varuṇa

Evidently dice were the symbol of ancient social justice and, as we shall see later, casting the lot was a means of equal distribution of wealth in early Vedic times. But before reaching this point we shall have to deal with some kindred subjects which are likely to substantiate our hypothesis as parts of circumstantial evidence. The *Akṣa* as we have seen above, is connected with *Ṛta* in the *Ṛgveda* as well as the *Atharvaveda*. But what is this Ṛta? According to Winternitz[63], *Ṛta* is the 'order of the Universe' while Macdonell[64] takes it to mean the 'physical and moral order'. Keith[65] thinks it to

62. P. V. Kane, *History of Dharmaśāstra,* II, p. 66.
63. *History of Indian Literature,* I. p. 154.
64. *History of Sanskrit Literature,* London, 1905, p. 75.
65. *Religion and Philosophy of the Veda*, p. 248.

be a term for the cosmic as well as the moral order. According to Radhakrishnan "*Ṛta* literally means 'the course of things'. It stands for law in general and the immanence of justice. This conception must have originally been suggested by the regularity of the movement of the sun, moon and stars, the alternations of day and night, of the seasons. *Ṛta* denotes the order of the world. Everything that is ordered in the universe has *Ṛta* for its principles. It corresponds to the *Universals* of Plato. The world of experience is a shadow or reflection of the *Ṛta*, the permanent reality which remains unchanged in all the welter of mutation."[66]

But such interpretations of the *Ṛta* are one-sided. There is no doubt that *Ṛta* stood for a peculiar complex of moral and physical laws. But this is not all. *Ṛta* also stood for other principles which all these great scholars have unfortunately overlooked. One point which should be stressed is that the Vedic poets eventually *felt the loss of Ṛta and strongly urged for its revival.* If it were exclusively the physical and cosmic laws, there was no need of such lamenting. At the same time it is interesting to note that in the post-vedic literature the conception of *Ṛta* is practically absent. In the principal Upaniṣads the word occurs only seven times.[67] This shows that *Ṛta* originally stood for a different set of principles which was consistent with the early Vedic way of life, but eventually those principles were undermined and annihilated and some poets dreamt of their revival in vain. Now, what were the principles for which *Ṛta* stood originally?

Chattopadhyaya tried to give an answer to this question having demonstrated the material basis of *Ṛta* from the Ṛgvedic passages. According to him, "the *Ṛta* assured the poets their cows, their water, their food, and in fact everything they considered as constituting material wealth. Being thus intimately connected with the essentially practical considerations, the concept of *Ṛta* was yet to acquire any spiritual significance. Ṛta, the order of nature, was also understood by the poets and their kinsmen as the most potent force assuring them of their means of subsistence."[69] How *Ṛta* assured the people their cows, their water, their food, their material wealth and other means of subsistence has been shown in numerous passages of the

66. *Indian Philosophy*, I. pp. 78-79.
67. *Taittirīya*, I. 1. 1; I. 9. 1; I. 12. 1; II. 4. 1; III. 1. 6; *Kaṭha*, III. 1; V. 2.
68. *Lokāyata*. pp. 622 ff.
69. *ibid.*, p. 628.

Ṛgveda.[70] 'The holdings of the *Ṛta* are fast, the manifold forms of the *Ṛta* are delightful, the praisers desire abundant food of the *Ṛta*; by virtue of the *Ṛta* cows are obtained, and they (the cows) enter into the *Ṛta.* Having pleased the *Ṛta* the praisers gain strength and water; the earth does yield the best cows only for the sake of the *Ṛta* and it is vast and incommensurable because of the *Ṛta.*'[71] There are many more passages like this.

Ṛgvedic passages relating to the *Ṛta* convincingly prove that the said concept had direct or indirect bearing on the process of obtaining means of subsistence. The moral aspects of *Ṛta* have been emphasised by the scholars and the source of this moral order has been traced to the physical order. But there is nothing in the *Ṛgveda* to prove that human morality has its roots in human reason and that the latter in its turn is a reflection of the law-governed universe. In the nineteenth century Europe it was believed that rising out of the background of the law-governed physical universe human being is essentially rational and hence moral. And this belief was artificiality imposed upon the Vedic conception of *Ṛta.* But if this artificially is withdrawn, there is no difficulty in finding the *Ṛta* in its real perspective and in its functional aspects.

We shall not therefore be wrong in assuming that the Vedic *Ṛta* must have originally been what Engels[72] called the *simple moral grandeur of ancient gentile society*, and this explains why the Vedic poets felt the loss of *Ṛta* for which the breakdown of ancient collective life was responsible. Of all the Vedic gods, Mitra and Varuṇa, especially the latter, had the closest connection with the *Ṛta.* Varuna is *Ṛtasya gopa*, the guardian of the *Ṛta,* who, as a moral governor stands far above any other deity. "His wrath is roused by sin, the infringement of his ordinances, which he severely punishes (*RV.* VII. 86. 3-4). The fetters (*pāśah*) with which he binds sinners, are often mentioned (I. 24. 15, etc). They are cast sevenfold and threefold, ensnaring the man who tells lies, passing by him who speaks truth (*AV.* IV. 16. 6).... On the other hand, Varuṇa is gracious to the penitent. He unites like a rope and removes sin (II. 28. 5; V. 85. 7-8). He releases not only from the sins which men themselves

70. I. 132. 3; I. 141. 1; I. 151. 3-8; II. 27. 12; III. 1. 11; III. 20. 4; III. 54. 3; III. 56. 2; III. 61. 6; IV. 2. 16; IV. 23. 8-10; IV. 51. 7-8; IV. 52. 2; V. 8. 1; V. 41. 1; VII. 66. 13.; etc.
71. IV. 23. 9-10.
72. *Origin of the Family, Private Property and the State,* Moscow 1952, p. 163.

commit, but from those committed by their fathers (VII. 86. 5)".[73] Evidently, more important than the physical attributes of Varuṇa "are his moral qualities, his control of the order of the world in its ethical aspect no less than in its physical, his connexion with the worshipper as the saviour in time of peril and distress, the freer from sin, the merciful god as well as the punisher of the sinner".[74] Thus the Varuṇa of the past was the guardian of truth and justice, and hence his ordinances were severe. "Varuṇa's ordinances are constantly said to be fixed, the epithet *Dhṛtavrata* being pre-eminently applicable to him... the gods themselves follow Varuṇa's ordinance.... Even the immortal gods cannot obstruct the ordinances of Mitra and Varuṇa.... Mitra and Varuṇa are lords of order (*Ṛta*) and light, who by means of order are the upholders of order."[75]

Thus we have tried to establish the tribal, and hence pre-class, basis of the conception of *Ṛta* and in this connection referred to the strictness of the character of Varuṇa as the guardian of *Ṛta*, the sacred and inviolable laws regulating the relations of the members of the pre-class society. We are to remember in this connection that the strictness and severity of Varuṇa was for the sake of truth and justice, for the sake of the inherent morality of tribal life. And with the growth of class society, when the lowest interests—'base greed, brutal sensuality, sordid avarice, selfish plunder of common possessions'[76]—dominated, the moral inspiration of Varuṇa's character naturally sank into oblivion. This moral basis being destoryed what remained in the character of Varuṇa was nothing but severity. Varuṇa in subsequent ages thus turned into a cruel god, a source of terror. In later literature, as we shall see in a subsequent section, his very presence was like a nightmare.

9. Relics of Ancient Equality

We are yet to answer another question to which we are automatically led by the preceding investigations. Is there any relic of pre-class society, of collective life, in the *Ṛgveda*? In

73. Macdonell, *Vedic Mythology*, Strassburg 1898, p. 26.
74. Keith, *op. cit.*, p. 97.
75. Macdonell, *op. cit.*, p. 26.
76. Engels, *op. cit.*, p. 163.

political and administrative spheres, as we have already seen, the institutions found in Vedic literature, are clear relics of pre-class tribal survivals. In the economic sphere, as regards production and distribution, the same also holds good. In RV. VII. 76. 5, a clear picture of primitive communism is found: 'being united with the *common cattle* they become of one mind they strive together as it were, nor do they injure the rituals of the gods: nor injuring each other they move with wealth'. Here are a few of other examples of collective ownership along with a significant reference to the past: '*As in the past* he (Agni) generated the *common wealth* (for the living beings)'.[77] 'Let the *common cow* be moving swiftly.'[78] 'We invoke Indra, the custodian of *common wealth* and the giver of wealth for protection.'[79] 'O Agni, your brilliance comes to us and you brought the cows of *Ṛta* equally to us'.[80] Such examples can be multiplied to show that the *Ṛgveda* during the long period of its composition witnessed the transition from pre-class to class society and that it actually contains the relics of ancient collectivity and equality. The concluding verses of the *Ṛgveda* are really significant. The poet is lamenting for the life that is lost, trying to revive the memory of the past, which is imagined to restore the bliss of *equality and unity* once enjoyed by the Vedic peoples of the earlier age.

10. Distribution: Casting the Lot

Now we are in a position to answer why the king in the Rājasūya had to mime an act of dicing. Casting the lot was one of the primi-the tive means of equal distribution of wealth, and the king of a later age—although he was too powerful—at least formally took an oath that he would maintain the inviolable *Ṛta*, the spirit of ancient equality and justice, and his taking part in ritual dicing can only be explained in this sense. Casting the lot was indeed the best means of distribution, because the commodities gathered as collective wealth of the tribe, to be distributed among the clans, had no *fixed value* in the modern economic sense, since costing was then unknown. Thus

77. *RV.* III. 2. 12.
78. VI. 26. 1.
79. VIII. 99. 8.
80. I. 141. 1.

bhāgya (lot) was a means of *bhāga* (share).

In Greek context George Thomson[81] has analysed the system of casting the lot as a means of equal distribution and his researches throw important light on what still remains obscure in Vedic literature. He shows that the ancient system of casting the lot gave rise to the conception of the goddess Moira. "The basic meaning of the word *moira* is a share or portion.... With *moira* is associated another word, *lachos*, a portion given or received by the process of casting lots. One of the Moirai (goddess of fate) bore the name of Lachesis, the goddess of Allotment. In this sense *lachos* is synonymous with *Kleras*, which, commonly used of a lot or holding of a land, originally denoted a piece of wood used for casting lots....The land was to be distributed by lot among the tribes, and the territory of each tribe was to be subdivided by lot among the 'families' or 'clans'.... Booty was distributed in the same way...... Plutarch goes on to remark that equality of the common meal was destroyed in course of time by the growth of luxury (he should rather have said the growth of private property) but persisted in the public distribution of meat at state sacrifices.... It may therefore be concluded that in its application to food, booty and land the idea of Moira reflects the collective distribution of wealth through three successive stages in the evolution of tribal society. Oldest of all was the distribution of food, which goes back to the hunting period. Next comes the distribution of chattels and inanimate movables acquired by warfare, which was a development of hunting, and, last, the division of land for purposes of agriculture."

Now let us view the Vedic system of distribution in view of what has been stated above. Chattopadhyaya[82] points out on the evidence of the *Nighaṇṭu* that words like *brahman*, etc., have originally meant food and material wealth at the same time, thus referring to a period, when the distinction between the idea of food and that of material wealth did not develop. The division of food, which goes back to the hunting period according to Thomson, is found in a few verses of the *Ṛgveda*. Indra is described as the divider of the shares (*bhāga*) of food (*vāja*),[83] and as such regarded as the mightiest among the gods.[84] But the most significant reference to the division of food

81. *Aeschylus and Athens*, pp. 38-44.
82. *op. cit.*, pp. 570-78.
83. *RV.* III. 49. 4.
84. 36.VI.1.

along with a distinct mention of *common meal* is found in the *Atharvaveda*: "Having superiors, intentful, *be ye not divided, accomplishing together, moving on with joint labour*; Come hither speaking what is agreeable one to another; I make you united, like-minded. Your drinking (be) the same, *in common your share of food*; in the same harness do I join you together; worship ye Agni united, like spokes about a name."[85]

Evidently these passages refer to a period of primitive communism when collective labour and common meal determined human relationships. The next stage was marked, according to Thomson, by the distribution of advanced wealth in the form of cattle, etc., and subsequently that of chattels and inanimate movables acquired by warfare. This type of wealth is indicated in the *Ṛgveda* by the term *vārya,* which has been interpreted by Sāyana as 'wealth in the form of cattle' (*gavādi dhanānām*) and also as 'wealth in the form of crops (*vrīhi-yavādinām*). Although wealth in the form of cattle or crops indicate an advanced, i.e., class-divided state of social development, the word for wealth still concealed within itself the old communistic conception. In its derivative meaning, *vārya* is that (coming from the root *Vṛṃ*) which is *by nature* divisible. Likewise the word *bhāga* stood at the same time for 'wealth' and 'share', thus indicating that there was originally no wealth that was not shared out. Division of wealth looted from the aliens occurs frequently in the *Ṛgveda,*[86] and in many such verses the ancient law of division is stressed. Thomson's third category, viz. the division of land, is practically absent in the *Ṛgveda* because, as we have said many times, the early Vedic peoples were predominantly pastoral. They were more interested in counting wealth in terms of cattle, and their attention to agriculture was drawn only at a later period.[87]

11. The Sabhāsthānu

In view of what we have stated above now it is not difficult to understand the function of the *Sabhāsthānu* or the dicer of the Vedic

85. III. 30. 5-6; Whitney's tr., I. pp. 138-39.
86. I. 20. 8; I. 73. 5; I. 102. 4; I. 103. 6; I. 112. 1; I. 135. 2-3; I. 162. 3; I. 183. 4; II. 10. 6; II. 19. 5; II. 23. 2; II. 24. 14; III. 28. 4; III. 30. 18; V. 42. 5; V. 86. 5; VI. 22. 4; VII. 56. 21; VIII. 36. 1-6; VIII. 96. 8; VIII. 96. 21; X. 51. 2; X. 114. 3; etc.
87. See Ch. I. Sec. 10, 12.

assembly. Macdonell and Keith[88] say: "*Sabhā* is the name of the assembly of the Vedic Indians as well as the hall where they met in assembly.... The hall was clearly used for dicing, presumably when the assembly was not transacting public business; a dicer is called *Sabhāsthānu,* pillar of the assembly, doubtless because of his constant presence there". But this interpretation of the *Sabhā* as the gambling house is misleading. As we have already noticed, the *Sabhā* was an assembly of tribal administration where the task of the division of wealth was carried out, and as such, it was the venue of casting the lot which was the technique of ensuring impartiality in the matter of distribution of wealth among the clans. This was the reason why the dicer was called *Sabhāsthānu,* (lit. 'the pillar of the assembly').

12. Annihilation of Ṛta: The Śunaḥśepa Legend

Indeed there was once a time, says *Ṛgveda*,[89] when the gods used to assemble together and accept equal shares. But this equality was not permanent. Eventually Indra demanded the lion's share of the booty.[90] This is a notable feature of the disintegration of tribal society everywhere in the world. "The robber wars increased the power of the supreme military commander as well as of the sub-commanders. The customary election of successors from one family, especially after the introduction of father-right, was gradually transformed into hereditary succession, first tolerated, then claimed and finally usurped. The foundation of hereditary royalty and hereditary nobility was laid. In this manner the organs of the gentile constitution were gradually torn from roots in the people, in gens, phratry and tribe and the whole gentile order was transformed into its opposite: from an organisation of tribes for the free administration of their own affairs it became an organisation for plundering and oppressing their neighbours; and correspondingly, its organs were transformed from instruments of the will of the people into independent organs for ruling and oppressing their own people".[91]

This also accounts for the fall of Varuṇa who was in the *Ṛgveda* the eternal bestower of wealth, the friend of mankind, the strict

88. *Vedic Index*, II. p. 426.
89. X. 191. 2. Cf. Ch. I. Sec. 10.
90. Cf. VII. 32. 12.
91. Engels, *op. cit.*, pp. 267-69.

upholder of moral laws. But when with the greed of wealth the basis of ancient *Ṛta,* of tribal morality, was destoryed, when property differences changed the original character of the community, the god was also transformed into a greedy one, a bad fellow, ugly in his insatiable demands. As Keith[92] rightly observes: "The figure of Varuṇa does not increase in moral value in the course of the development of the Vedic religion.... Varuṇa is remembered as the god who has fetters and becomes in the Brāhmaṇas a *dreaded god* whose ritual in some measure is assimilated to that of the demons and the dead. After the performance of the bath, which ends the Agniṣṭoma sacrifice, the performer turns away and does not look back *to escape from Varuṇa's notice,*[93] and in the ceremony of that bath when performed after the horse sacrifice, a man of peculiar appearance is driven into the water and an offering made on his head, as being a representative of Varuṇa[94]: this form of the expulsion of evils shows Varuṇa reduced to a somewhat humble level, and degraded from his Ṛgvedic eminence."

This Varuṇa is really the ghost of the Ṛgvedic Varuṇa. In the Śunaḥśepha legend of the *Aitareya Brāhmaṇa,* which reflects the ugliest aspects of class society, this friend and benefactor of human beings is transformed into an importunate creditor. King Hariścandra was sonless. He was very eager to have children and desperately promised that if a son was born to him he would sacrifice that child to Varuṇa. Accordingly a son, Rohita by name, was born to him and at once Varuṇa demanded his due. Hariścandra requested him to wait for ten days. Ten days over, Varuṇa reappeared with his claim. This time the king said that a victim is not fit for sacrifice until its teeth appear, and in this way he was able to befool Varuṇa again and again till Rohita became an adult. But Varuṇa was an importunate creditor. He again appeared with his uncanny demand. Rohita who had by this time become adult did not want to get himself killed at the sacrifice. He took his bow and left the palace. The angry and disappointed god, unable to get Rohita in his grasp, sent waters into the belly of the king.

Rohita then began to wander in the forests. In the forest he suddenly came across a poor person, Ajīgarta by name, who had

92. *op. cit.,* pp. 247-48.
93. *Taittirīya Saṃhitā,* VI. 6. 35; *Maitrāyaṇī Saṃhitā,* IV. 8. 5.
94. *Āpastamba Śrauta Sūtra,* XIII. 19. 1.
95. VII. 13 ff.

three sons—Śunaḥpuccha, Śunaḥśepa and Śunolāṅgula. Rohita purchased Śunaḥśepa having given one hundred cows to Ajīgarta. Varuṇa had no objection in accepting Śunaḥśepa as a substitute for Rohita. As none was found to bind Śunaḥśepa to the sacrificial post, his greedy father Ajīgarta performed that task when he was offered one hundred cows in addition to the one hundred he had already received. And for another one hundred he did not even hesitate to undertake the task of slaughtering his own son.

The story, however, did not end in complete tragedy. Śunaḥśepa was saved by the grace of the ancient Vedic deities whom he invoked when he was bound to the sacrificial post. What we learn from this story is that Śunaḥśepa was not the victim of a simple sacrifice. He was, in fact, the victim of the greed, selfishness and cruelty of class society. It was a society where the gods, like their human prototypes, were merciless monsters; men with wealth could do anything and everything; a father, driven by hunger, would sell his son for a hundred cows, bind him for another hundred and slay him for another. This was what the Vedic poets categorically said: *fall from the Ṛta—Nirṛti*. The sacrificial victim, rather the victim of circumstances, could only thus desire in vain: keep us away from Nirṛti.[96] Maddened by the grim forces of this *Nirṛti*, the poet exclaims: I ask thee, O Yajña,. . . where is the *Ṛta* of the past gone? Who is the new one that holds it? Where is the *Ṛta* of yours gone? Where, O gods, is the holding of the *Ṛta*? Where is the watchfulness of Varuṇa?[97]

The priests of the Rājasūya were also slaves of king's wealth, unable either to get rid of the regime of *Nirṛti* or to bring back the old days of *Ṛta*, and what they could do under such circumstances was to recollect the events through which the annihilation of the *Ṛta* was complete.

96. *RV.* I. 26. 9.
97. *ib.*, I. 105. 4-6.

III

FOOD AND DRINK

A Study in the Rituals of the Vājapeya

1. Prologue

The rituals of the Vājapeya sacrifice, although represented in a very sophisticated way in later Vedic literature, are really important for the study in the prehistory of the sacrifical cult itself. Elsewhere[1] we have argued that the principles underlying the Vedic sacrifices were not basically different from those of magic and that the latter was neither a pseudo-science nor an abortive art but a direct means of food production, 'an illusory technique complementary to the deficiencies of the real technique'.[2] In fact, the relations between the principles of magic and those of the Vedic rituals have long been recognised and commented on. Winternitz, for example, has remarked the following with reference to the hymns of the *Atharvaveda:* "Indeed, many of these magic songs, like the magic rites pertaining to them, belong to a sphere of conceptions which, spread over the whole earth, even recur with the most surprising similarity in the most varying peoples of all countries. Among the Indians of North America, among the Negro races of Africa, among the Malays and Mongols, among the ancient Greeks and Romans, and frequently still among the peasantry of present-day Europe, we find again exactly the same views, exactly the same strange leaps of thought in the magic songs and magic rites, as has come down to us in the *Atharvaveda* of the ancient Indians. There are, then, numerous verses in the *Atharvaveda,* which according to their character and often also their contents, differ just as little from the magic formulas of the American-Indian medicine-men and Tartar shamans, as from the Merseburg magic maxims, which belong to the spare remains of the

1. Ch. I. Sec. 8; Ch. II. Sec. 1.
2. G. Thomson, *Studies in Ancient Greek Society,* London 1949, I, p. 38; *Aeschylus and Athens,* London 1941, pp. 13-14.

oldest German poetry".[3] But what has not been demonstrated by Winternitz is the social basis of this identical pattern of tribal beliefs and practices. This we want to do here with special reference to the rituals of the Vājapeya, an agricultural affair which was later transformed into one of the principal ceremonies of royal inauguration. In order to account for this transformation we are led by the proposition that man's consciousness of the external world is determined by the relation which he establishes with his fellow beings *in the development of production,* and this alone explains why the external world appears so differently to peoples belonging to different levels of culture and even to different classes of a given society.

2. The Vājapeya and the Rājasūya

According to the existing tradition, the Vājapeya was one of the principal ceremonies of royal inauguration which bestowed upon the performer a superior kind of monarchy called *Sāmrājya.* According to Eggeling,[4] the reason why this sacrifice had received a special treatment is that, unlike other forms of Soma-sacrifice, it had some striking features indicating its political character. According to the later Sūtra literature,[5] the performance of the Vājapeya should be arranged in much the same way as that of the Rājasūya. The *Śatapatha Brāhmaṇa* indicates that the Vājapeya is a ceremony of superior value which has probably led Kātyāyana[6] to note that the Rājasūya may be performed by a king who has not yet performed the Vājapeya. According to the evidence furnished by the Brāhmaṇa literature, the Rājasūya confers upon the sacrificer royal dignity (*rājya*) and the Vājapeya paramount sovereignty (*sāmrājya*). It is also to be noticed in this connection that while the Rājasūya was entirely a Kṣatriya ceremony, the Vājapeya might be performed even by the Brāhmaṇas. This implies an original non-royal character of the ceremony, and that is why Āśvalāyana[7] says that after performing the Vājapeya a king may perform Rājasūya and a Brāhmaṇa the Bṛhaspatisava. "With this rule would seem to accord the

3. Winternitz, *History of Indian Literature,* Calcutta 1927, I. p. 128.
4. Eggeling in *SBE,* XLI, *intro.*
5. For details see P. V. Kane, *History of Dharmaśāstra,* Poona 1941, pp. 1206 ff.
6. *Kāt. S. S.,* XV. 1. 1-2.
7. IX, 9. 19.

relative value assigned to the two ceremonies in the *Taittirīya Saṃhitā* (V. 6. 2. 1) and *Brāhmaṇa* (II. 7. 6. 1), according to which the Vājapeya is a *Samrātsava* or consecration to the dignity of a paramount sovereign, while the Rājasūya is called a *Varuṇasava,* i.e., according to Sāyana, a consecration to the universal sway wielded by Varuṇa. In much the same sense we have doubtless to understand the rule in which Lātyāyana defines the object of the Vājapeya (VIII. II. I), viz. 'whomsoever the Brāhmaṇas and kings (or nobles) may place at their head, let him perform the Vājapeya'. All these authorities, with the exception of the *Śatapatha Brāhmaṇa* and Kātyayāna, are thus agreed in making the Vājapeya a preliminary ceremony, performed by a Brāhmaṇa who is raised to the dignity of a purohita, or head-priest or by a king who is elected paramount sovereign by a number of petty rājās; this sacrifice being in due time followed by the respective installation and consecration ceremony, viz. the *Bṛhaspatisava,* in the case of the Purohita, and the Rājasūya, in that of the king. In regard to the *Bṛhaspatisava,* which these authorities place on an equality with the Rājasūya our Brāhmaṇa (i.e., *Śatapatha*) finds itself in a somewhat awkward position, and it gets out of its difficulty (V. 2. 1. 19) by simply identifying the *Bṛhaspatisava* with the Vājapeya, and making the Vājapeya itself to be 'the consecration of Bṛhaspati' and Kātyāyana (XIV. 1. 2) compromises matters by combining the two ceremonies in this way that he who performs the Vājapeya is to perform the Bṛhaspatisava for a fortnight before and after the Vājapeya".[8]

3. The Essentials of the Vājapeya[9]

The first important ritual of the Vājapeya is that of collective drinking, a continuation of the preceding *Ṣoḍaśī* rite in which the sacrificer offers five Vājapeya cups to Indra (uttering *Vāj. Saṃ.* IX. 2-4) and also seventeen cups of Soma and seventeen cups of Surā to thirtyfour gods (the traditional thirty three and Prajāpati as the thirtyfourth) deposited on earth-mounds situated in front of or behind the axle. This is a type of *Ekāha* sacrifice consisting of three services or pressings (*savana*) at each of which certain cups of liquor are drawn, to be ultimately consumed by the priests and sacrificer after

8. Eggeling, *op. cit.*, p. XXV.
9. *Śat Br.*, X. 1. 2-5; V. 2. 1-2.

libations to the respective deities. At certain stated times during the performance, hymns are chanted by the Udgātṛ followed by an appropriate recitation of verses by the Hotṛ or his assistant. The *Vājapeya-sāman,* the seventeenth chant in addition to the sixteen of the *Ṣoḍaśī,* is sung in the *Bṛhati*-tune and in *Saptadaśa* (Seventeen) *stoma.*

As a form of Soma-sacrifice, animal sacrifice (*paśubandhu*) is an integral ritual of the Vājapeya. Over and above the three victims of the *Ṣoḍaśī* rite, the Vājapeya requires not only a fourth one, dedicated to Sarasvatī, the goddess of speech and a fifth one for the Maruts, but also a set of seventeen victims for Prajāpati, the god of creatures and procreation. The one for the victorious Maruts must be a spotted sterile cow and those for Prajāpati must be all hornless, all dark grey and all male animals. Before their ceremonial slaughter the Hotṛ would recite the *Vāmadevya Sāman,* and after the offerings are made the omenta of the victims are to be taken.

Then the ritual of the consecration of the sacrificer takes place which begins with a chariot race. The chariot itself is conceived as Indra's thunderbolt which is seized by the pole and turned from left to right with *mantras* (*Vāj. Saṃ.* IX. 5. ff.) addressed to Aditi, the Great Mother. Four horses are then anointed and yoked to the chariot. Then wild-rice is cooked and served in seventeen plates which the horses are made to smell. The *Vājināṃ Sāman* (*SV,* I. 435) is sung which says: 'The fiery steeds have gathered fiery mettle, the impulse of the god Savitṛ; win ye the heaven, O coursers'! (cf. *Lāt. S. S.,* V. 12. 14). Seventeen drums are beaten. Besides the sacrificer's chariot inside the *Vedī,* sixteen others, each drawn by four horses, are got ready, outside the Vedī, for the race to the *Uḍumbara* branch as its goal and turning-point. The *Uḍumbara* branch which serves as the goal is planted at the end of the seventeenth arrow's range, shoot by the sacrificer northwards through the space between the *utkara* and *cātvāla.* Then the sacrificer steps on the chariot with a hymn (*Vāj. Saṃ.* IX. 13; cf. *Taitt. Saṃ.* 1. 7. 7. 2) addressed to Savitṛ. While the cars are on move the Adhvaryu utters verses from the *Ṛgveda* (IV. 40. 3-4; VII. 38. 7-8; X. 64. 4) and the *Vājasaneyi Saṃhitā* (IX. 15-18). After the cars have come back with the sacrificer keeping ahead of the others, the victorious horse is again anointed.

The race over, the priest takes the sacrificer to the Āhavanīya fire in which offering of clarified butter is made. He utters twelve *Apits,* formulas congratulating individuals (cf. *Vāj. Saṃ.* IX. 20), or makes the sacrificer pronounce them. The priest then utters six *Kliptis*, formulas praising the sacrificial cult itself (cf. *Vāj. Saṃ.* IX. 21), or makes the sacrificer pronounce them.

The eight-cornered sacrificial post is then wrapt up or bound up in seventeen cloths. There is a *wheaten* head-piece. Instead of the ordinary mortar-shaped top-piece, fixed on the post, here it is made of wheaten dough. The post has a hollow at the top and it is not pointed at the end. It is seventeen cubits long. The priest then brings the sacrificer's wife, makes her wrap round herself a garment of *Kuśa* grass[10] and causes her to propitiate the sacrifice. A ladder is fixed up on the post, and the sacrificer says: 'Come, wife, ascend we the sky'. 'Ascend We,' also says the wife. The sacrificer and his wife then ascend and touch the wheaten top-piece. According to the ritual of the Black Yajus,[11] the sacrificer, having ascended, lifts up his arms to heaven, praying 'we have gone to the light, to the gods; we have become immortal; we have become Prajāpati's children'. Men standing below then throw up to him seventeen small packets of salt made in *Aśvattha* leaves, and he sprinkles the salt as homage paid to Mother Earth.

The sacrificer descends on a piece of gold and steps upon a piece of skin spread out by the priest. A throne, made of *Uḍumbara* wood, is placed for him in front of the *Havirdhāna* (cartshed) behind the *Āhavanīya* (fire). The priest placing him on the throne says: 'This is thy kingship; thou art the ruler, the ruling lord; thou art firm and steadfast; thee for the tilling; thee for peaceful dwelling; thee for wealth; thee for thrift'.

Seated on the throne the sacrificer offers seven *Vāja-prasavanīya* oblations. Seventeen kinds of food are brought in a vessel made of *Uḍumbara* wood by which the oblations are made. Hymns from the *Vājasaneyi Saṃhitā* IX. 23-29 are uttered in praise of Soma, Agni, Aryaman, Bṛhaspati, Indra, Viṣṇu, Puṣan, Aśvins, Savitṛ and Vāk (Sarasvatī). The sacrificer then is made to sit on a black antelope skin, with his face to the east and with a small gold and silver plate placed on either side of him. Having got himself anointed in that position, he pronounces the formulas of the *Ujjiti* (victory) oblations and says: 'With the (word of) one syllable Agni won the breath: may I win that; with the (metre of) seventeen syllables Prajāpati

10. In the ceremonial of the Black *Yajus* the sacrificer himself has to put on a *tārpya* garment. See *Taitt. Br.*, 1. 3. 7. 1.
11. Sāyana on *Taitt. Saṃ.*, I. 7. 9.

won the seventeenfold *stoma*: may I win that'.

4. Keith on the Popular Character of the Vājapeya

The aforesaid rituals, to be performed by the kings, are presented in a very sophisticated way in the Brāhmaṇa and the Sūtra texts. But, as Keith[12] has rightly pointed out, "in sacerdotalizing the rite the priests have still retained its popular features.... (1) There is a race of seventeen chariots in which the sacrificer is victorious. The purpose of this rite is doubtless, as stated by Oldenberg, to secure the sacrificer by magic the swiftness of the victorious steeds as strength. (2) The sacrificer with his wife mounts on a chariot wheel, obviously a symbol of the sun, which is placed on the top of a long pole. The joint action of the two is significant of the popular character of of the rite, and the act is again a magic device to secure the exaltation of the sacrificer. (3) After his descent from the pole the sacrificer is anointed and proclaimed as victor. The anointing is intended to confer on him the power of oblation which is used for the anointing. (4) Before the descent the priests of the people touch him with bags of salt earth in *Aśvattha* leaves or in *Aśvattha* boxes, clearly as a means of securing fertility, showing that the offering is more than a mere piece of magic for the glorification of any individual person. With this is in harmony the insistence of the *Śāṅkhyāyana* (XV. 1. 1) on the fact that the rite is available to any one who desires *annādya*, (i.e., the eating of the food) and the name is explained as 'food and drink'.... Moreover, this accords with the Mantras used in touching the sacrificer, *annāya tvā* (i.e., to you for the sake of food) etc. and the rule in *Śāṅkhyāyana* (XVI. 17. 4) that the offering can be made for a Vaiśya, to which may be added the consecration of the sacrificer for *Kṛṣī* in the *Vājasaneyi* (IX. 22) and possibly the connection of the Maruts, the 'people among the gods', with the rite". Accepting these views as dependable working hypotheses we shall now turn our attention to the particulars of the aforesaid rituals and the range of their suggestivity.

5. The Ritual of Collective Drinking

Drinking had always been an essential feature of the Vedic

12. *Veda of the Black Yajus School*, HOS, 1914, pp. CX-CXI.

sacrifices and hence it must have a great ritual significance, the nature of which we are expected to discover. The common form of wine used by the Vedic people was called *Soma* which occupied a very important place in Vedic literature, being considered as the means through which men could overcome death and attain immortality.[13] Soma was also a Vedic god and the important rituals centering round this god (*Somayāga*-s) are quite well known. Two other kinds of wine, *Surā* and *Pariśrut,* were also known to the Vedic peoples and these two kinds were used especially in the Vājapeya sacrifice.

In later Tantric tradition the use of wine is also well known. Wine is one of the five *Pañcamakāras* of the Tantric cults. What, therefore, does the ritual use of wine really mean? Scholars who have tried to rationalise or justify Tantra have resorted on the one hand to the mystic interpretations of such rituals, and on the other, tried their best to find out a suitable Vedic basis for them. But this approach goes against all canons of historical enquiry. On the basis of some valuable data, we have, however, come to the conclusion that ritual use of wine is a very primitive practice, originally connected with fertility magic, and that this old practice under different historical conditions made its way into the patriarchal Vedic tradition and also in the matriarchal Tantric tradition. Interestingly enough, this argument finds support in Keith's interpretation of the Vājapeya in which he says that wine in the said function was clearly related to 'the ceremonial rituals in connexion with fertility magic'.[14]

William Crooke[15] has shown that the idea that liquor is the vehicle of magical power lies at the root of the tribal rituals all over India. He has cited numerous examples of the ritual use of liquor for the purpose of ensuring the fertility of the fields. As for example, the Oraons before transplanting of the rice-seedlings make a libation of wine on the ground; the Baigas before cultivation scatter a line of wine along the boundary of the cultivable land. It is due to the fact that in primitive thought wine was regarded as a life giving principle. Chattopadhyaya[16] has furnished two sets of examples to show that (1) liquor is resorted to for the purpose of overcoming death and that (2) the use of liquor is designed to ensure birth. That wine

13. Cf. *RV*. IV. 48. 3.
14. *Religion and Philosophy of the Veda*, p. 91.
15. *Religion and Folklore of Northern India*, Oxford 1926, pp. 100 ff.
16. *Lokāyata*, Delhi 1968, pp. 309 ff.

overcomes the contamination of death (cf. the Ṛgvedic passage: We have drunk the Soma and have become immortal) is evidenced from the funeral rites among backward people in different parts of the world. "The Irish wake is a familiar example of the practice of drinking to celebrate death. In West Africa the Tshi people drink heavily during the fast which follows a death.... The same is the case among the Yorubas.... At funerals among the Woolwa Indians there is much drinking of *mishla*.... As soon as a Bangala man dies, the family gets in large supplies of sugarcane wine.... The Guina Indians drink and dance at the funeral feast.... Among the Tshinyai of the Zambesi the native beer, *pombe*, plays a considerable part in post-funeral rites...."[17] Similar use of wine in the funeral rite is not at all uncommon in India. One of the commonest name for locally made wine in India is *mṛtasañjivanī*, that which restores life.[18] The same belief probably explains the use of wine in the puberty rites, the essence of which is death and rebirth.[19] Wine plays an important part in the marriage rituals all over the world as an agent of procreation.[20] One of the best known examples of the belief in wine inducing the reproductive urge in the human being is retained in the creation legend of the Santals.[21] So in primitive thought wine is the agent that helps man not only to overcome death but also to create new life, and it is here that the ritual use of wine for enhancing fertility of the earth is to be sought.

6. The Chariot Race

As regards other rites peculiar to the Vājapeya, the most interesting is the chariot race in which the sacrificer is made victorious. Professor Hillebrandt claims for this feature of the sacrifice the character of a relic of an old national festival, a kind of Indian Olympic games.[22] Oldenberg says that the purpose of this rite is to secure the sacrificer by magic the swiftness of the victorious steeds as strength, and Keith accepts this interpretation without any modification.[23]

17. *Encyclopaedia of Religion and Ethics*, V. pp. 79-80. See ch. VIII. pp. 153-54.
18. Chattopadhyaya, *op. cit.*, p. 310.
19. See my *Indian Puberty Rites*, Calcutta 1968, pp. 5 ff.
20. *ERE*, V. p. 80.
21. *JASB* (SC) XIX, pp. 12-14; Chattopadhyaya, *op. cit.*, pp. 310-11.
22. Eggeling, *op. cit.*, p. XXIV.
23. *Veda of the Black Yajus School*, p. CX.

But this rite can not be dissociated from the previous rite of collective drinking as regards the question of purpose. It is also a clear fertility rite. Sir James George Frazer has drawn our attention to the tradition that the great games of Greece originated in funeral celebrations and that the tradition is confirmed by the Greek practice. Thus in the Homeric age funeral games including chariot-races, foot-races, wrestling, boxing, spear-throwing, quoit-throwing and archery were celebrated in honour of the dead heroes at their barrows.[24] Frazer gives plenty of examples to show that these funeral games were supposed to ensure plenty of corn, fruit, milk and fish.[25] As is known to all, funeral rites and fertility rites are closely linked up all over the world. The death and revival of plant life have not only given us a good number of primitive myths but also have contributed to the growth of the ideas of resurrection and rebirth and given rise to numerous cults and rituals. The primitive female figurines in many cases are grim embodiments of the Mother or Earth Goddess who is also the guardian of the dead—'an underworld deity connected alike with the corpse and the seed-corn buried beneath the earth'.[26] One should not fail to recall in this connection that *a cult of Mother Goddess* is conspicuously present in the section dealing with the ritual of the Chariot race.[27]

Later on, however, the original purpose of the Chariot race became somewhat changed, and like the Akṣa of the Rājasūya, it came to be used as a means of the distribution of wealth. In the Vājapeya, the king's participation in the chariot race is a symbolic miming of this old custom. That the chariot race had something to do with the ancient system of distribution is evident from the Vājapeya legend which says: "*The gods went on making offerings unto one another. Prajāpati gave himself up to them: then the sacrifice became theirs; and indeed the sacrifice is the food of the gods. They then spake, 'To which of us shall this belong?' They did not agree together, saying, 'To me; To me'; 'Not being agreed', they said, 'Let us run a race for it: Whichever of us shall win, to him it shall belong;'—'So be it;' So they ran a race for it*".[28]

24. *Iliad*, XXIII. 255 ff.; 629 ff.; 657 ff.
25. *The Golden Bough*, Part III, 1966 edition, pp. 92-105. See ch. VIII. pp. 152-55.
26. Cf. Piggott, *Prehistoric India*, p. 127.
27. *Śat. Br.*, V. 1. 4. 4.
28. *Ib.*, V. 1. 1. 2-3.

7. Food and Drink

According to Eggeling Vājapeya means 'drink of strength' or the 'race cup', but he has overlooked the most simple meaning which is *Food and Drink*.[29] In fact every line of the *Śatapatha Brāhmaṇa* clearly suggests that originally the Vājapeya was a simple magical performance employed as a productive technique to obtain food and drink. Here we are quoting a number of passages from the said *Brāhmaṇa* in order to substantiate our assumption.

"Thereupon he seizes a spotted sterile cow for the victorious Maruts; for the spotted sterile cow is this (earth): Whatever food, rooted or rootless, is here established on her, thereby she is a spotted cow. Now, he who offers the Vājapeya wins food, for Vāja-peya doubtless means the same as *anna-peya*(food and drink); and the Maruts are the *peasants,* and the *peasants* are *food* (for the nobles)."[30]

"He now takes out material for *wild rice* of seventeen plates for Bṛhaspati; for he who offers the Vājapeya wins food,—Vāja-peya being doubtless the same as *anna-peya*: thus whatever *food* he has thereby won, that he now prepares for him".[31]

"He then steps over against (the horses) with the Bārhaspatya pap, and touches it; for he who offers Vājapeya wins *food* since Vāja-peya is the same as *anna-peya:* whatever Food he has thus gained that he now, having reached the goal, brings in contact with himself, puts within himself."[32]

"And as to why he touches the *wheat:* wheat is food, and he who offers the Vājapeya, wins food, for Vāja-peya is the same as *anna-peya:* thus whatever food he has thereby won, therewith now that he has gone to that supreme goal, he puts himself in contact and possesses himself of it,—therefore he touches the wheat (top piece)."[33]

"They throw up to him bags of salt; for *salt means cattle, and cattle is food;* and he who offers the Vājapeya wins food, for Vāja-peya is same as *anna-peya:* thus whatever food he thereby has gained, therewith now that he has gone to the supreme goal, he puts himself in contact, and makes it his own—therefore they throw bags of salt

29. Kane, *op. cit.*, p. 1206.
30. *Śat. Br.,* V. 1. 3. 3.
31. *ib.*, V. 1. 4. 12.
32. *ib.*, V. 1. 5. 25.
33. *ib.*, V. 2. 1. 13.

up to him."[34]

"He now proceeds with the Bārhaspatya pap. Its *Sviṣṭakṛt* remains yet unoffered when he (the Adhvaryu) brings him (the Sacrificer) some food; for he who offors the Vājapeya wins food, *Vāja-peya* being the same as *anna-peya:* thus whatever food he (the Sacrificer) has thereby gained, that he (the Adhvaryu) now brings to him."[35]

"May the Lord of Speech render our meat palatable, hail: For the Lord of Speech is Prajāpati, and meat means food: May Prajāpati this day make palatable this our food."[36]

"That chariot, seized by the pole, he turns (from left to right) so as to make it stand inside the *Vedī*, with, 'in the winning of wealth, the *Great Mother*'—Wealth means food: in the winning of *food*, the *Great Mother*."[37]

"O Divine waters, what rushing, high-peaked, wealth-winning wave ye have, therewith may this one win wealth; *Wealth is food:* he thus says, May he thereby gain food".[38]

"With that strength be thou strong and wealth-winning for us, O Courser, and victorious at the gathering: Wealth means food: he thus means to say, '*And be thou a food-winner for us at this our sacrifice*, at the gathering of the gods win thou this sacrifice, Prajāpati."[39]

"May gain of wealth come to me; Wealth means food; he thus says: May gain of food come to me: May these two, Heaven and Earth, the all-shaped, come to me; for Prajāpati is Heaven and Earth."[40]

8. The Sāmans

The above citations sufficiently reveal the original purpose of the Vajāpeya. That the Vajāpeya primarily stood for a magical performance as a technique of food production is also proved by the *Sāmans* associated with it. The word *Sāman* is generally interpreted as 'melody', although not in the modern sense of the term. To quote Winternitz[41]: "The priests and theologians certainly did not invent

34. *ib.*, V. 2. 1. 16.
35. *ib.*, V. 2. 2. 1.
36. *ib.*, V. 1. 1. 16.
37. *ib.*, V. 1. 4. 4.
38. *ib.*, V. 1. 4. 6.
39. *ib.*, V. 1. 4. 10.
40. *ib.*, V. 1. 4. 26.
41. *op. cit.*, I, pp. 167-168; italics added.

all these melodies themselves. The oldest of them were presumably popular melodies to which in very early times semi-religious songs were sung at solstice celebrations and other national festivals, and yet others may date back as far as that noisy music with which pre-brahmanical wizard-priests—not unlike the magicians, shamans and medicine-men of the primitive peoples—accompanied their wild songs and rites. Traces of this popular origin of the *Sāman*-melodies are seen already in the above-mentioned *stobhas* or shouts of joy, and specially in the fact that the melodies of the *Sāmaveda* were looked upon as *possessing magic powers* even as late as in the brahmanical times. There is a ritual book belonging to the *Sāmaveda,* called *Sāmavidhāna-Brāhmaṇa,* the second part of which *is a regular handbook of magic, in which the employment of various Sāmans for various purposes is taught.*"

The *Sāmans* are therefore primitive songs intended to achieve some definite purpose. "The common speech of the savages," writes Thomson,[42] "has a strongly marked rhythm and a lilting melodic accent. In some languages the accent is so musical, and so vital to the meaning, that when a song is composed the tune is largely dictated by the natural melody of the spoken words.... And if their common speech is poetical, their poetry is magical. The only poetry they know is song, and their singing is nearly always accompanied by some bodily action, designed to effect some change in the external world—to impose *illusion* on *reality*". Winternitz[43] points out that one of the main characteristics of the *Sāmans* is that when these are chanted the priests have to make some bodily actions. Moreover, the *Sāmans* are of two kinds—*Grāmageya* (to be sung in the villages) and *Araṇyageya* (to be sung in the forests). The purpose of chanting them outside the locality was certainly magical. Otherwise there was no need of chanting them in the forests.

Sri B. P. Mishra in an informative article[44] has shown that each of the *Sāmans* of the *Pañcaviṃśa Brāhmaṇa* was employed for a material purpose. Many of these *Sāmans* also occur in other texts including the *Śatapatha Brāhmaṇa* and, in connection with the Vājapeya, we have referred to some of them. The *Pañcaviṃśa Brāhmaṇa,*[45] which

42. *Studies in Ancient Greek Society,* I. pp. 439-40.
43. *Loc. cit.*
44. *Religious Life in Ancient India,* (ed. D. C. Sircar), Calcutta 1971.
45. XVIII. 6.

insists specially on the symbolic identity of Prajāpati and the Vājapeya, states that the latter consists of seventeen *stotras* and has for its characteristic mode of chanting the *Saptadaśa-stoma* or seventeen-versed hymn. For example, the *Bahiṣpavamāna-stotra,* which in the oridnary *Agniṣṭoma* is chanted in nine verses is at the Vājapeya made to consist of seventeen verses. Again, the *Mādhyandina-pavamāna,*ordinarily chanted in fifteen verses, here consists of seventeen. Likewise, the *Ārbhava-pavamāna* has been made so. The *Vājapeya-sāman,* otherwise called *Bṛhat-stotra,* also consists of seventeen verses.

However, the most important of all these is the *Vāmadevya-saman.* One should not fail to recall in this connection that this particular *Sāman* is specially described in the *Chāndogya Upaniṣad*[46] as a sexual rite identified with the *Yajña* itself. Every part of this *Sāman*—*Hiṅkāra, Prastāva, Udgītha, Pratihāra, Nidhāna*—is identified in this Upaniṣad with different modes of sexual intercourse. In the *Bṛhadāraṇyaka Upaniṣad*[47] these sex rites are elaborated and it is clearly stated that by performing sexual intercourse one acquires the merit of the *Vājapeya* sacrifice. The part played by sexual acts in agricultural rites is well known to all.[48] The *Vāmadevya Sāman*[49] is chanted during the Vājapeya celebration in connection with the offerings of animal victims to Prajāpati. The passage of the *Śatapatha Brāhmaṇa,*[50] which refers to the chanting of the *Vāmadevya,* undoubtedly presupposes the sexual rites of the *Chāndogya Upaniṣad.* It frankly states that *Vāmadevya* means *productivity.*

9. Yajña As the Productive Technique

In view of what we have stated above we are now in a position to assert that the Vājapeya was originally an agricultural magic performed exclusively for the purpose of food and drink. "Indeed the sacrifice is the food of the gods",[51] for Prajāpati told the gods: "The sacrifice (shall be) your food, immortality your sustenance (*ūrj*) and the sun of your light."[52] The relation between the Vāja-

46. II. 13. See Ch. I, Sec. 7.
47. VI. 4; etc.
48. See Ch. I, Sec. 7, 9.
49. *SV.* II. 32-34.
50. V. 1. 3. 12.
51. *Śat. Br.,* V. 1. 1. 2.
52. *ib.,* II. 4. 2. 1.

peya and agriculture is clearly demonstrated in the Vājapeya-hymn offered to the Maruts in which it is stated beyond all doubt that the Maruts are *peasants* and the peasants are food.[53] Equally significant is the ritual of the cooking of wild rice[54] which refers to the *collectional stage* of social evolution and thus pushes back the origin of the Vājapeya to a remote antiquity.

That the Vedic *Yajñas* were originally inseparable aspects of the primitive productive technique has been admitted even by the Vedic tradition itself. The *Aitareya Brāhmaṇa*[55] says that once the *Yajña* went away from the gods. At this the gods became very anxious and made desperate attempts to bring it back, because the loss of yajña meant a threat to the means of subsistence of the gods. This is proved by the following passage of the same text[56]: "The *Yajña* went away from the gods (saying) 'I shall not be your food'. 'No' replied the gods, 'Verily thou shalt be our food'. The gods crushed it; it being taken apart was not sufficient for them. The gods said, 'It will not be sufficient for us, being taken apart; come, let us gather together the yajña. (They replied) 'Be it so'. They gathered it together: having gathered it together they said to the Aśvins, 'Do ye two heal it'."

The gods crushed the *yajña* by violence on its refusal to serve them. They reduced it into shattered pieces to utilise its parts individually, but this attempt proved futile. Hence they called the divine physicians, the Aśvins, to revive the shattered pieces once again in the original undivided form. Although in the said myth forced after-thoughts were added by the priests, its significance is clear enough to assure us at least of two points that the *yajña* was originally connected with the mode of obtaining food and that it was of collective service, not to be appropriated by individuals in parts and portions.

Other passages of the *Aitareya Brāhmaṇa* also show that the *yajña* had originally been a vital aid to food production. "The *Yajña*, as food departed from the gods; the gods said, 'The *Yajña* as food hath left us; this *yajña*, food, let us sarch for'. They said, "How shall we search? 'By the *brahman* and the metres (*Chandas*); they said. They consecrated the Brāhmaṇa with the metres; for him they performed the *yajña* up to the end; they also performed the joint

53. *ib.*, V. 1. 3. 3.
54. *ib.*, V. 1. 4. 12-14.
55. III. 9.
56. I. 18; Keith, *Religion and Philosophy of the Veda*, p. 121.

offerings to the wives (of the gods). Therefore now also in the consecration offering they perform the *yajña* right up to the end, they also perform the joint offerings to the wives.... They performed the guest reception; to him with the guest reception they came nearer; they hastened with the performance. They made it end in the sacrificial food. Therefore now also the guest reception ends in *iḍā*....Having obtained him (*yajña*) they (the gods) said, 'Serve us for food'. 'No', he replied, how can I serve you? 'Then he only looked at. To him they said, 'with the *brahman* and the metres becoming united do thou serve us as food'. 'Be it so' (he replied). Therefore now also the *yajña* becoming united with the *brahman* and the metres bear the *yajña* to the gods".[57]

10. Yajna and Magic: The Collective Approach

The passage of the *Aitareya Brāhmaṇa,* quoted above, shows that the gods, evidently the remote ancestors of the Vedic peoples, revived sacrifice by *brahman* and *chandas*. The latter denotes metre or rhythm, but the significance of the former is misled by various interpretations. In the Upaniṣads, *brahman* is a term for the Absolute. Elsewhere *brahman* is the name of a god who is equated with Prajāpati. In the early Vedic texts *brahman* signifies a class of priests and also holy power, and as such it has a direct biaring on the term brāhmaṇa. But *brahman* is also a term for food and also for wealth in the *Ṛgveda.* The etymology of the name Brahmaṇaspati, as suggested by Sāyana,[58] is striking: *Brahmaṇaḥ annasya parivṛḍhasya karmaṇaḥ vāpate pālayati,* one that nourishes the activity of food production. According to the *Nighaṇṭu*[59] the word *brahman* is synonymous for *anna* (food) and wealth. Commenting upon the said interpretation Yāska has foreshadowed the *Taittirīya Upaniṣad* passages like *Jātāni Annena Vardhante,* etc.[60] Hence there is no doubt that, despite later interpretations, the word brahman originally stood for *anna* or food, which is recorded in the Vedic tradition itself. Likewise the word Brāhmaṇa, as is now evident, originally denoted the primitive magicians whose ritual assistance was required for producing and procuring *brahman.* According to Sāyana the word

57. III. 45; Keith, *op. cit.*, pp. 193-94.
58. On *RV*. II. 23. 1.
59. II. 7; II. 10.
60. II. 2.

brahman also stood for *stotra* or hymns, and this is also significant for our purpose.

The *Yajña* was restored also by *Chandas*. While dealing with the *Sāmans* we have seen that rhythm and metre, song and melody, were imagined as having magical efficacy in obtaining food. According to the *Bṛhadāraṇyaka Upaniṣad*,[61] in the beginning the world was covered over with death and hunger and these were overcome only by speech—the hymns (*ṛk*), the formulas (*yajus*), the chants (*sāman*), the metres (*chandas*) and the rituals (*yajña*). In many passages of the *Chāndogya Upaniṣad*[62] songs are clearly associated with food production. It is also said that the gods, being afraid of death, evidently from hunger, took shelter under the *Chaṇdas* or metres.[63] The importance attached to various metres like *gāyatrī, anustubh, bṛhatī, tristubh, jāgatī, virāj,* etc. in the Vedic literature is not therefore without any significance. That they were evidently meant to fulfil the desire of food has been shown by Chattopadhyaya[64] who has cited a number of significant verses from the *Ṛgveda*. "Then take they seat with us amidst the *gaṇa* and *sing that we may obtain food*—we who are singing (VI. 40. 1). "(O Agni) thou *with those songs bring the wealth attended with food;* we shall serve thee with our service (II. 6. 1)". "That Indra inspired and fulfilled the *desires of the Aṅgirasas expressed in songs for food* (II. 20. 5)". "Through Yajña the seer with desire got the cows with *songs* from the giver of water (II. 21. 5)." "The Agni Vaiśvānara, being realised as such in mind, we invoke *with songs* in the yajña, being desirous of food and wealth (III. 26. 1)". "The *haviḥ* offering placed on the *Kuśa*-grass and the *songs* make thee (the Aśvins) come to us with food in accordance with our wish (I. 117. 1)". "O Maruts, this panegyric is for thee: this *song* came to us who respect thee and melt thee (to charity) that *we may know the food,* as the spoils of victory, and meant for the (nourishment of the) body (I. 165. 15; I. 166. 15; I. 167. 11; I. 168. 10)".

One point which we must not overlook as regards the aforesaid verses is the collective approach. In every case we have *we* and *us* and not *I* or *me*. In *RV*. VI. 40. 1. quoted above, Indra is invoked to take his seat amidst the *gaṇa* and participate in the

61. I. 2. 1-5.
62. I. 3. 7; I. 13. 4; II. 8. 3; etc.
63. I. 4. 2.
64. *Lokāyata*, pp. 108 ff.

singing ritual for the purpose of obtaining food. Since *gaṇa* means tribe, the question of collective approach to material desires rises automatically. Those who sang the songs for food belonged to a stage of society at which the community was still an undivided whole. It was the proper environment for magic which rested entirely on collective psychology. Jane Harrison[65] observes: "One element in the rite we have already observed, and that is, that it must be done collectively, by a number of persons feeling the same emotion.... Collectivity and emotional tension, two elements that tend to turn the simple reaction into a rite, are—especially among primitive proples—closely associated, indeed scarcely separable. The individual among savages has but a thin and meagre personality; high emotional tension is to him only caused and maintained by a thing felt socially; it is what the tribe feels that is sacred, that is matter for ritual.... Intensity then and collectivity go together...."

Traces of this collectivity are found in the *Sattras*. The *Atharva-veda*[66] appears to regard the *Sattras* as *utsanna* (gone out of vogue) and this shows that these rituals were very ancient. The *Sattras* were sacrificial sessions, the duration of which varied from twelve days to a year or more. The *Sattras* were to be performed by many sacrificers (*Kātyāyana S. S.*, I. 6. 14; *Jaimini* VI. 6. 16. 23). There were no separate priests but the Yajamānas themselves were the priests (*Jaimini* X. 6. 45-59). A text quoted by Śabara on *Jaimini* VI. 2. 1. says that the persons who engaged together in a *Sattra* must be at least 17 and no more than 24, and each of the performers secured the same regard for which the *Sattra* was performed. There was no choosing of priests and no question of their remuneration (*Jaimini* X, 2. 34-38).[67] One of the most interesting days of this collective ritual in which all were Yajamānas was the *Mahāvrata* which was the last day but one in a *Sattra*. One should not fail to recall in this connection that *Mahāvrata* clearly means *anna* or food.[68] In this, besides the offering of a *mahāvratīya* cup of Soma in addition to the usual ones to Prajāpati, a harlot (?) and a brahmacārin abused (?) each other on the northern hip of the altar and *sexual intercourse between a man and a woman* took place in a

65. *Ancient Art and Ritual*, London 1935, pp. 36-37.
66. XI. 7. 7-8.
67. Kane, *op. cit.*, II. pp. 1241-42.
68. *Tāṇḍya Br.*, IV. 10. 2; *Śat. Br.*, IV. 6. 4. 2.

screened shed to the south of the *mārjālīya* shed.[69] Drums were beaten and songs were sung in which the wives of the performers and maidens also took active part. Girls, placing water-jars on their heads, danced thrice with the *mārjālīya* seat, striking the ground with their right feet and singing popular songs.[70]

Although from the later texts it is very difficult, rather impossible, to reconstruct the original *Sattra* rituals, which were so primitive that even in the days of the *Atharvaveda* they were regarded as things of hoary antiquity, the features which we have chalked from the later texts give us some idea of a primitive fertility rite in a primitive set up. There was no single yajamāna like a king or a wealthy person for whose welfare the sacrifice was to be performed. There were no priests who would perform the acts against sacrificial fees. The *Sattra* rituals were thus basically collective in which all were Yajamānas and priests at the same time. The *Mahavrata* was the ritual of food production in which natural fertility was viewed, as happened in the case of many primitive tribes all over the world,[71] in terms of human fertility, as the primitive peoples wanted to increase the generative powers of nature by sexual acts or their mimings.[72]

11. Metamorphosis of the Yajamāna

Now we are in a position to trace the process through which the primitive rites of food production like the Vājapeya were gradually transformed into the mechanical secerdotalism of the priestly class designed exclusively for the interest of the king or the ambitious individuals. We have seen that there was a plurality of the Yajamānas in the *Sattras*. According to Monier-Williams[73] a Yajamāna denoted "the person paying the cost of a sacrifice, the institutor of sacrifice (who, to perform it, employs a priest or priests, who are often hereditary functionaries in a family), any patron, host, rich man, head of a family or tribe". Evidently this is true so

69. *Kāt. S. S.*, XIII. 3. 9.
70. *Jaiminī*, X. 4. 8; *Āpastamba* S. S., XXI. 17. 15. 16.; XXI. 19. 17-20; XXI. 20; *Aitareya Āraṇyaka*, V. 1. 5.
71. J. G. Frazer. *The Golden Bough* (ab), pp. 136 ff.; R. Briffault, *The Mothers*, London 1952, III, pp. 3 ff.; 197 ff.
72. N. N. Bhattacharyya, *Indian Mother Goddess,* Calcutta 1970, Chs. II-III.
73. *Sanskrit-English Dictionary,* p. 839; Cf. Bloomfield in *JAOS*, XIX, p. 13; Keith, *Religion and Philosophy of the Veda*, p. 289.

far the later *Yajñas* in their sophisticated forms are concerned. But the etymology of the word yajamāna goes against such an impression. The word is derived from the root *yaj* to which the suffix *śānac* is added. According to Paṇini,[74] when the person derives the benefit of an action performed by himself, the suffix *śānac* is added to the root. Therefore etymologically *yajamāna* means, 'he who performs the sacrificial act for his own interest.' In later age, the Yajamāna was still the enjoyer of the fruit of sacrifice, but instead of performing it himself he got it done by the priests, and for this he had to pay a huge sum of money to them.

Chattopadhyaya[75] shows that in fact there are many indications in the *Ṛgveda* to confirm the etymological evidence that originally the Yajamānas themselves were the performers of the sacrificial acts in which the formidable array of priests was not required. Numerous examples from the *Ṛgveda*[76] can be cited to show that the important functions of the sacrifice were performed by the Yajamānas themselves without any aid of the priestly class. In a verse it is stated that on the banks of Asiknī the Yajamāna is, as it were, the Hotā.[77] Moreover, in an overwhelmingly large number of passages a pronounced collective bias is attributed to the functions of the Yajamānas, and we have not only the mention of a collective body of Yajamānas but also of their identity with the common tribesmen. "We, the Yajamānas, with favourable *mantras* (spells) invoke you (Agni)....One who fulfils the desire of the people (*Viśaḥ*)...."[78] "O Agni, the Yajamānas daily hold towards you all the best wealth—along with you, desiring wealth, the intelligent people opened wide the stall full of cows."[79] "The gods and the Yajamānas, the protector of the wind ask for the goddess *Śraddhā*; calling her with intense longing they gain wealth through Śraddhā."[80] "Sarasvatī, whom the fathers invoked and who, coming from the south, pervades the *Yajña*—may she give to the Yajamānas the shares (*bhāgam*) of the food, fostering wealth a thousand fold."[81]

74. I. 3. 72.
75. *Lokāyata.*, pp. 606 ff.
76. I. 24. 11; I. 51. 8; I. 81. 2; I. 83. 3; I. 92. 3; I. 138. 4; etc.
77. *RV.* IV. 17. 15.
78. I. 127. 2.
79. X. 45. 11.
80. X. 151. 4.
81. X. 17. 9.

"O Agni, the possessor of food, the expert sons of Vasiṣṭha invoked you in the assemblies (*Vidathesu*) with praises; do give us, the Yajamānas, increasing wealth and protect us always with well-wishes".[82]

Since it took a long period of time for the composition of the *Ṛgveda*, it is not difficult to find out passages indicating the functional differences between the Yajamānas and the priests. But originally there was no such difference as we have seen in connection with the *Sattras*. Keith[83] quotes the view of Oldenberg to show that the *Sattras* contain relics of primitive collective endeavour. Ganganath Jha[84] found it necessary to use the term 'communistic sacrifice' to denote the *Sattras*. Even the etymological meaning of the word *Yajurveda* is significant in this respect: '(They) performed the Yajña in the hoary past, *Yaj lit us*'. Thus, along with a reference to the past, there was, in the use of the plural, also a reference to the ancient collective functioning.[85]

In later times, with the emergence of class division, this collectivity was lost. The Yajamānas were no longer a collective entity, but wealthy individuals, usually Kṣatriya chiefs, and the task of performing the *Yajñas* rested essentially on the professional priests. In a passage of the *Aitareya Brāhmaṇa*[86] it is stated that the *Yajña* deserted the gods and it was pursued by the Brāhmaṇas and the Kṣatriyas. The Kṣatriyas, symbolising the lordly power, could not get hold of it by their weapons. But the Brāhmaṇas could, because, being blocked by them, the *yajña* recognised its own weapons of holy power in them. Hence it agreed to return to the Brāhmaṇas, and also to the Kṣatriyas, provided that they would resort to the holy power of the Brāhmaṇas. "From them the *Yajña* departed; it the holy power and the lordly power pursued: the holy power pursued with the weapons of the holy power; the lordly power with those of the lordly power. The weapons of the holy power are the weapons of the *Yajña*; the weapons of the lordly power are the horse chariot, the corslet, the bow and arrow. The lordly power returned without attaining it; from its weapons it turned away trembling. The holy power followed it and obtained

82. X. 122. 8.
83. *Religion and Philosophy of the Veda*, p. 290.
84. *Pūrvamīmāṃsā and its Sources*, Benaras 1942, p. 318 f.
85. Chattopadhyaya, *op. cit.*, p. 614.
86. VII. 19.

it; having obtained it, it kept blocking it from above; it being obtained and blocked from above standing, recognising its own weapons, went up to the holy power. Therefore even now the *Yajña* finds support in the holy power and in the Brāhmaṇa. The lordly power then followed it; it said, 'Do thou call upon me in this *Yajña*'. 'Be it so', it replied, 'lay aside thine own weapons, and with the weapons of the holy power, the form of the holy power, becoming the holy power, do thou come to the *Yajña*".[87]

12. Conclusion

This is how, with the growth of class society, the *Yajña* could be protected and performed by the priestly and royal classes. What was *Vājapeya,* technique of obtaining the means of subsistence, the collective magic rituals to ensure the primitive labour process of food production, in the pre-class society, was later transformed into a royal or aristocratic function. Now it is to be performed by a Brāhmaṇa or a Kśatriya desirous of the position of 'a super-eminently learned or prosperous man'. Now the king is believed to have gained identity with Prajāpati, the lord of creatures. The primitive equality was no more. This is reflected in a legend found in the *Jaiminīya Brāhmaṇa,*[88] according to which, formerly king Varuṇa was the equal of other gods, but desirous of becoming the lord of the gods he resorted to Prajāpati and eventually became the king of the gods. Special features of the Vājapeya, in its sophisticated form, especially insist upon the king's identity with Prajāpati. "When the race starts the *brahman* priest ascends on to an Uḍumbara Chariot-Wheel (which is revolved from left to right) pronouncing formulas in which he expresses his intention to win *vāja* and to ascend into the highest firmament of Indra. Uḍumbara wood (ficus glomerata) represents food and procreation, Prajāpati the nobility (Cf. *Ait. Br.,* V. 24; VII. 32; VIII. 8) the wheel, the sun and universal dominion: the king is to become a *Cakravartin.* By pronouncing in this way, these formulas, he wins the atmosphere. This race, like the cow raid and a dice play in other inauguration ceremonies, represents a test for the ruler's superiority in valour and physical prowess, and a means of enabling him to prove himself the fittest man for kingship,

87. Keith, *op. cit.*, pp. 309-10.
88. III. 152; J. Gonda, *Ancient Indian Kingship from the Religious Point of View,* Leiden 1966, pp. 86-87.

as well as magical devices to achieve the defeat of his adversaries in prowess, segacity, etc".[89]

The above quote is from Gonda who is one of the recent authorities on the Vedic sacrifices. Like the earlier authorities—Oldenberg, Keith and others—he has also insisted upon the magical element of the sacrifices. But what he has clearly ignored is the social basis of such magical elements, characteristic of all the *Yajñas*, their reality and illusion in pre-class and class societies respectively. The three grand sacrifices of the Vedic texts—the Aśvamedha, the Rājasūya and the Vājapeya—reveal how the real techniques of *Yajña* were replaced by illusory techniques, how they, being divorced from the primitive social reality, ultimately culminated into meaninglessness and gross absurdity, according to the logic of the pure illusion itself.

89. *Ibid.*, pp. 84-85.

IV

THE TWICE-BORN

A Study in the Rituals of Tribal Initiation

1. Prologue: Birth and Rebirth

"From the cradle to the grave", writes E. O. James, "human existence has seemed to be in a state of flux, 'never continuing in one stay', a dying to be born again, exemplified in the decay and regeneration in nature. This has called forth a series of *rites de passage* at the critical junctions to obtain a fresh outpouring of life and power." Among the primitive tribes the members of a community are found graded, according to age, as children, adults and elders, the transition from one grade to another being effected by the rites of initiation, the most important of which is that at puberty which is nothing but an introduction to full tribal status and a pre-condition of marriage or sex life. The qualification for admission in the adult group is not birth, but rebirth (cf. the Sanskrit term *dvija* or twice-born), restricted only to those who have undergone the appropriate rites and customs.

The significance of the puberty rites is therefore expressed in primitive thought by the idea that at initiation the individual dies and is born again. Kartsen writes: "When a child is born, the life thus brought into being is not a new life. . . . It is simply one of the forefathers that reappears in the new-born."[1] Frazer says that the new-born is conceived as a re-incarnation of clan-totem. That is why, all over the world, it is or has been the custom to name the child after one of its predecessors.[2] Just as the ancestor is born again as an infant, so at puberty the child dies and is born again as a man or a woman, and the occasion is marked by giving him or her a new name. The rebirth of the initiate is often represented dramatically by a magical representation of the act of dying and

1. R. Kartsen, *The Civilization of South American Indians,* London 1926, p. 416.
2. *Totemism and Exogamy,* London 1910, II, p. 302, 453, III, p. 298.

being born from the womb.[3] Here is an example from the *Aitareya Brāhmaṇa* (I. 3).'

"Him whom they consecrate the priests make into an embryo again". He should be bathed in water (equated with *retas*), anointed with *navanīta* or clarified butter (symbol of embryo according to the text) and purified with *darbha* or *kuśa* grass. Then collyrium is to be given in his eyes, just as it is put in the eyes of the new-born. After this, the candidate will have to enter and stay in a hut shaped like a female organ (*yoni*). He should not come out of the hut and must not see the sun. He is to be covered at first with a cloth (symbol of the *ulva* or the placenta) and then with the skin of a black antelope (*Kṛṣṇājina*, symbol of uterus). So long as he stays into the hut, he will have to keep his hands clasped (*muṣṭi*), just as a child remains in the womb. When all this is done, he will have to come out of the hut still covering the body with that piece of cloth symbolising the *ulva* because the baby comes out of the mother's womb under the coating of the placenta.

Many features of the said ritual are still found in the *Upanayana* ceremonies which are frankly the sophisticated developments of the primitive tribal rites of initiation. In this connection it should also be pointed out that the concept of rebirth, which was originally derived from the observation of plant life and was responsible for the later development of the ideas of the transmigration of soul and the doctrine of *Karma,* held good also in other stages of human life. Not only an individual was expected to have rebirth during his initiation into maturity, in other stages of his life he was also to have the same. Thus, if he wanted to become a recluse, he had to declare the death of his past life by performing his own *Śrāddha* or funeral rites, and then he had to adopt a new name. The Śūdras were deprived of this *dvijatva* or second birth. But there were many rulers, royal officers and landlords belonging to the Śūdra community. If they wanted to have a higher social rank they could have it through a process of rebirth by performing the *Hiraṇyagarbha Mahādāna* sacrifice. The performer of this *Mahādāna* ceremony uttered a *mantra* in adoration of the god Hiraṇyagarbha (Viṣṇu) and entered into a *hiraṇya-garbha* or 'golden-womb' which was a specially prepared gold vessel, 72 *aṅgulis* in height. The Brāhmaṇas then performed the *Garbhādhāna, Puṃsavana* and *Sīmantonnayana* ceremonies of the

3. Cf. H. Webster, *Primitive Secret Societies,* New York 1932, pp. 38 ff.

'golden womb', and the performer of the *mahādāna* had to sit with his head between his knees and holding his breath for some time. Then he was taken out of the womb and his *Jātakarman* and other ceremonies were celebrated as if he was a newly born child. He was then regarded as having assumed *divya-deha* (celestial body), as a result of his re-birth from the 'golden womb', after having discarded his *martya-deha* (earthly body) which he was carrying after his birth from his mother's womb.[4]

With these few words, we shall now turn our attention to a brief description of some of the leading features of the *Upanayana* ceremony.

2. The Ritual of Upanayana

The auspicious time for the *Upanayana* is autumn, spring or summer, the fruitful seasons of the year. It should be performed in the bright half of the month. A Brahmacārī has to wear two garments, *vāsas* and *uttarīya*. The upper garment (*uttarīya*) for a Brāhmaṇa should be the skin of a black deer, for a Kṣatriya that or a *ruru* deer and for a Vaiśya that of a cow or goat. The initiated one must keep a *daṇḍa* or a staff which should be made of the *palāśa* or *bilva* wood in the case of a Brāhmaṇa, of the *nyagrodha* or *aśvattha* or *rauhitaka* or *vaṭa* or *khadira* wood in the case of a Kṣatriya and of the *badara* or *uḍumbara* or *nyagrodha* or *pilu* wood in the case of a Vaiśya. The length of the staff should be as high as the head in the case of the Brāhmaṇas, forehead in the case of the Kṣatriyas and tip of nose in the case of the Vaiśyas.

A girdle made of *muñja* grass should be tied round a Brāhamaṇa boy's waist, one made of *mūrvā* grass for a Kṣatriya, and one of hemp for a Vaiśya. The girdle is called *mekhalā*. Some of the Gṛhyasūtras like *Āśvalāyana, Āpastamba,* etc. do not say any word about the sacred thread while others say that the boy already wears the *yajñopavīta* before the *homa* begins. It seems that threads of cotton were not invariable in the days of the Gṛhyasūtras. The student may take a *yajñopavīta,* a cord of threads, a garment or a rope of *kuśa* grass. Manu says that the *upavīta* of a Brāhmaṇa should be made of cotton and it should have three threads. Generally the *Yajñopavīta* has three threads of nine strands. The *yajñopavīta* for Brāhmaṇas, Kṣatriyas and Vaiśyas should respectively be of

4. D. C. Sircar, *Successors of the Sātavāhanas*, pp. 50 ff.

cotton, hemp and sheep wool.

Sometimes a feast is given to the Brāhmaṇas before the ceremony begins. The boy also has to take food. He has to tread on a stone to the north of the fire with his right foot after *homa*. He has also to taste curds thrice after repeating the verse *dadhikrāvno akāriṣam*. On the fourth day after *Upanayana*, a rite is performed called *medhāyajña* by virtue of which it is supposed that the student's intellect is made capable of mastering the *Vedas*. The student has to water the root of a *palāśa* tree or anoint it with *ājya* (clarified butter). The fire kindled at the time of *Upanayana* is to be kept up for three days. The student is required to offer every day after *Upanayana* a *samidh* into the fire in the morning and in the evening. After giving the student the staff the teacher gives him a bowl for collecting alms. The student should first beg of a man or a woman who will not refuse. He should then beg of three women or of six or of twelve. Manu says that he should first beg of his mother, sister or mother's sister. Food obtained by begging is supposed to be pure. The initiated one has to perform *sandhyā* or daily prayer at least twice. The principal features of the prayer called *sandhyā* are *ācamana* (sipping water), *prāṇāyāma* (restraint of breath) *mārjana* (sprinkling water by means of *kuśa* grass), *arghya* (offering water out of respect to the sun) *upasthāna* (worship of Mitra and Varuṇa) and recitation of *Gāyatrī* hymn.[5]

3. The Problem of its Original Contents

The ritual of *Upanayana* as found in the Gṛhya and Dharma sūtras reveals a sophisticated stage of development, the essential features of which consist of the formal acceptance of the pupil by the teacher, the entrusting of the pupil to the care of certain gods, the duties to be discharged by the pupil like putting fuel on the fire, begging alms, etc., the garments to be used by the pupil and so on. The earlier ritualistic texts like the Brāhmaṇas also bear similar contents (cf. *Śat. Br.* XI. 3. 3), although here and there, like the

5. *Āpastamba Gr. Sū*, 1. 1; X. 5; X. 9; XI. 15-16; XI. 22; *Āpastamba Dh. Sū*, 1. 1; *Āśvalāyana Gr. Sū.*, I. 19-22; III. 6; *Hiranyakesin Gr. Sū*, I. 1; I. 2; *Bhāradvāja Gr. Sū.*, I. 1 ff.; *Pāraskara Gr. Sū.* II. 2; II. 5; *Vasiṣṭha Dh. Sū.*, XI. 55 ff.; *Baudhāyana Gr. Sū*, II. 5; *Kāth. Gr. Sū.*, XLI. 10 ff.; *Gaut. Dh. Sū*, I. 15 ff.; *Mānava Gr. Sū.*, I. 22 ff.; *Gobhila Gr. Sū.*, I. 2 ff.; *Khadira Gr. Sū.*, II. 4 ff.; *Śān. Gr. Sū.*, II. 1 ff.; *Manu*, II. 41 ff.; *Yājñavalkya*, I. 18 ff.; etc.

Aitareya passage (I. 3) quoted above, we came across more primitive forms in which the method of obtaining a second birth through initiation is described. The *Atharvaveda,* although refers to the Brahmacārin gathering fuel and begging alms for the teacher and also to prayers for liturgical employment at the ceremony of initiation, does not throw any light on the primitive forms of Upanayana. Nor does the *Ṛgveda,* the oldest of our materials, in which we come across no explicit reference to the ceremony of the Upanayana.

We find that instead of giving any description of the original rituals of the Upanayana, the earlier texts only prescribe some codified rules. The tradition behind such codification is practically absent in all the texts. This silence requires an explanation. The word *Upanayana* literally means 'the drawing near or leading forth (of a boy for study under the teacher)'. The prefix *upa* is significant which also denotes something 'secret' and which has often some bearing on matters sexual. So many words beginning with *upa* are found in Sanskrit having both the senses contained in them. It appears that the present grammatical derivation of the word Upanayana is based upon the changed significance of the original rite which had some esoteric elements. One should not fail to recall in this connection that in tribal initiation, it has been observed that, the whole ceremony is secret, performed at a distance from the settlement, and often preceded by a probationary period of seclusion. When the novice returns to the settlement he is strictly forbidden to reveal to the uninitiated anything that he has done or heard or seen.[6] From this point of view if we are inclined to think that originally the Upanayana ceremony, quite in accordance with the tribal mode of initiation, contained some esoteric rituals and that they were not recorded either because they were esoteric or because in subsequent ages with the change in the social values they lost their importance, we shall not be wrong, so far as formal reasoning is concerned. But to establish this from the view point of material logic, it is necessary at first to prove that the Upanayana is definitely a modification of tribal puberty rites and that many features of the latter form integral part of the former.

4. Upanayana and Puberty

Manu (II. 36) says that a Brāhmaṇa boy should undergo through

6. Webster, *op. cit.,* pp. 49-50.

the ceremony of *Upanayana* in the eighth year from birth or from conception, a Kṣatriya in the eleventh year and a Vaiśya in the twelfth year respectively. In the *Gṛhyasūtras,* however, we come across a variety of views regarding the age of the Upanayana.[7] In some of them, the Upanayana is allowed to be performed even earlier or at different ages. This anomaly is also found in the Smṛtis, in some of which it is stated that if the spiritual eminence for the boy is desired, it may be performed on the fifth year for a Brāhmaṇa, on the sixth year for a Kṣatriya and in the eighth year for a Vaiśya. Sometimes the fifth, eighth and ninth years from conception are prescribed for a Brāhmaṇa, while in some earlier works (cf. *Āpastamba Dh. Sū.* I. 1. 1. 21 *Baudh. Gṛ. Sū.* II. 5) are prescribed seventh to twelfth years.

This inconsistency in relation to the age of initiation provides us with a hope to explain the whole matter in terms of puberty rites. It is to be marked that the age of the Upanayana as we come across in the law books is the lowest age limit. In fact the highest age limit even according to Manu II. 38, for the Brāhmaṇa is sixteen years, for the Kṣatriya 22 years and for the Vaiśya 24 years. Kautilya (III. 59) categorically says that a girl attains maturity at twelve while a boy at sixteen.

Now, since the law-books hold that the Upanayana is a *second birth* through which the initiated one has the right over the Śrauta and Smārta works,[8] he should at least belong to such an age-group in which he is competent to have some access in those subjects. Secondly it is important to note that supreme importance has been attached to the question of celebacy or *Brahmacarya,* and the initiated one has to follow a number of sexual taboos. He must avoid love affairs; he should not touch a girl and play with her;[9] he should observe complete celebacy and must not be auto-erotic; even night-emissions are to be penalised;[10] even he must not clasp the feet of his teacher's wife or assist her in her toilet and bath.[11] In fact a boy of eight years does not require any sexual taboo, since his impulses are not matured, but in the case of a boy attaining the age of puberty

7. *Āśvalāyana,* I. 19. 1-6; *Āpastamba,* X. 2; *Śāṅkhyāyana,* II. 1; *Baudhāyana,* II. 5. 2; *Bhāradvāja* I. 1; *Gobhila,* II. 10. 1; *Mānava,* I. 22. 1; *Kāṭhaka,* XLV. 1-3; etc.
8. Cf. *Manu,* II. 169-71.
9. *Gaut. Dh. Sū.,* II. 13-25; etc.
10. *Manu,* II. 180-81, 198.
11. *Āpastamba Dh. Sū.,* I. 1. 2. 26-30.

such restrictions are needed.

Thirdly, the knowledge which the initiated one is expected to have is mainly religious in character. Every religious system prescribes some sort of initiation at puberty as an introduction to the system of religious life. Even, in many a backward society, still surviving in different parts of the world, a man cannot have any religious function unless he has undergone the necessary initiatory rites at puberty. Among the natives of South East Australia an uninitiated person is thought to be a stupid, idiotic sort of man, unworthy of receiving the honours of their ceremonies, and frequently addressed as a boy although he is an oldish man.[12] "When an individual reaches the full development of puberty, he or she undergoes a ceremony which entitles him or her on its successful completion to a certain social rank or status in the community. As life progresses, other and higher ranks are progressively attainable for each sex,[13] until the highest and the most honourable grade that enjoyed by an old man, or an old woman, is reached."[14]

5. Buddhist and Jain Initiation

Let us now view the whole thing in terms of the methods of religious initiation. We begin with Jainism. One of the leading features of this religion is that there is a close union between the laymen and monks in matters of religious life. This is proved by the similarity of their religious duties which differ not in kind but in degree. This has enabled Jainism to avoid fundamental changes within. The followers of Jainism have to undergo initiatory rites at puberty. Many of their rites resemble those of the Brāhmaṇas and Buddhists, since all these have been inherited from the tribal rites practised from time immemorial. The Jain Saṅgha like that of the Buddhists was modelled after the surviving tribal organisations of the sixth century B. C. The head of the Jain Saṅgha was called *Gaṇadhara*, 'one who holds the tribe', i. e. tribal chief. The order of the monks is recruited chiefly from novices entering it at puberty. A monk entering the order takes the five great vows (*vratas*) which were originally nothing but close adherence to some strictly tribal values

12. A. W. Howitt, *Native Tribes of South East Australia*, London 1904, p. 530.
13. Cf. *māturagre adhijananaṃ dvitīyaṃ mauñjivandhane|*
tṛtīyaṃ yajñadīkśāyāṃ dvijasya śruticodanāt||
14. H. L. Roth, *Natives of Sarawak and British North Borneo*, London 1896, p. 169.

which were trampled and undermined in reality during the time of Buddha and Mahāvīra. Instructions and taboos for the novices are furnished in details in the Jain *sūtras*[15] and they are surprisingly similar to those found among the Brāhmaṇas and Buddhists. The initiation of the monks generally takes place under a banian tree. An ascetic can only retain five garments (three upper and two lower ones), the colours of which vary according to his sect. The next step in the initiation is the removal of hair, after which a mixture called *vāsakṣepa* is applied to the man's head. Then sacred *mantras* are whispered in his ear. If he belongs to the Digambara sect, he must have to take an *entirely new name.* If a Śvetāmbara, he might either *change his name or add a new one* to his old one. But a Sthānakavāsī retains his original name intact. The rules for the initiation of the nuns are also the same.

Admission to the Buddhist Order (Saṅgha) is gained by two forms of initiation, Pravrajyā (Pali *Pabbajjā*) and Upasampadā. The former means 'going out' from one state of life to another. This ceremony is in a certain way analogous to the Brahmanical initiation by virtue of which a layman is admitted to the order, and is henceforth obliged to live with a preceptor. The lowest age limit is eight. The initiated one begins his life as a pravrajita (*pabbajita,* homeless one) and is called Śrāmaṇera (*sāmanera*), that is, a 'novice'. The period of novitiate generally lasts for twelve years. The *Upasampadā* may be conferred on all who have previously been admitted to Pravrajyā.[16] The difference between these two modes of initiation becomes quite clear on account of the fact that twenty years is the lowest age at which a man is qualified for Upasampadā and it follows that a boy who has become a Śrāmaṇera at eight will have to wait twelve years before he can receive Upasampadā.[17] But this rule was not hard and fast. It appears that the disciples of Buddha were allowed to confer Pravrajyā and Upasampadā simulataneously on candidates. Even in the days of Aśoka, the lay devotee Bhaṇḍuka received Pravrajyā and Upasampadā simultaneously.[18] It seems that in the earlier phases of Buddhism, initiation was given at puberty, and later, probably on account of Brahmanical influence,

15. *Uttarādhyayana,* I. 1-18; *Sūyagaḍa,* II. 2; etc.
16. The circumstances disqualifying persons on admission and ordination are minutely expounded in *Mahāvagga,* I. 29-76.
17. S. Hardy, *Eastern Monachism,* London 1860, pp. 45 ff.
18. *Dipavaṃsa,* XII. 62 f.

the lowest age limit was fixed at the eighth year of the boy. This assumption can be substantiated by the fact that in one of his discourses Lord Buddha expressly forbids to confer pravrajyā on a boy under fifteen years of age.[19]

In Tibet, a Śrāmaṇera can receive a second initiation in his sixteenth year; in China the ceremony of hair-shaving is performed usually at the same age. The 'pagan accrescences', in the language of Kern, are due to influences of the local initiatory rites.[20] The Śrāmaṇera, male or female, might undergo some sort of specialisation, if they desired.[21] They have to learn the ten *Śikṣāpadas.*[22] The rule now followed in Ceylon[23] is exactly the counterpart of the Brahmanical Upanayana.[24] The rite of Pravrajyā is very simple. The boy desirous to be initiated will first choose a *vihāra* and approach the elder. He has to shave his hairs, wear the yellow robe and make a declaration of the *Triśaraṇa* or three refuges.

In Nepal, the initiation is called *abhiṣeka* in which primitive elements can easily be detected. The teacher in charge of the candidate prepares a pot (*kalasa*) full of water and puts into it a lotus made of gold; five brands of sweetmeats, five drugs, five flowers and threads of five colours are provided. On the first day the student has to sit on *Vajrāsana* and recite the three refuges. On the second day, the teacher gives three protections: The first is Vajrarakṣā which the teacher provides him by placing a *vajra* (symbolised by a flower) on the head. The second is Loharakṣā or protection from or by iron which is performed by placing three iron padlocks on the belly and shoulders of the boy. The third is Agnirakṣā or protection from fire, and this is performed by placing a wine-pot on the head. Then is performed *Kalasa-abhiṣeka* which is sprinkling of holy water from a *Kalasa* or vessel. Then comes the head priest and gives a silver ring to the boy. On the third day the boy's hairs are shaved and then he is favoured with the *triratna* and the precepts.[25]

19. *Mahāvagga,* I. 50.
20. H. Kern, *Manual of Indian Buddhism*, Strassburg 1898, p. 78 n; S. Hardy, *op. cit.*, pp. 45 ff.
21. *Sutta-vibhaṅga,* II. 139.
22. *Mahāvagga,* I. 56.
23. Hardy, *op. cit.*, p. 23.
24. Kern, *op. cit.*, p. 78.
25. B. H. Hodgson, *Religion and Literature of the Nepalese Buddhists,* London 1874, p. XV, 212.

6. Tribal Character of Buddhist Initiation

The Buddhist and Jain Saṅghas, as we have remarked above, were modelled on tribal organisations. Every member of the Saṅgha had equal right and the state of affairs was managed in a purely democratic way. There was no such thing in the Saṅgha as private property. Referring to the monks of the modern Jain Saṅghas, Mrs. Stevenson made this interesting comment: "He is now to be a homeless wanderer, possessing nothing and dependent for his very subsistence on the alms of the charitable. He may possess no metal of any sort: even a needle, if borrowed, must be returned at sunset, and his spectacles, if he wears them, should be framed in wood".[26] In India Buddhist communities do not exist now, but from the surviving literary evidences it is quite clear that the functioning of the earlier Buddhist Saṅghas was guided by the tribal principles of equality and democracy and the absence of private property.[27] These questions, however, do not concern us at present. Here we are only to see how throughly did Buddha imitate the tribal model in laying down the principles of initiation, i.e. the procedure of entry into the order.

We have seen that in tribal society one's initiation as a full member of the tribe is preceded by a puberty rite, the essence of which is the simulation of death and rebirth, departure from one life and coming into another. These ideas find expression in the Buddhist concepts of *prabrajyā* (going out) and *upasampadā* (arrival). The former is 'going out' from the worldly life, marked by the tribal custom of shaving the head and other minor features like changing into the yellow robe and so on. But more important is *upasampadā* which is an elaborate method of obtaining the sanction of all the full-fledged members of the *saṅgha* for getting the candidate admitted into it.

In tribal society such sanction is given by the elders. Being essentially a kinship organisation, the claim to the tribal membership is determined by descent. But since the Buddhist Saṅgha was not a kinship organisation, the procedure of admission into the Saṅgha must follow a slightly different method. And in this case the method followed by Buddha was nothing but what is known as

26. S. Stevenson, *Heart of Jainism* (1915), Indian ed. New Delhi 1970, p. 226.
27. R. C. Majumdar, *Corporate Life in Ancient India*, Calcutta 1919, pp. 310 ff., 316-18.

tribal adoption. The tribes often grant membership to persons who are not their natural kinsmen. How this adoption takes place may be illustrated with reference to the adoption of Morgan by the Hawk clan of the Seneca tribe: "After the people had assembled at the council house, one of the chiefs made an address giving some account of the person, the reason for his adoption, the name and gens of the person adopting, and the name bestowed upon the novitiate. Two chiefs taking the person by the arms then marched with him through the council house and back, chanting the song of adoption. To this the people responded in musical chorus at the end of each verse. The march continued until the verses were ended, which required three rounds. With this the ceremony concluded."[28]

This ritual of tribal adoption is expected to throw some light on the Upasampadā ceremony as found in the *Mahāvagga* (I. 28; I. 76; etc.). "Then the Blessed one....thus addressed the Bhikkhus: I prescribe, O Bhikkhus, that you confer the *Upasampadā* ordination by a formal act of the order in which the announcement (*natti*) is followed by three questions. And you ought, O Bhikkhus, to confer the *Upasampadā* ordination in this way: Let a learned, competent Bhikkhu proclaim the following *natti* (announcement of a resolution) before the Saṅgha: Let the Saṅgha, reverend Sirs, hear me. This person N. N. desires to receive the *upasampadā* ordination from the venerable N. N. (i.e. with the venerable N. N. as his *upājjhāya*). If the Saṅgha is ready, let the Saṅgha confer on N. N. the *upasampadā* ordination with N. N. as *upājjhāya*. This is the *natti*....And for the second time I am speaking to you: Let the Saṅgha....(etc. as before). And for the third time I thus speak to you: Let the Saṅgha (etc. as before). N. N. has received the *upasampadā* ordination from the Saṅgha with N. N. as *upājjhāya*. The Saṅgha is in favour of it, therefore it is silent. Thus I understand".[29]

7. Primitive Rituals Connected with Upanayana

From the fragmentary nature of the materials themselves it is rather impossible to come to any definite conclusion in the case of

28. Chattopadhyaya, *Lokāyata,* p. 478, Cf. Morgan, *Ancient Society,* pp. 80-81.
29. *Sacred Books of the East,* Vol. XIII, p. 169-70.

things ancient Indian. And that is not our purpose also. Here we are tapping different types of materials in order that they might themselves offer some suggestivity. Whatever we have collected in the preceding sections somehow suggests a basis for our understanding of the ancient Upanayana ceremony in terms of the tribal rites of initiation. There are some other features forming part of the Upanayana ceremony which may rightly be regarded as legacies of more primitive rituals connected with tribal initiation. We are mentioning them one by one.

In Bengal, during Upanayana, a boy must remain in seclusion for three days. During this period he must not see the sun or touch the earth. It is interesting to note that these two rules are observed either separately or conjointly by girls at puberty in many parts of the world. Frazer suggests more than one hundred such examples and concludes that the general effect of these rules is to keep the initiated one suspended, so to say, between heaven and earth. Being shut off both from the earth and from the sun, he or she can poison neither of these great sources of life by his or her contagion.[30] The Zulu girls believe that they would shrivel to skeletons if the sun were to shine on them at the time of their puberty rites.[31]

According to the *Gṛhyasūtras,* "for three nights or twelve nights after Upanayana, the initiated one should not taste *kṣāra* or *lavana* (salt).[32] It is interesting to note that abstinence from salt is one of the leading features of the puberty rites among many African tribes.[33] Another important form of taboo is in relation to speech. After the Upanayana, the boy must not speak during his meal times at least for one year. Spencer and Gillen inform us that among some of the northern tribes of Central Australia the novices are kept for a certain period under a ban of silence.[34] A similar prohibition prevails at Torres Straits,[35] Papan Gulf[36] and in many other places. It appears that the vow of silence which is employed for the purpose of religious merit and is found in various scattered passages of the

30. *Balder the Beautiful,* London 1913, Part I, pp. 22 ff.
31. Macdonald in *Journal of the Anthropological Institute,* Vol. XX. p. 209.
32. *Āśvalāyana,* I. 22. 27; *Baudhāyana,* II, 5. 55; *Bhāradvāja* I. 10; *Pāraskara,* II. 5; *Khadira,* II. 4, 43; *Hiraṇyakeśi,* I. 8. 2.
33. Cole in *Journal of the Anthropological Institute,* Vol. XXXII, pp. 309 ff.
34. B. Spencer and F. Gillen, *Northern Tribes of Central Australia,* London 1904, pp. 334 ff.
35. C. Seligmann, *Expedition to Torres Straits,* Vol. V, Cambridge 1904, p. 210.
36. Holmes in *Journal of the Anthropological Institute,* XXXII, pp. 419 ff.

Mahābhārata and other texts, and which is still performed in India by the wandering ascetics, is perhaps a development of the ancient puberty rites in which speech was tabooed to a limited extent among certain social groups.

The rite of hair-shaving, which is a prominent feature of the Omahas, Pawness, Dakotas, Peublos and other tribes,[37] forms a significant part of the ceremony of Upanayana. The Buddhist initiation (*Pravrajyā*) also requires hair-shaving as an integral part of the ceremony. This holds good also in the case of the Jains. There is also a rite of the same nature called *caula* or *cuḍākarma* or *cuḍākaraṇa* which is to be performed on the first or the third year of the boy, according to the rules prescribed by the Gṛhyasūtras. Now-a-days, the said rite generally takes place on the day of Upanayana. But this rite appears to be the development of an older puberty rite called *Keśānta* or *Godāna* which was to be performed in the 16th year for the Brāhmaṇas, 22nd year for the *Kṣatriyas* and 24th year for the Vaiśyas (cf. *Manu*, II. 5). Traces of this rite are found in the *Śatapatha Brāhmaṇa* III. 2. 4, the *Śāṅkhyāyana Gṛhyasūtra* I. 28. 20-22 etc. and also in the Smṛtis. Bhavabhūti in the first act of the *Uttararāmacarita* says that Rāma and Sītā had also to perform this rite. According to the Gṛhyasūtras like *Āśvalāyana* I. 17, 18 and later texts like *Saṃskāraprakāśa* 317 or *Saṃskāranamālā* 904 the rites of Keśānta or Godāna and Cuḍākaraṇa may also be performed by the girls. According to Frazer, some races think that the spirit lives in the head and it is important not to disturb this spirit more than is necessary. As among the Greeks, the hair is itself regarded as the seat of life. The Biblical story of Samson suggests a widespread belief that the hair itself as a source of mysterious power. The same belief prevails in the Semitic countries also.[38] In different parts of South India, hair is regarded sacred and the burning of an enemy's hair is an interesting feature of the black magic.[39] The Spartan women used to cut their hair at puberty.[40]

Like hair-shaving, *Karṇavedha* or ear-piercing forms an essential part of the puberty rites of tribal India.[41] It is interesting to note that earlier Indian texts are silent about this rite. It is only mention-

37. *Encyclopaedia of Religion and Ethics*, Vol. VI, p. 477.
38. W. Robertson Smith, *Religion of the Semites*, London 1899, pp. 337 ff.
39. E. Thurston, *Omens and Superstitions of South India*, London 1912, pp. 53, 115.
40. Plutarch, *Lykurgus*, XV. 4.
41. Crooke in *Journal of the Anthropological Institute*, XXVIII, p. 246.

ed in the *Vyāsa Smṛti* and in the *Kātyāyana sūtra*, a supplement to the *Pāraskara Gṛhyasūtra*. The *Smṛti-candrikā* of Devanna-bhaṭṭa gives a brief note on Karṇavedha. A faint reference of this rite may be traced in *Nirukta* II. 4. Referring to the rite of ear-piercing observed by the Gond and other Central Indian tribes Russel says that this particular rite should be explained in terms of fertility magic since the lobe made in the ear is supposed to have some sympathetic effect in opening the womb and making the child-birth easy.[42] Jevons considers it to be a survival of offering of blood to the deity.[43] Crawley thinks it to be a relic of the physical mutilations performed by the savages and holds that "when we find that the mouth and lips, teeth, nose, eyes, ears and genital organs are subjected to such processes, we may infer that the object is to secure the safety of these sense organs by what is practically a permanent amulet or charm.".[44] It is clear, therefore, that such rites as ear-piercing have a magical or mysterious significance in the outlook of our primitive ancestors, and this has been revealed in certain features of puberty rites and in the rituals of the Upanayana.

According to the Dharmasūtras[45] and also the Smṛtis,[46] the initiated one has to observe a number of taboos, the most important of which is that he should observe complete celebacy. He must not masturbate and if he suffers from night emissions he should make a penance. He should not indulge in sexual affairs and speak with women. He must not clasp the feet of his teacher's wives, assist them at their toilet, wash their feet and shampoo them. Abstinence from taking ịntoxicating drinks, dancing, singing and sexual enjoyments is also demanded in the ten precepts of the Buddhists. These taboos, especially in sexual matters, have been interpreted by various scholars from different viewpoints. In my *Indian Mother Goddess* (Calcutta 1970) I have tried to explain these in terms of the patriarchal values which were being aggressively imposed upon Indian life with the growth of private property as the driving force of society and which therefore demanded absolute chastity of women. These taboos are in striking agreement with those found among various

42. R. V. Russell, *Ethnological Survey of the Central Provinces,* Allahabad 1911, VII, pp. 99 ff.
43. F. Jevons, *Introduction to the History of Religion,* London 1896, pp. 171 ff.
44. A. E. Crawley, *The Mystic Rose,* London 1902, p. 135.
45. *Āpastamba,* I. 1. 2. 21-30; *Baudh,* I. 2. 34-37; *Gaut,* II. 13 ff.; etc.
46. Cf. *Manu,* II. 181 ff.; *Yājñavalkya,* I. 33; etc.

tribes of India who have developed a *patriarchal* form of social organisation. This also holds good in case of some peoples outside India. In Bengal, there is a custom that when the ceremony of Upanayana takes place, no woman is allowed to be present on that spot. Among the Thongas the site where the initiatory ceremony takes place is not to be seen by the women.[47] In Australia, it is the general custom that the novice must avoid women during the rites; among the Narrinyeris, he should not take food from a woman; among the Kanaris, he must not even eat a female animal.[48]

8. Conclusion

That the Upanayana ceremony through which the initiated one is expected to have a rebirth to obtain full manhood is originally a development of the primitive tribal puberty rites intended for the same purpose has been supposed by most of the scholars who have worked on this subject. But there has been no attempt to substantiate this supposition, which is likely to be quite correct, by evidence from different sources scattered around us. We have taken this subject not with the purpose of establishing anything but, as we have stated above, with that of tapping different sources in order that they might themselves offer some suggestivity. Whether they really do so depends on the nature of the evidences we have been able to derive from the ritualistic contents of the Brāhmaṇa literature, of the Dharma and Gṛhya Sūtras and of the Smṛtis and to correlate them with the surviving tribal rites of India and elsewhere. But something must have transpired which may be utilised as clues to the understanding of the social processes through which the traditional norms and institutions of ancient India came into existence, and in the remaining chapters our attempt will be to make these clues more explict by studying the essentials of other kindred rituals which we consider to be of greater historical significance in the social context of India.

47. H. Junod, *Life of a South African Tribe,* London 1927, Vol. I, p. 77.
48. A. W. Howitt, *Native Tribes of South East Australia,* London 1904, pp. 670-74.

V

SACRED AND ACCURSED

A Study in the Menstrual Rites of Ancient India

1. Prologue: Initiation into Womanhood

Initiation into womanhood is of more far-reaching significance than that into manhood in primitive belief. In fact, the signs of puberty are more explicit in the girls than in the boys. The rites of the first menstruation are the most invariable and the most strictly observed of all the rites of primitive humanity. All the world over, not only among the primitive peoples, but also among peoples on a far higher cultural plane, the forms of rites attaching to the first menstruation are similar. In primitive belief, menstruation was thought to be the effect of sexual intercourse, and the latter was, therefore, accounted necessary for the establishment of the physiological function.[1] Hence precocious sexual intercourse was not merely looked upon as permissible, but as indispensable, and was encouraged and enjoined. This may explain why ceremonial defloration is in many cases an important feature of the puberty rites of the girls. Among the Nayars, for example, defloration had to take place before puberty 'in order that the girl may not be deflowered by the regular operation of nature'.

2. The Universal Dread

There is a deeply ingrained dread which the primitive man universally entertains of menstrual blood. The Australian tribes strictly seclude their women at their monthly courses.[2] Among the Bagandas, a menstruating woman cannot drink milk, come into contact with any milk-vessel and touch anything belonging to her husband. They believe that if a menstruating woman handles

1. R. Briffault, *The Mothers,* London 1952, Vol. II, p. 447.
2. Howitt, *op. cit.*, pp. 776 ff.

anything of her husband, he will surely fall ill; if she touches his weapons, he will certainly be killed in the next battle; if she touches a well, it will surely go dry.[3] Among the Bhuiyas of South Mirzapur, menstrual blood is dreaded much.[4] Among the Kharwars of the same region, a menstruous woman is kept in outer house; she is not allowed to enter the kitchen or cowshed, nor can she touch the cooking vessels.[5] The South Indian women generally seclude themselves at their monthly periods and observe a number of rules such as not to drink milk, not to milk cows, not to touch fire, not to lie on a high bed, not to walk on common paths, not to walk by the side of flowering plants and not to observe heavenly bodies.[6]

Pliny's account of the dreadful effects produced by a menstruating woman expresses substantially the beliefs which are current among most of the rural populations of Europe (*Natural History*, VII. 64 f.; XVII, 226; XXVIII. 38, 44, 65, 67, 73, 77, 81, 82, 84, 85; cf. Columella's *De re Rustica* X. 358 ff.; XI. 3, 38, 50, 64; Cassinus Bassu's *Geoponica,* I. 15; X. 2, 3, 14, 64; XII. 2, 5, 8, 20, 25; XVI. 2. 10; Porphyry's *De abstinentia* III. 3; Dioscorides' *Materia Medica,* II. 99). Menstrual blood is also dreaded in the Mosaic Law Book of the *Holy Bible* (*Leviticus* XV) as well as in the *Quran* (II. 122; II. 228). The Brahmanical Law Books hold that the menstruating woman must be dreaded.[7] A woman during her menstrual period must remain untouched by anyone (*Atri*, 27-80; *Yama,* 54-62), unseen by any Brāhmaṇa engaged in dinner (*Manu* III. 229), be treated on the first day as *cāṇḍālī,* on the second as *brahmaghātinī* and on the third as *rajakī* (*Aṅgiras* 35-39, *Āpastamba* VII. 4; *Parāśara* VII. 19) and be excluded from all sorts of religious, social and even funeral rites.

The Purāṇas also attach great importance to the menstrual flow of women. In the *Varāha Purāṇa* there is a full chapter (CXLII) devoted to the menstrual taboos. One must not talk with her (*Agni,* CLV. 25, *Kūrma* II. 16. 36) nor eat anything offered by her (*Kūrma,* II. 92. 30). *Mantras* should not be recited before

3. J. Roscoe, *The Baganda,* London 1911, pp. 96, 419, 459.
4. W. Crooke, *Tribes and Castes of the North Western Provinces and Oudh,* Calcutta, 1896, II, p. 87.
5. *North Indian Notes and Queries,* I, p. 57.
6. L. K. A. K. Iyer, *Cochin Tribes and Castes,* Vol. I, p. 201 ff.
7. *Manu,* IV. 40-42; *Āpastamba,* VII; *Viṣṇu* XXII. 71-72; XXXVI. 7; LXXXI. 6; *Parāśara,* VII. 13-20; *Dālavya,* 146-54; *Bṛhat-parāśara,* VII, 226-36; *Laghuyama,* 12-17; etc.

her (*Śiva*, Sanatkumāra, XXIII. 34) and to make sexual intercourse with her is regarded as one of the greatest sins (*Vāmana* XIV, 40). If she touches anyone she has to perform a number of penances (*Agni*, CLXX. 34, 42). Menstruating women are also dreaded in the older works. Thus, in the Gṛhyasūtras we find that a student must not see a woman in her courses (*Śāṅkhyāyana* II. 12. 10; IV. 11. 6). After the Samāvartana (graduation) he must be careful at least for three days so that he may not come across a menstruating woman (*Pāraskara* IV. 7. 48). Vedas must not be recited before her (*Śāṅkhyāyana* IV. 7. 48). Those who have retired from family life should not also see a woman in this condition (*ibid*, VI. 1. 3). A student must not talk or play with girls in their menses (*Khadira* III. 1. 36; *Gobhila* III. 5. 6).

3. The Sanctifying Significance

This terror attaching to the primitive taboo on the menstruating woman was not, in the primitive and original form of the conception, the deeply ingrained dread for impurity and unholiness. As I have already pointed out in my *Indian Puberty Rites*, this attitude was a subsequent development which was caused by the imfluence of patriarchal values. There are also many instances in which menstrual blood had developed a sanctifying and purifying influence. Thus in the matriarchal Tantras it is regarded so sacred that it is prescribed as an offering to the Great Goddess and her consort. In some of the Purāṇas it is stated that the monthly periods of women must not be misused (*Viṣṇu*, III. 8; *Garuḍa* I. 95. 20). According to the *Vāyu* (VIII. 42, 84-85) and the *Brahmāṇḍa* (VIII. 82-84) Purāṇas, in olden times women used to menstruate only once in their life and it is in the *Kali* age that the present system of monthly courses has been introduced. The *Garuḍa-Purāṇa* (I. 95. 20) says that a woman cannot become pure until she has her monthly courses and the view is also found in the *Mahābhārata* (XII. 35). In the *Arthaśāstra* of Kauṭilya (III. 153) it is explicitly stated that the menstruation of a woman should be properly utilised. In case of the husband's concealing the fact of his wife's being in menses or neglecting to lie with her after her menses, he shall pay a fine of 96 *paṇas*. In many scattered passages of the *Mahābhārata* it is stated that a woman's courses should be rendered fruitful. In the story of Utaṅka we find how a woman intending to commit adultery with her husband's disciple makes the plea of her menstruation. In the Pāṇḍu-Kuntī discourses we find that if a woman had sex relation with a man other than her husband it was regarded as an act of adultery, but if she did so in order to make her menstruation fruitful it was no crime at all.

The primitive people instinctively projected their own experiences into the objects around them and thus associated various ideas so as to constitute a practical philosophy of life, making unconscious use of the principle of analogy. This empiric approach led them to think that natural productivity should be viewed in terms of human productivity, earth-mother in terms of human-mother. The same preconditions which fertilise women are also thought to fertilise Mother Earth. As for example, in Bengal, it is believed that, at the first fall of the rains, Mother Earth menstruates in order to prepare herself for her fertilising work. A stone is set up on the ground, the top of which is smeared with vermilion, a mark of the menstrual blood of the goddess. During this menstrual period, there is an entire cessation of all ploughing, sowing and other farm work.[8] In the Deccan, after the *Navarātra,* her temple is closed from the tenth to the full-moon day while she rests and refreshes herself.[9] In the Punjab Mother Earth sleeps for a week in each month.[10] A similar rite of purification is also made in the case of the goddess Bhagavatī in her temple at Kerala.[11] In the Malabar region Mother Earth rests during the hot weather until she gets the first shower of rain.[12] In many parts of India great importance is attached to the menstruation of the goddess Pārvatī.[13] Reference must be made in this connection to the menstruation of the goddess Kāmākhyā of Assam.

4. The Life-Giving Power

Thomson writes: "It is important to observe that the magic of human fecundity attaches to the process, not to the result. . . . to the lochial discharge, not to the child itself; and consequently all fluxes of blood, menstrual as well as lochial, are treated alike as

8. E. A. Gait, *Census Report* 1901, *Bengal*, Vol. I, p. 189.
9. M. M. Underhill, *Hindu Religious Year,* Calcutta 1921, p. 34.
10. *North Indian Notes and Queries,* II, p. 172.
11. V. Nagam Aiya, *Travancore State Manual,* Vol. II, Trivandrum 1906, pp. 89 ff.
12. L. K. A. K. Iyer, *op. cit.*, Vol. II, pp. 78 ff.
13. *Indian Antiquary,* Vol. XVIII, pp. 159 ff.

manifestations of the life giving power inherent in the female sex. In primitive thought, menstruation was regarded, quite correctly, as the process of the same nature as childbirth."[14] Before the Bhils begin to sow they set up a stone in the field and smear it with vermilion.[15] As vermilion stands for menstrual blood, the act of smearing it on the stone implies the infusion of productive energy into the earth. The relation between vermilion or red ochre and the productive aspects of nature has been brilliantly shown by Robert Briffault.[16] To quote Thomson again: "Aristotle, Pliny and other naturalists, ancient and medieval, believed that the embryo is formed from the blood retained in the uterus after the stoppage of menstruation. (The same was also the wrong belief in ancient India, and hence the law makers advised that on the fourth day of menstruation, when the blood would cease to come out, the woman concerned must take bath and unite with her husband to make her menstruation fruitful. NNB). This is the blood of life. Hence the commonest method of placing persons or things under a taboo....menstrual, lochial or any other interdict formed on this original pattern...is to mark them with blood or the colour of blood. And in keeping with the ambivalent nature of the taboo itself, this sign of blood has the double effect of forbidding contact and imparting vital energy... There is no sphere of human life in which a greater uniformity can be observed than in the treatment of menstrual and puerperal women[17]....Its potency makes it something to be dreaded....From one aspect the woman who may not be approached is inviolable, holy; from another aspect she is polluted, unclean. She is what the Romans called *Sacra*, sacred and accursed. And hence in patriarchal society, after woman has lost her control of religion, it is the negative aspect that prevails."[18]

5. Menstrual Rites

Almost in every place of the world, the first menstruation of a girl is observed by certain rites and customs of which the most marked is seclusion in a hut specially constructed for this purpose.

14. G. Thomson, *Studies in Ancient Greek Society*, Vol. I, London 1949, p. 205.
15. W. Crooke, *Religion and Folklore of Northern India*, Oxford, 1920, p. 250.
16. *The Mothers*, London 1952, Vol. II, pp. 412-17.
17. G. Thomson, *op. cit.*, p. 209.
18. *ibid.*, p. 205. cf. *infra*, pp. 120-21.

The well known examples come from South Africa, found among the Zulus and Awa-nkondes, the Barotses of Upper Zambesi, the Thongas of Delagoa Bay, the Caffre tribes, and the Basutos and the Bavili tribes of Lower Congo. The Americas provide examples of first menstrual rites observed by the Chinook Indians, Nukta Indians, Hadia Indians, Tlingit or Kolash Indians of Alaska, Tinne Indians of Columbia, Thompson Indians, Lillooet Indians, Shuswap Indians, Guaranis of Southern Brazil, Chiriguanos and Yuracares of Bolivia, Matacos of Granchaco, Macusis of Guiana, Koniagas, Malemuts, Unalits, Hupa, Wintun, Pend' Oreilles and Musquakie Indians and many other tribes.[19]

In Torres Straits, when a girl shows signs of her initial bleeding, a circle of bushes is made in a dark corner of the house and the girl is secluded there for three months. She must not see the sun and be seen by any male member of the house. She is forbidden to eat turtle or turtle-eggs. At the end of three months she becomes free again through a grand ceremony.[20] In Kabadi, a district of British New Guinea, "daughters of chiefs, when they are about 12 or 13 years of age, are kept indoors for two or three years, never being allowed, under any pretence, to descend from the house, and the house is so shaded that the sun cannot shine on them".[21] In Cambodia a girl at her first menstruation has to stay under a mosquito curtain for a hundred days, though at present four, five, ten or twenty days are thought enough. She has to observe a number of rules such as not to be seen by a stranger, not to eat flesh or fish, not to go to the pagoda and so on.[22] In Ceylon, when the girl has her first monthly course, she has to undergo a confinement

19. D. Kidd, *The Essential Kaffir*, London 1904, pp. 209 ff; G. Gouldsbury and H. Sheane, *The Great Plateau of Northern Nigeria*, London 1911, pp. 158-60; H. H. Johnston, *British Central Africa*, London 1917, p. 411; L. Decle, *Three Years in Savage Africa,* London 1898, p.78;H. Junod, *Life of a South African Tribe,* London 1927, Vol. I. p. 178; E. Casatis, *Thé Basutos,* London 1861, p. 268; R. E. Dennet, *At the Back of the Black Man's Mind*, London 1906; S. Powers, *Tribes of California,* Washington 1877, pp. 85, 265 ff.; F. Boas, *Chinook Texts,* Washington 1896, pp. 246 ff.; J. R. Swanton, *Ethnology of the Hadia*, London 1905, pp. 110 ff.; H. H. Bancroft, *Native Races of the Pacific States,* London 1885, Vol. I, pp. 110 ff.; H. W. Bates, *The Naturalist on the Amazons,* London 1973, p. 382; G. E. Church, *Aborigines of South America,* London 1912, pp. 207-27; etc.
20. *Jour. Anthro. Inst.*, Vol. XXIX, pp. 212 ff.
21. J. Chalmirs and W. Gillen, *Works and Adventures in New Guinea,* London 1885, p. 159.
22. J. Moura, *La Royaume du Cambodge,* Paris, 1883, Vol. I, p. 377.

of two weeks. During this period of seclusion, she must remain unseen by the males. When the period of seclusion is over, she comes back with her face covered by hands. A ceremonial bath of purification is then followed under a *jak* tree. Sometimes the hut, in which she was confined, is burnt.[23]

6. The Indian Context

In 1891, S. C. Bose wrote that when a Hindu maiden reached maturity she was kept in a dark room for four days, forbidden to see the sun, regarded unclean and untouchable, fed on boiled rice, milk, sugar, curd and tamarind, led to neighbouring tank on the fifth day accompanied by five married women and smeared with turmeric water.[24] He evidently thought of Bengalee women only when he generalised the custom.

However, we find that menstrual rites, observed on the attainment of a girl's puberty, are in vogue among the backward tribes and castes of Bengal, Madhya Pradesh, Orissa, Madras, Andhra, Mysore, Kerala and also among some matrilineal tribes scattered in different parts of India. In the case of some higher castes also the menstrual rites hold good. Thus, the Rarhi Brahmins of Bengal compel a girl at puberty to live alone, and do not allow her to see the face of any male. For three days she remains shut up in a dark room and has to undergo some penances. She must not eat fish, flesh, egg or sweetmeat; she must live on rice and clarified butter.[25] Among the Deshast Brahmins, the first menstruation of a girl is celebrated. The secluded girl sits on a little throne and is attended constantly by a Maratha maid servant. The neighbours and relatives pay visits, bring presents for her and wash her in oil.[26] The Aradhya Brahmins of Mysore observe the first menstruation with a ceremonial bath.[27] The Dikshitar Brahmins of South India also perform the first menstruation celebration with pomp and splendour, the rites being essentially similar to those of the Nayars.[28] The

23. *Indian Antiquary,* Vol. XXXI, p. 380.
24. S. C. Bose, *The Hindus as They Are*, London 1891, p. 86.
25. H. Risley, *Tribes and Castes of Bengal,* Calcutta 1891, Vol. I, p. 152.
26. H. Risley, *Census of India,* 1901, I. B. Ethnographic Appendices, p. 118.
27. H. V. Nanjundayya and L. K. A. K. Iyer, *The Mysore Tribes and Castes,* Mysore, 1928-35, Vol. II, p. 36.
28. E. Thurston and K. Rangachari, *Castes and Tribes of Southern India,* Madras 1909, Vol. I, p. 340.

Malayalam-speaking Kṣatriyas of the same region also seclude their girls at the first menstruation.[29]

The Kadirs of Kerala and other regions of South India seclude their girls in a hut during the commencement of their first menstruation.[30] Among the Pulayans or Cherumans, the girl has to remain secluded for seven days. With her seven friends she has to dip in a river and then paint her face in yellow. In the period of her seclusion no one else may enter the hut, not even her mother. Women stand a little way off and lay down food for her. At the end of the time she is brought home, clad in a new clean cloth, and friends are honoured with betel nut, *toddy* and *arack*.[31] Among the Tiyans of Madura, a girl is thought to be polluted for four days from the beginning of her first menstruation. She has to reside in the northern side of the house and sleep on a grass mat. Another girl keeps her company and sleeps with her, and the girl concerned must not touch any person, tree or plant and see the sky. Her diet must be strictly vegetarian, without salt. She has also to keep a knife with her.[32] More or less similar puberty rites are found among the Kappilions of Madura and Tinnevelly[33] as well as among the Parivarams of Madura.[34] The menstrual rites of the Parayans or Malas are similar to those of the Pulayans described above.[35]

The puberty rites of the Nayars are called *thirandukuli*. The girl concerned has to remain secluded in a room. In the room there must be a lamp, a brass pot, a bundle of cocoanut blossoms and other things. The girl holds a handled mirror made of a round brass plate. The event is properly announced among the relatives. The neighbouring women visit the girl and dress her in new garments. On the third day the relatives and friends are invited. The *Manans* and *Velans* arrive on the fourth day. The menstruating girl along with her other girl friends undergoes a ceremonial bath. The whole party then returns in procession. The ceremony is followed by a great feast. The *Velans* sing before the assembly.

29. N. K. Pillai, *Census of India: Travancore,* 1931, Vol. XXVIII, p. 374.
30. L. K. A. K. Iyer, *The Cochin Tribes and Castes,* Vol. I, p. 5, II, p. 11.
31. Thurston and Rangachari, *op. cit.*, II, p. 65; Iyer, *op. cit.*, I, pp. 98-99; Pillai, *op. cit.*, p. 161; S. Mateer, *Native Life of Travancore*, London 1883, p. 45.
32. Thurston and Rangachari, *op. cit.*, VII, pp. 63 ff.
33. *ibid.*, III, p. 218.
34. *ibid.*, VI. p. 157.
35. Iyer, *op. cit.*, I. p. 76.

Sometimes the girl is led to a neighbouring house. On her return, drums are beaten and shouts of joy are given. Sometimes the feast is postponed to a more suitable day before the completion of which the girl is not allowed to enter the kitchen or go to the temple for worship.[36]

Similar rites are observed among such southern tribes and castes as the Haddi, Jalari, Jogi, Kapu, Karna-sale, Kuruba, Muka Dora, Mutracha, Maravan, Mala, Toreya, Tsakala, Bili Magga, Budubuduki, Darizi. Dasari, Domb, Gangadikara Okkalu, Ganiga, Golla, Halepaik, Halikar Okkaliga, Hasalar, Helava, Holeya, Idiga, Jain, Jangala, Jetti, Kacha Gauliga, Kare Okkalu, Kille-Kyata, Komati, Koracha, Kumbara, Kunchitiga, Ladar, Mediga, Meda, Mondaru, Nagartha, Nattuvan, Nayinda, Patvegara, Reddi, Sadaru, Salahuva Vakkalu, Padma Sale, Saniyasi, Satani, Tigala, Togata, Uppara, Wodda and so on.[37]

The first menstruation is also regarded as an occasion of ceremonial importance among some tribes and castes of Central India like the Gonds, Halabas, Kaikaris, Marathas, Kamars, Koshtis, Kunbis, Kurmis, Lodhis, Pardhis, etc.[38] Among the Gonds, there is, or was till lately, a building, out of the sight of the village, to which women in this condition retired. Their relatives brought them food and deposited it outside the hut, and not until they had gone away did a woman dare to come out and take it. It was believed that the greater evil would befall any one who looked upon a woman during her state of impurity.[39] Similar precautions are also taken by the Santals and the Mundas.[40]

7. The Ceremonial Defloration

Another form of puberty rites of the girls is ceremonial defloration which is closely connected with the menstrual rites. Previously it was widely current in different parts of India and the custom is still surviving among a good number of backward tribes. It seems

36. Thurston *op. cit.*, VI, p. 316; Iyer, *op. cit.*, II, pp. 27-30; Pillai, *op. cit.*, p. 162.
37. Thurston, *op. cit.*, Vols. I-VII, *Passim*; Nanjundayya and Iyer, *op. cit.*, Vols. I-IV, *passim*.
38. R. V. Russell and Hiralal, *Tribes and Castes of the Central Provinces*, London 1916, Vols. I-IV, *passim*.
39. *ibid.*, III, p. 83; IV, p. 67.
40. E. T. Dalton, *Descriptive Ethnology of Bengal*, Calcutta 1872, pp. 191, 214, 279.

probable that the *talikettu* or marriage ceremony existing among the Nayars of Kerala is a relic of ceremonial defloration. Captain Hamilton referred to the ceremonial defloration of the queen of Zamorin by the Namboodri priest. Duarte Barbosa recorded incidents of ceremonial deflorations through which the Nayar maids were introduced into womanhood.[41] The custom of ceremonial defloration by the family priest was also current in different parts of Bengal which was known as *Guruprasādī*.

These customary rites were not codified due to the increasing influence of patriarchy which demanded absolute chastity of women. Thus, in the law books the function of ritual defloration was entrusted to the husband. In the Gṛhyasūtras[42] there is a rite called *Caturthīkarma* (rite on the fourth day after marriage) which was nothing but a rite of ceremonial defloration. The Gṛhyasūtras explicitly say that on the fourth night the bridegroom must deflower the bride with the recital of a number of *mantras*. It was originally a puberty rite, but as the marriageable age of the girls came down, it appears that the rite of *Caturthīkarma* was discontinued and that the rite was performed long after the ritual of marriage and appropriately named *Garbhādhāna*. There is another rite called *Ṛtusaṅgamana*, also called *Niṣeka*[43] as distinct from *Garbhādhāna* which may be a relic of some older forms of ceremonial defloration on or before the commencement of the first menstruation. It is interesting to note that while performing the sexual act according to the rules prescribed in the *Caturthīkarma*, the husband had to recite those passages from the *Bṛhadāraṇyaka Upaniṣad* which identify sexual union with sacrifice. (For details see Kane, *History of Dharmaśāstra*, 11 pp. 203 ff.). Relics of menstrual rites are also found in the *Strī-ācāra*, in the *Snāpana*, *Paridhāpana* and *Saṃnāhana* rites,[44] in the *Tailaharidrāropaṇa* and others.

Among the several requirements of the bride to be chosen, the Gṛhyasūtras lay down that she must be a *nagnikā*. The word

41. See H. Risley, *Peoples of India*, p. 200; M. Billington, *Woman in India*, London 1895, p. 80; G. Panikkar, *Malabar and Its Folk*, Madras 1900, p. 143; D. Barbosa, *Description of the Coasts of East Africa and Malabar*, Hakluyt Society, p. 126; L. Moore, *Malabar Law and Custom*, Madras 1905, p. 70.

42. *Gobhila*, II. 5; *Sāṅkhyāyana*, I. 18-19; *Khadira*, I. 4. 12-16; *Pāraskara*, I. 11; *Āpastamba*, VIII. 10-11; *Hiraṇyakeśi*, I. 23-24.

43. Cf. *Vaikhānasa*, I. 1; III. 9; VI. 2.

44. *Āpastamba G. S.*, IV. 8; *Kāṭhaka*, XXV. 4; *Pāraskara*, I. 4; *Gobhila*, II. 1. 10-18; *Mānava*, I. 11. 46.

Nagnikā is variously explained by the commentators. Mātṛdatta, the commentator on the *Hiraṇyakeśi Gṛhyasūtra,* holds that *nagnikā* means 'one whose menstrual period is near' i.e., one who is fit for sexual intercourse. But Aṣṭāvakra, the commentator on the *Mānava Gṛhyasūtra,* says that *nagnikā* means one who has not yet experienced the impulses and emotions of the new stage of life (cf. *Vasiṣṭha Dharmasūtra* XVII. 70). In the *Gautama Dharmasūtra* (XVIII. 20-23) it is said that a girl should be given in marriage at puberty; she is allowed to remain virgin until her third menstruation. Manu holds three contradictory opinions, the first of which is that a maiden may rather live unmarried, but the father should never give her to one who is devoid of good qualities (IX. 89). But in some of the Dharmasūtras and Smṛtis it is stated that the father incurs the sin of destroying an embryo at each appearance of menses as long as the girl is unmarried.[45] Again, Manu says that a maiden after attaining puberty may wait for three years but after this period she may find out a man for her (IX. 90). This also finds support in the Dharmasūtras.[46] In another place Manu explicitly says that a man of thirty should marry a girl of twelve while a man of twenty four should marry a girl of eight years (IX. 94). This view is shared by the *Mahābhārata* though in some parts of the same text quite a different view is expressed.

From the time of the *Ṛgveda* (X. 85. 40-41) there was a mystical belief that Soma, Gandharva and Agni were the divine guardians of a girl, and according to the *Gṛhyasaṃgraha,* quoted in the commentary on the *Gobhila Gṛhyasūtra* III. 4. 6 and the *Pāraskara Gṛhyasūtra* (I. 4. 16), Soma enjoys a girl when she developes her pubic hairs, Gandharva enjoys her when she develops her breasts and Agni enjoys her when she menstruates.[47] This is frankly a mythological expression of the primitive puberty rites pointing to ceremonial defloration of a girl by at least three individuals. And this myth was subsequently utilised by patriarchal law makers in order to explain and support the cause of child marriage and to declare that a girl must be married before she develops the signs of maturity.

45. *Vasiṣṭha,* VII. 70-71; *Baudhāyana,* IV. 1. 12; *Yājñavalkya,* I. 64; etc.
46. Cf. *Baudhāyana,* IV. 1. 40.
47. Cf. *Saṃvarta Saṃhitā,* 64-67.

8. Remarks

In India, puberty rites are found not only among the backward peoples surviving in tribal stage, but also among peoples belonging to the higher grades of culture, though, with the rapid growth of industrialisation and urbanism, these rites are fading away fast. It is found that in many cases the rituals of a particular group are adopted, either in the original or in a changed form, by another group often belonging to a higher level of culture. As for example, relics of tribal menstrual rites, the most invariable and the most strictly observed of all the rites of primitive humanity, are abundantly found in the marriage rituals of the higher castes. Traces of ceremonial defloration may also be found in the now-obsolete ritual called *Caturthīkarma*. The Brahmanical Upanayana has retained traces of the primitive initiatory rites. Many of its leading features are in close agreement with the fundamentals of puberty rites performed by the tribes of various orders.

The adoption of the ritual of a particular group of people by another group is essentially connected with the social changes caused by the 'shifting tensions' in the primitive mode of food production. The pastoral tribes must have borrowed or inherited many of their ritual features from the hunting tribes, since hunting led to the domestication of cattle. In the second pastoral grade, as the case is with the so called Vedic Indians, when stock-raising was supplemented by agriculture, some agricultural features were also incorporated in the pastoral rituals. In the later Saṃhitās and the Brāhmaṇas, for example, we have reference to agricultural rituals while they are conspicuously absent in the earlier portions of the *Ṛgveda*. The same process holds good in the case of the agricultural tribes. Of the three agricultural grades, as is well known, the third is supplemented by stock-raising. As is evident, the rites of the first menstruation, etc. were obviously connected with agricultural tribes, since the relation between the processes of birth and generation and those of fertility in general appeared to be very intimate in primitive thought. In the next chapter we shall see how the two aspects of the same mystery found very similar modes of ritual expression.

VI

EARTH AND WOMAN

A Study in the Cults and Rituals of Fertility

1. Prologue

In the first chapter of this work we have seen how sexual acts were intimately connected with primitive religious rituals and cited a few passages from the ancient Vedic texts in which sexual union was identified with the performance of Vedic sacrifices like the *Vājapeya,* etc. In the fourth and fifth chapters we have held that the reason of establishing such relation between the sexual and religious aspects of human life must be traced to the primitive beliefs centering round the ideas of fertility and procreation. The ritualistic contents of the Brāhmaṇa literature, of the Dharma and Gṛhya Sūtras, of the Smṛtis and Purāṇas, are sophisticated developments and codifications of the ideas arising out of such primitive beliefs and this can be shown if we take into consideration the *rites de passage* marking separation from childhood and entrance into manhood or womanhood and the beliefs clustering round the physical features of women as well as their application in determining the sexual relation by which the social processes were on the move.

Rituals based upon fertility magic must have played a very significant part in the agricultural societies. "The fertility of the soil retained its immemorial association with the women who had been the tillers of the earth and were regarded as the depositaries of agricultural magic."[1] The following beliefs are universal: Women cause the fruits to multiply because they know how to produce children. Whatever is shown or planted by a pregnant woman will grow and increase as the foetus in her womb. A sterile woman is injurious to the garden; a barren woman makes the fields barren. Thus "the identification of earth with woman pervades the thought of all stages of culture and pages could be filled with the illustrations

1. R. Briffault, *The Mothers,* London 1952, Vol. III, p. 117.

of the universal equation."[2] Numerous such examples can also be furnished from ancient Indian literature. The word *Kṣetra* (seed-field) applies to woman in all the cases. In the law-book of Manu (IX. 33) man is identified with seed and woman with seed-field: *Kṣetrabhūtā smṛtā nārī pumn. aḥha ātsmṛ vījabhūt.*

Behind the universal conception of the fruit bearing Mother Earth as the *Great Goddess* how the ancient beliefs relating to pro-ceation and fertility worked out, we propose to deal with in the present chapter with the help of a few surviving or now-obsolete rituals.

2. A Sculpture from Nagarjunikonda

From Nagarjunikonda has been found a piece of sculpture which depicts the lower portion of a female figure in a sitting posture with legs doubled up and wide apart and feet pointing outwards. The bifurcated lower portion of the *vulva* is very prominently indicated, while the area between the broad belt below the navel and the upper portion of the vulva is used to make a *Pūrṇaghaṭa* (vessel) highly decorated with an ornamental belt around it.[3] In other words it depicts the lower portion of a nude pregnant woman and the elevation of the womb is represented by the *ghaṭa* or jar.

In the *Śatapatha Brāhmaṇa*,[4] *Ghaṭa* or *Kumbha* is equated with the womb of the Mother Goddess, if not with the Mother Goddess herself. The *Kathāsaritsāgara*[5] identifies *kumbha* and *ghaṭa* explicitly with uterus. "The equivalence may explain why the *Navarātra*, 'nine night' fertility festivals to all Mother Goddesses begins on the first Āśvina by establishing a fertility-jar (*Ghaṭasthāpana*).[6]

The *kumbha* or jar as representation of Mother Goddess still survives in many festivals. In different parts of the country the rite of infusing by means of spells (*mantra*) the spirit of the goddess into an earthen jar is performed. A place within the temple is purified by plastering the surface with mud and cowdung. The jar is filled with water and covered with the shoots of the mango

2. *ibid.*, p. 56 f.
3. *Epigraphia Indica,* Vol. XXIX, pp. 138-39.
4. XIII. 8. 3. 3.
5. LXX. 112.
6. D. D. Kosambi, *Myth and Reality,* Bombay 1961, p. 73.

tree, and over it is placed an earthen saucer containing barley and rice, which is covered with a yellow cloth. The priest recites verses, and sprinkling water on the jar and its contents with a few blades of sacred *Kuśa* grass, he invites the goddess to enter it. As a sign that she has occupied it, the outside of the jar is sprinkled with red powder. During the period occupied in the rite the priest practises abstinence, eating only roots and fruits. The service concludes with a fire-sacrifice in which barley, sugar, butter and sesamum are burnt before the jar which holds the goddess.[7]

The most popular Mother Goddess of Bengal is Durgā, whose worship consists of the rituals of *Navapatrikā* or nine plants—*rambhā, kaccvī, haridrā, jayantī, bilva, dāḍima, aśoka, mānaka* and *dhānya*—which reveal her association as earth and corn mother with the vegetative forces of nature. In one such ritual, a *Yantra* called *Sarvatobhadramaṇḍala* is drawn upon the ground. It is simply a Tantric diagram showing the pictures of the female generative organ. Then a *pūrṇaghaṭa* or *pūrṇakumbha* is to be placed on the said diagram. The *Pūrṇaghaṭa* is an earthen vessel filled with water. It is nothing but a symbol of the female womb. The figure of a baby called *Sinduraputtalī* is drawn on the surface of the vessel. The open mouth of the *pūrṇaghaṭa* is covered with five kinds of leaves, and a cocoanut, smeared with vermilion, is placed on it. It is a simple fertility rite by which the plants are brought into contact with the female reproductive organ, evidently to ensure multiplication.[8]

3. Linga and Yoni

Thus in primitive magico-religious rites the importance of human generative organs was a significant feature. Briffault provides us with numerous examples in which the exposure and worship of the generative organs form an important feature of the religious rites all over the world.[9] Pausanias observes that at Cylbene "the image of Hermes which the people of the place revere is nothing but the male organ of generation erect on the pedestal".[10] At Syracuse, on the day of Thesmophoria, cakes of sesame and honey representing

7. *North Indian Notes and Queries*, IV, p. 19 f.
8. Chattopadhyaya, *Lokāyata*, pp. 294 f.
9. *The Mothers*, Vol. III, pp. 207 ff.
10. J. E. Harrison, *Prolegomena to the Study of Greek Religion*, Cambridge 1908, p. 122.

the female organ were offered to Demeter.[11] At Roman marriages, the bride was required to sit upon the image of Priapus (Mutunnus), the phallic god.[12] Even in the middle ages phallic worship was practised in France and Belgium.[13] At Mohenjodaro we come across the models of *liṅga* and *yoni* which were used probably as life-bestowing amulets,[14] while at Harappa a number of conical *liṅgas* representing the male organ, and large undulating rings of stones, thought to symbolise the female principle, have been recorded.[15]

The origin of the *yoni* cult of the later Tantras must therefore be sought in the prehistoric ruins of Harappa and Mohenjodaro. The Tantric *Śrīcakra* is nothing but the representation of female generative organ.[16] Primarily the *liṅga* was the symbol of the act of cultivation while the *yoni* represented Mother Earth. This finds support in a statement of Manu: *iyaṃ bhūmirhi bhūtānāṃ śāśvatī yoniru-cyate.*[17] One should not forget to recall in this connection that the primitive hoe was designed to resemble the male organ, while the word *lāṅgala* (plough) is closely associated with *liṅga.*[18] Later on, when metaphysical values were attributed to them, the principles of the cult of *liṅga* and *yoni* came to be interpreted in terms of a dualistic philosophical outlook.

4. Sacred Prostitution

The sacred prostitution practised in various parts of the ancient world was therefore a custom based upon some objective understanding, a custom quite in accordance with the primitive beliefs in the identical relation of earth and woman. Prostitution was an essential feature in the cults of the Goddess Mylitta of Babylon, Venus of Cyprus, Aphrodite of Corinth, Anitis of Armenia and other gods and goddess of Western Asia.[19] Every woman was bound, at least once in her life, to offer her body to strangers before the

11. L. R. Farnell, *Cults of the Greek States,* Edinburgh 1896-1909, Vol. III. p. 99.
12. O. Keifer, *Sexual Life in Ancient Rome,* London 1963, pp. 114 ff.
13. E. S. Hartland, *Primitive Paternity,* London 1909, Vol. I, p. 63.
14. J. Marshall, *Mohenjodaro and the Indus Civilization,* London 1931, pls. XIII. 1. 7; XIV. 2. 4.
15. M. S. Vats, *Excavations at Harappa,* Delhi 1950, pp. 51, 53, 55 ff., 140.
16. R. G. Bhandarkar, *Collected Works,* Poona 1936, Vol. IV, p. 209.
17. Manu, IX. 37.
18. P. C. Bagchi, *Pre-Dravidian and Pre-Aryan in India,* Calcutta 1929, pp. 10, 14.
19. For references see my *Indian Mother Goddess,* pp. 31-39.

deity. Religious prostitution was current among the women of Heliopolis or Baalbec in Syria. In a Lydian inscription, belonging to the second century, a lady called Aurelia Aemilia declares that she had prostituted herself in the temple service in the same way as her mother and grandmother had done. In the epic of *Gilgamesh,* Ishtar is represented as gathering round her unchaste girls and harlots, and as a goddess of prostitution the epithet 'consecrated' is applied to her.[20] Lactantius (*Divinae institutiones,* I. 7) says that Aphrodite or Venus who is generally identified with Ishtar or Astarte instituted the art of courtesanship. Prostitution has something to do with the goddess cult also in India. Even today 'the sacred earth' to be collected from the door of a prostitute is required in Durgā worship. Relics of sacred prostitution are also found in a Jātaka story,[21] while in Southern India religious prostitution in the temples was legally abolished only a few years ago.

Various theories have been set forth to explain this custom, but those offered by Manhardt and Frazer are generally accepted. The latter concludes that a great Mother Goddess, the personification of all the reproductive forces of nature, was worshipped under different names but with a substantial similarity of myth and ritual by many peoples of Western Asia; that associated with her was a lover, or rather a series of lovers, divine yet mortal, with whom she mated year by year, their commerce being deemed essential to the propagation of animals and plants, each in their several kind; and further, the fabulous union of the divine pair was stimulated and, as it were, multiplied on earth by the real, though temporary, union of the human sexes at the sanctuary of the goddess for the sake of thereby ensuring the fruitfulness of the ground and the increase of man and beast".[22]

5. Ritual and Myth

There is no need, at present, to take Frazer's view as absolute. Let us see what the other data suggest by themselves. From the ancient texts we find that the Egyptian Isis was originally a Corn Mother who was not only the creatress of the fresh verdure of vegetation that covered the earth, but the green corn-field itself,

20. N. K. Sanders, *Epic of Gilgamesh,* Pelican, pp. 83 ff.
21. E. B. Cowell, *Jātakas,* Cambridge, 1895-1913, V. No. 141.
22. J. G. Frazer, *Adonis Attis Osiris,* London, 1907, pp. 34-35.

personified as a goddess. Cybele, the Phrygian Mother of the Gods, was also originally a Corn Mother. The union of Cybele and Attis, like that of Aphrodite and Adonis, or Ishtar and Tammuj, was marked by sex festivals. The union of Demeter and Zeus was also imitated by men and women in the sex festivals at Eleusis in order to make the fields wave with yellow corns.

Of the influential gods, worshipped in different countries in Western Asia and Egypt with a variety of rituals including sacred prostitution, special mention should be made of Adonis (Tammuj), Attis and Osiris. They were the sons (sometimes also conceived as brothers) and lovers respectively of the goddesses Aphrodite (Ishtar), Cybele and Isis. According to the existing myths, these gods would die every year, causing the goddesses to mourn, and would then be brought back to life once again. We have seen that the said goddesses were the personifications of the green-corn-fields, the Mother Earth. The said gods likewise were the personifications of corns, the sons and mortal consorts of the goddess, and the theme of their annual death and revival symbolised the annual facts of plant-life in relation to the field. In the first chapter we have seen how the killing of the king or priest (impersonating the dying gods) was originally nothing but an incident in the ritual cycle of the queen (impersonating the goddess). It is ritual that generates and sustains myth.

6. An Indian Cult of the Prostitutes

It is against this background that we are now going to introduce the readers with the rituals of an Indian god of the Adonis type. This god is Kārtikeya, a well known deity whose legends are found in the epics and the Purāṇas. The worship of Kārtikeya is a living feature of modern Hinduism in different parts of India. There are a few works on this god dealing with his characteristics as found in ancient literature and inscriptions, his iconographical peculiarities and sacred places associated with his name. Only two features of the Puranic Kārtikeya which should be remembered in this connection are that he was brought up by the Divine Mothers and that he came out piercing the body of another semi-divine being called Skanda with whom he came to be identified later.

But here I am describing a local form of his cult which has nothing to do with his traditional mode of worship. At Chinsurah in the

Hooghly District of West Bengal, about 40 KM to the north of Calcutta, where I live and where I was born and brought up, this god, i.e. Kārtikeya, is worshipped specially by the prostitutes. Of course it is now a dying cult. In my early years I saw many images worshipped by different groups and now there is only one. Even this one, although still worshipped by the prostitutes, bears no speciality. Other images of this god are also worshipped at Chinsurah in different localities by collecting subscriptions from the peoples. These public-worships have nothing to do so far as the present study is concerned.

What I remember and what I have gathered from the old persons of this place regarding the Kārtikeya of the prostitutes are the following. The image of the god, though he is seated on the peacock, looks more like an amorous gentleman of the nineteenth century than a god with his usual emblems. This figure is popularly known as *Bābu-kārtik,* the prefix *bābu* being indicative of the usual epithet of the occasional consorts of the prostitutes. But this has very little to do with the original cult of the god. Of the rituals connected with his worship, two deserve special mention which are still remembered by many of us. One was the dance of the eunuchs and the other was the digging of a trench in which rice, pulses, barley and various seeds were sown and allowed to sprout. The dance of eunuchs reminds us of the ancient cult of Attis, the god who was emasculated and in whose worship the eunuchs had a significant part to play. *It is to be remembered in this connection that in Bengal if not in the whole of India, the eunuchs earn their livelihood by dancing in such houses where a baby has recently been born and that their presence and blessings are considered auspicious to the new-born, pointing to their ritual connection with childbirth.*

The other ritual may be called the ritual of the *Garden of Adonis.* This is done by digging a trench on the earth or by sowing seeds in an earthen pot. Numerous examples of such rituals of the *Garden of Adonis* have been collected by Frazer,[23] and in the next section we shall furnish a few Indian examples. The ritual use of the *Garden of Adonis* in the cult of Kārtikeya at Chinsurah and his association with the eunuchs suggest that he was primarily a god of vegetation and fertility. His association with pregnancy and childbirth is also indicated by the fact that the Puranic tradition

23. *ibid.*, p. 194 ff.

makes him the husband of Ṣaṣṭhī, the protectress of children.

In different parts of East Bengal we have Kārtikeya *Vratas* (rituals) performed by married women for the purpose of offspring and vegetation, and in these rituals *Gardens of Adonis* are cultivated in earthen pots. Sometimes an image of Kārtikeya is placed in the centre of a small paddy-field specially made for this purpose, and the area is surrounded in a circular fashion by smaller images of the said god. The performers of this *Vrata* have to hear a legend, which is a Puranic story that runs as follows. A Brāhmaṇa couple in their sorrowful state of mind for not having any issue of their own, gave up their social life and began to live in a forest. One day they came across a number of women in that forest performing a rite which appeared to the Brāhmaṇa as strange. Asked by him, they answered that they were performing the ritual of Kārtikeya by sowing seeds in earthen pots. They also assured him that if his wife would perform the same rite with them, she must bear good children. Accordingly the Brāhmaṇa's wife performed the ritual and in return she gave birth to nice children.

Thus Kārtikeya is a god of fertility, both natural and human, and we find that, on the one hand, he is worshipped by the housewives desirous of good offsprings, while on the other, by a special class of women, the purpose of which we do not know, not even they. One of my informants who is now a woman of eighty and once who had the occupation of prostitution, told me that the purpose was to get customers like Kārtikeya, a nice, healthy and wealthy person and at the same time licentious. I do not know why, when and how the god Kārtikeya came to be conceived as a class one debauch, but there are some references in the *Brahma Purāṇa* which show that such a tendency to characterise him in this way began to develop as early as the tenth century A. D. It is also to be remembered that in popular belief Kārtikeya is supposed to be unmarried and the epithet *Āibuḍo,* i.e. unmarried, is attributed to him. The consort of the Kārtikeya of Chinsurah is Sarasvatī who was also worshipped especially by the prostitutes, not because she is the goddess of learning but because, in popular belief, though not in actual condition, she is unmarried and of doubtful moral character. To me, however, it appears that Sarasvatī is traditionally associated with the courtesans for her being the presiding deity of the sixty four arts which the learned courtesans should master according to the *Kāmasūtra* of Vātsyāyana which also describes the public worship of this goddess by the wealthy Nāgarakas with vocal, musical and dramatic performances. In any case, it is interesting to note that in some South Indian sculptures the goddess is represented as seated on a peacock which is the vehicle of Kārtikeya.

But my informant's professional interpretation cannot explain the association of Kārtikeya with such primitive rituals as the dance of the eunuchs or making of the *Garden of Adonis*. It therefore appears that a very primitive god of vegetation and fertility, whose cult was an offshoot of primitive Mother Goddess cult, was later symbolised by Kārtikeya and that the original worship of this primitive deity was marked by indiscriminate sexual acts. But in course of time, with the gradual development of patriarchal values, when the concept of female chastity for the purpose of inheritance of property became the driving force of society, the task of performing and maintaining the ancient sexual rites fell on a special class of women, the prostitutes, who were the natural production of the demoralised, patriarchal, property-oriented social system. In the initial stage of this later development, they had some prestige and social position, owing to their traditional association with religious cults and arts, which can be proved by ancient literary references, but this also declined in course of time, and they lost even their hold on religious affairs. A few rituals, however, survived among them, but these were purely insignificant mechanical survivals, completely meaningles to them.[24] An isolated relic of such survivals is the Kārtikeya of Chinsurah.

An interesting feature of the Kārtikeya cult is that it follows the solar calendar, while other cults of India mostly follow the lunar. It is performed on the last day of the month of Kārtika. Two other rituals are known to follow the solar calendar. One is the ritual of *Ambuvācī* which is observed by the Bengalee women from the 7th to 11th day of the month of Āṣaḍha (the third month of the Hindu year). It is a fertility rite. In Bengal, it is believed that, during the four days of the said ritual, Mother Earth menstruates in order to prepare herself for her fertilising work. During this period there is an entire cessation of all ploughing, sowing and other farm work. Widows have to undergo a number of taboos since procreation is forbidden to them. The second ritual which follows the solar calandar is that of *Itu* performed exclusively by Bengalee women on

24. See my *History of Indian Erotic Literature*, Ch. 12.

every sunday of the eighth month known as Mārgaśirṣa or Agrahāyana. She seems to be a goddess since the epithets *Lakṣhmī*, *Ṭhākurāṇi*, etc. are attributed to her. The most striking feature of the ritual of Itu is the *Garden of Adonis.* In an earthen pot various seeds are sown and tended for a month, and this is the symbol of the goddess. Four small vessels (*ghaṭas*) filled with water which represent the female womb are placed on the pot. On each sunday a ceremonial fast is observed by women, and on the last sunday the *Gardens of Adonis* are carried to a river or tank by the women and thrown into the water. Since the rituals of Ambuvācī, Kārtikeya and Itu are all concerned with vegetation, fertility and childbirth and since all of them strictly follow a solar calendar, can we not suppose that they are inter-connected revealing a very primitive ritual cycle constituted by them?

7. The Gardens of Adonis

We have seen that the rituals of Kārtikeya and Itu are characterised by the *Garden of Adonis* by which we understand the sowing of different corn-seeds on earth or earthen pots. This ritual is not an isolated feature. In different parts of Rajasthan, Gaurī is worshipped as the goddess of vegetation and fertility. The meaning of Gaurī is 'yellow', emblematic of the ripened harvest when the votaries of the goddess adore her effigies which are those of a matron painted the colour of ripe corn. An image of the goddess and a smaller one of her husband are placed together. A small trench is then dug and barley is sown in it. The women dance round it, hand in hand, invoking the blessing of the goddess. The young corns are taken up from the *Garden of Adonis* and distributed by the women to the men, who wear them in their turbans.[25]

In these rites the distribution of the barley-shoots to the men point clearly to the desire for offspring along with the rapid growth of vegetation. The same motive probably explains the use of the *Gardens of Adonis* in the marriage rituals. In Madras, seeds of five or nine sorts are mixed and sown in earthen pots; the bride and bridegroom water the seeds for four days and on the fifth day the seedlings are thrown into a tank or river.[26] In the Himalayan

25. J. Tod, *Annals and Antiquities of Rajasthan* (ed. W. Crooke) London 1920, I, pp. 570 ff.
26. *Indian Antiquary*, XXV, p. 144.

districts of North Western India the cultivators sow barley, maize, pulse or mustard in a basket of earth on the 24th day of the fourth month of Hindu calendar and on the last day of the month they place the new sprouts among small clay images of Śiva and Pārvatī and worship them. Next they cut down the green stalks and wear them in their head-dress.[27] At the temple of Padmāvatī, near Pandharpur in Maharashtra, during the *Navarātra,* a *Garden of Adonis* is cultivated in front of the pedestal of the goddess.[28] A similar rite is observed before the images of two other goddesses, Ambābāi and Lakhubāi, who also have temples in the same region.[29]

In many parts of Northern India we have a festival, the *Jayi* or *Jawara* of Upper India, and the *Bhujaria* of Madhya Pradesh, in which, on the seventh day of the bright half of *Śrāvaṇa,* grains of barley are sown in a pot of manure and on the first day of the next month, the women and girls take the yellowish-green stalks out and distribute the plants to their male friends who bind them in their turbans.[30] At Sargal this ceremony is observed about the middle of September. On the last day of the function, the women of every family bring their own pots and having laid them on the ground they dance around them. Then taking the pots of sprouting corn they descend to the edge of the water, wash the soil away from the pots, and distribute the young plants among their friends.[31]

The Garo priest, at sowing time, invokes Rohimi or Rokeme the goddess of vegetation.[32] In Western India various kinds of grain are worshipped in honour of the Mother Goddess, and the mother is invoked to enter the seedlings which are worshipped and finally thrown into water.[33] In Uttar Pradesh, on one of the *Navarātra* days sacred to Devī Durgā, special agricultural rites are performed.[34] Among the Oraons, it is believed that the Corn Mother watches over the threshing-floor until the next

27. E. T. Atkinson, *Himalayan Districts of the North Western Provinces of India,* Allahabad 1884, Vol. II, p. 870.
28. *Bombay Gazetteer,* Vol. XX, p. 454.
29. *ibid.,* pp. 443, 460.
30. W. Crooke, *Popular Religion and Folklore in North India,* Westminister 1896, p. 294.
31. Murray Aunsley in *Folklore,* Vol. V, pp. 253 ff.
32. A. Playfair, *The Garos,* London 1909, p. 93.
33. *Bombay Gazetteer,* Vol IX(1), p. 392.
34. B. A. Gupte, *Hindu Holidays and Ceremonials,* pp. 181 ff.

harvest.[35] Among them and also among the Mundas, *Gardens of Adonis* are specially cultivated by women in the sowing season.[36] The Bhuiyas, Kols and Binds of Uttar Pradesh also worship Hariāri Devī, Mother of Greenery, during the rainy season in a similar way.[37] In Kashmir and Punjab, during the *Navrātra,* plants of barley and wheat are placed in an earthen pot and offered to the Mother Goddess.

In Bengal the Goddess Lakṣmī is symbolised by a certain quantity of rice kept in a basket, and on the basket over the heap of rice a wooden pot, popularly known as *Gāchkauṭā* on tree-case, is placed. It is shaped like a womb and smeared with vermilion. The basket itself is decorated by cowrie-shells, the universal symbol of female generative organ. On the appointed days the pot is installed on a wooden throne or platform by the oldest lady of the house. The said ritual is performed four times in a year in connection with sowing and reaping. On the full moon day, immediately after the worship of the goddess Durgā, the ritual of Kojāgarī Lakṣmī takes place. According to popular belief, the goddess comes at night and knocks at the door of every house. Probably this Lakṣmī is an offshoot of the goddess Durgā and in the capacity of a Corn Mother her relationship with the latter resembles that of Persephone with Demeter. On the last day of the month of Kārtika, we have the ritual of Muṭh-Lakṣmi in which a few stalks of rice are carried from the field to the house. One should not fail to note in this connection that the vegetation god Kārtikeya is also worshipped on that very day. In the next month the same stalks are worshipped in connection with Navānna-Lakṣmī or the Lakṣmī of New Rice.

8. Sītā and Persephone

The myth of Demeter is very significant to the study of the original character of the Mother Goddess. One day while Persephone, daughter of Demeter, was wandering, the earth opened suddenly, and Pluto, god of Hades, forcibly carried her off. When Demeter heard that Pluto had carried off her daughter with the consent of Zeus, she withdrew herself from Olympus and also cast a blight

35. S. C. Roy, *Oraons of Chotanagpur,* Ranchi 1915, pp. 441 ff.
36. Dalton, *op. cit.*, p. 259.
37. W. Crooke, *Tribes and Castes of the North Western Provinces and Oudh,* Calcutta 1896, Vol. I, p. 83.

upon the earth as a result of which no barley grew nor did trees yield fruit. The goddess then retired to Eleusia where the king Celeus received her cordially and she became nurse of his sons, Triptolemus and Demophon. She desired to make Demophon immortal, and put him on one night into a fire. But his real mother screamed aloud as a result of which the spell was broken, and the boy perished. Demeter, however, made up for the loss by instructing the other son in the art of agriculture. Meanwhile the blight remained upon the earth, and mankind was perishing from famine. Thereupon a compromise between the parties was arranged and Zeus declared that Persephone would spend one third of each year on earth with her mother, and the remaining two thirds with Pluto.

According to Frazer, the myth reveals that Demeter and Persephone are personifications of corns. The former is the ripe corn and the latter, the seed-corn.[38] Persephone's stay in the underworld is certainly suggestive of the seed-corn staying under the earth. Pausanias (VIII. 42) writes that he saw a cave sacred to Black Demeter at Phigalia. The Black Demeter appears to have been the personification of the barren winter earth; the Green Demeter, the goddess of green plants; and the yellow Demeter, the deity of ripe harvest. The Indian Buddhist goddess Tārā is also blue, green and yellow.[39] Kālī the black and naked goddess, might also represent the barren and naked winter-earth in her original character. In the month of Boedromion (September-October) the *Eleusiana* took place which was a mystic ceremony of initiation performed during the festival of Demeter. The idea of the dying away and the subsequent revival of seed grain, which had its mythical counterpart in the story of Persephone, abducted by Pluto in the underworld, developed into a secret cult into which persons were initiated through special mysterious usages, the secret of which no one was allowed to reveal.[40]

The myth of Demeter and Persephone may have some bearing on the myths and legends which formed the basis of Vālmīki's *Rāmāyaṇa*, one of the two celebrated epics of India. The similarity of the Demeter-Persephone myth with the main story of the *Rāmāyaṇa*

38. J. G. Frazer, *Spirits of the Corn and the Wild*, London 1913, pp. 37 ff.
39. B. T. Bhattacharyya, *Indian Buddhist Iconography*, Calcutta 1958, pp. 306 ff.
40. See Chs. IV and V. For the Greek rituals of initiation see Thomson, *Aschylus and Athens*, pp. 97 ff.

is too striking to be ignored. The heroine of the epic is born of a field-furrow, abducted by a Pluto (Rāvaṇa of Laṅkā), and after all her adventures she returns to the earth. The story of the quest of Sītā by Rāma and his troops reminds us of Demeter's quest for Persephone or the quest of Isis for the body of Osiris. In the ancient hymns of the Vedas Sītā is simply the furrow which bears crops for men.[41] The word *Rāma* is derived from root *ram* which means ploughing as well as the act of sexual intercourse. In the *Arthaśāstra* of Kauṭilya (I. 24), Sītā is conceived as residing in seeds and plants; the superintendent of agriculture is mentioned as *Sītādhyakṣa.* The *Harivaṃśa* (Viṣṇu, III. 14) also identifies Sītā with fields for ploughmen. Hence it appears that in hoary antiquity the myths of Sītā evolved out of agricultural rituals and that one such myth was rendered into the form of an epic by the great poet Vālmīki.

9. Earth Goddess of Harappa Culture

In a passage of the *Mārkaṇḍeya Purāṇa* the Devī says: "Next O Ye gods, I shall support the whole world with the life-sustaining vegetables which shall grow out of my own body during a period of heavy rain. I shall gain fame on earth then as Śākambharī."[42] Thus this goddess is no other than Mother Earth from whose body grow the life-sustaining vegetables. In this connection we may refer to a seal unearthed at Harappa which, on the obverse, shows a nude female figure, head downwards and legs stretched out upwards, with a plant issuing out of her womb.[43] This may be regarded as a primitive prototype of the aforesaid Earth Mother Śākambharī. There are many other seals in which trees and plants are associated with the goddess.[44] Many of the Mother Goddess figurines from Mohenjodaro are painted with red slip or wash, the significance of which we have discussed above. The goddesses wear a distinctive head-dress which rises from the back of the head, in some cases directly from the head, while in others it forms part of the coiffure. They are significantly nude save for a very short skirt round the

41. *Ṛgveda,* IV. 57; *Atharvaveda,* III. 17. 4; *Yajurveda,* XII. 69-72; *Gobhila Gṛ. Sū.,* IV. 4. 27-30; *Pāraskara Gṛ. Sū.,* II. 17. 9-10; etc.
42. XCII. 43 f. (Pargiter's tr.).
43. J. Marshall, *Mohenjodaro and the Indus Civilization,* London 1931, Vol. I, p. 52.
44. *ibid.,* 63 ff., Mackay, *Further Excavations at Mohenjodaro,* Vol. I, pp. 337-38.

waist secured by a girdle.[45] Terracotta figurines from Southern Sind along the Indus are similar to those found at Harappa and Mohenjodaro.[46] The figurines of the Mother Goddess from Chanhudaro are also of Mohenjodaro type, the only difference being that they stand upon a flat, more or less open, base which recall the figurines from the pre-Harappan sites of Northern and Southern Baluchistan. The figurines of the Kulli culture finish at the waist in a splayed pedestal, arms bent with hands on the hips, breasts usually shown, eyes fashioned from small stones, hair elaborately dressed, ornamented by oval pendants resembling cowrie-shells, and bangles on arms and wrists. In the Zhob valley sites the same type of female figures recurs with necklaces, large and beak-like noses, and slit mouths and bangles. Stuart Piggott rightly observes that they are "a grim embodiment of the Mother Goddess who is also the guardian of the dead—an underworld deity connected alike with the corpse and seed-corn buried beneath the earth. The fertility aspect so often connected with such underworld gods is indeed represented by other models".[47]

10. Earth and Woman

We shall conclude this chapter with reference to an interesting ritual connected with earth and woman. Frazer referred to a curious custom of rain-making which prevailed in different parts of Europe. When people suffered from drought, rain was invoked by a number of women who stripped themselves naked. Referring to this custom he remarked that "such attempts are by no means confined, as the cultivated reader might imagine to the naked inhabitants of those sultry lands like Central Australia and some parts of Eastern or Southern Africa where for months together the pitiless sun beats down out of a blue and cloudless sky on the parched and gapping earth. They are, or used to be, common enough among outwardly civilised folk in the moist climate of Europe."[48]

The motive behind this curious rite may easily be explained in terms of imitative magic. Earth requires seed in the form of water, just as a woman requires seed or semen to produce a child. During

45. Marshall, *op. cit.*, p. 341; Mackay, *op. cit.*, p. 349.
46. N. G. Majumdar, *Exploration in Sind* (MASI, 48), Delhi 1934, pp. 38, 68.
47. S. Piggott, *Prehistoric India*, p. 127.
48. *The Golden Bough* (ab), pp. 62-78.

the Gorakhpur famine of 1873-78, there were many accounts of women stripping themselves naked at night and dragging the plough over the fields.[49] Of regular nudity rites in case of the failure of rains we have an instance from Chunar: "The rains of this year held off for a long period and last night (24th July 1892) the following ceremony was performed secretly. Between the hours of 9 and 10 P. M. a barber's wife went from door to door and invited all the women to join in ploughing. They all collected in a field from which all males were excluded. Three women of a cultivator's family stripped off all their cloths; two were yoked to a plough like oxen, and the third held the handle. Then they began to imitate the operation of ploughing. The woman who had the plough in her hand shouted, 'O Mother Earth: Bring parched grain, water and chaff. Our bellies are bursting to pieces from hunger and thirst."[50]

The same rite was performed in a village near Lucknow on the 30th of July 1963, and the news appeared in the newspapers with funny journalistic notes and comments. However, what we find in this case is that it is a simple rite of rain-magic in which Mother Earth is associated with woman. Probably the curious marriage rite called *Matamangara* of North India is based upon the said idea of communicating the fertility of the earth to the bride.[51] In the Telugu country, five women are sent to the clay pit to bring the earth for the seats of the bride and bridegroom.[52] The first act done when a child is born among the Nayars is to beat the earth with a cocoanut leaf and in the puberty rites of the Parayans the mother strikes the ground behind the child with a flail.[53] The Oraon girls, during the time of sowing, pat the earth to render her fertile.[54]

It appears from what we have seen above that the Earth Mothers came into being when people began to settle down in agricultural communities. The connection between the growth of agriculture and the origin of the village communities may account for the emergence of Earth and Corn Mothers on the basis of the identical nature of earth and woman. All over the world, the earth-spirit

49. Crooke, *op. cit.*, p. 69; see also *Journal of Royal Anthropological Institute,* Vol. XIX, pp. 231 ff.
50. *North Indian Notes and Queries,* Vol. I, p. 210.
51. Crooke, *Religion and Folklore of North India,* p. 51.
52. J. E. Padfield, *The Hindu at Home,* Madras 1896, p. 144.
53. Thurston, *op. cit.*, V, p. 344; VI, p. 93.
54. S. C. Roy, *op. cit.*, p. 142.

is generally regarded as female and the presiding deities of agriculture are mainly goddesses, because the idea of fertility and reproduction is concerned with woman. The fact that agriculture among primitive races was the business of women rather than of men probably meant that the goddesses were at first worshipped by women rather than by men.

VII

DEATH AND RESURRECTION

A Study in the Rituals of Dewali and Holi

1. Prologue

All the world over, rituals have been classified into various types according to their nature. At the simplest level of life the rituals are instinctive in character, and many of them have developed out of a primitive conception of death and rebirth. This conception owed its origin probably to the observation of the functioning of plant life, its death and revival. The idea of life after death was the natural conclusion of this observation. In a preceding chapter we have seen that among the ancients every significant turning point of life has been equated with death. As for example, the *upanayana* is a rite of puberty which sanctions a new life, a second birth, to the initiated one. We have seen that, among primitive tribes, the person to be initiated has to pretend as if he is dead. His kinsmen make a ritual lament. Then he has to pretend as if he is born again, toss his hands and feet, like a new-born babe. Likewise when a man becomes a recluse, he has to change his name and make his own funeral rites. He is considered to be a new man whose past life is dead for ever. Evidently these ideas, especially the idea of death and rebirth in every turning point of an individual's life, contributed to the growth of the concepts of *Karma*, transmigration of soul, metempsychosis, and so on.

Robertson Smith has shown that in the primitive religion, it is ritual that generates and sustains myth. On the basis of Semitic studies he points out that a comprehension of Hebrew ritual is essential to the understanding of Hebrew mythology.[1] In fact divinities are born of ritual, as is correctly held by Jane Harrison. "The May-pole or harvest sheaf is half a way to a harvest-maiden; it is thus that a goddess is made. A song is sung, a story told, and

1. W. Robertson Smith, *Religion of the Semites*, London 1899, p. 17.

the very telling fixes the outline of the personality".[2] The rites of the annual decay and revival of plant life, current in olden days, as we have seen in a preceding chapter, undoubtedly gave rise to the myths of Osiris and Isis in Egypt, Attis and Cybele in Phrygia, Tammuj and Ishtar in Syria and Babylon, and Adonis and Aphrodite in Cyprus and Greece. Herein one has to seek the root of the Christian concept of resurrection. The story of the death and resurrection of Christ was probably based upon the myths of the death and revival of Adonis, Attis and Osiris.[3] This does not, however mean that Christ was a mythical figure. It is everywhere a common practice to ascribe mythical elements to historical personalities. Here we may refer to the Buddha-legends which have thoroughly converted a historical personality into a divine figure.

That the festivals of Holi and Dewali (Dīpāvalī), celebrated now-a-days in different parts of India with so much pomp and splendour, were originally the rituals of death and resurrection, may appear strange and even fanciful, but there are indeed grounds to believe that they were so. However, before dealing with the essentials of these festivals, it is necessary to introduce our readers with some allied facts and concepts which are expected to serve as keys to our understanding.

2. The Cult of the Dead among the Buddhists

The ancient Buddhist monuments may be divided into five groups according to their object: Stambha, Stūpa, Caitya, Vihāra and Sucaka.[4] Of these, the Vihāras were monasteries for the accommodation of monks living together in communities, and were mostly, *if not always*, connected with Caityas. The Sucakas were ornamental rails mostly employed as the enclosures of Stūpas, or to surround a terrace on which stood a sacred tree, etc. The Stambhas were pillars on the capital of which a religious symbol is represented.[5] Some scholars believe that the conception of Stambha derived its main impulses from the ancient phallic cult. It is a development of the primitive custom of erecting a monolith as a symbol

2. J. E. Harrison, *Prolegomena to the Study of Greek Religion*, Cambridge, 1908, pp. 64, 187, 304.
3. J. G. Frazer, *Adonis, Attis, Osiris*, pp. 182-93, 219-34, 269-77.
4. Cf. J. Fergusson, *History of Indian and Eastern Architecture*, London 1876, p. 50.
5. A. Grünwedel, *Buddhist Art in India*, London 1901, pp. 20-21.

of human generative organ (cf. the erection of *dhvaja* mentioned in the third chapter) on a buried dead-body as a symbol of regeneration. This is quite likely.

The term Stūpa applies to any mound, as a *funeral pile* or tumulus, and hence to domical structures over sacred relics of Buddha and other Buddhist saints. "When they preserved relics, the shrine in which these were kept was the *Dhātugarbha* (Pali, *Dhātugabbha;* Singhalese *Dāgaba;* Japanese *Tō*); and as most Stūpas were erected over relics (*dhātu*), the whole structure a Dāgaba (*Dhātugarbha*). A Stūpa consists of a circular or square base supporting a dome (*garbha*), on which stands a square block or neck (*gala*) representing a box to hold a relic, crowned by a capital consisting a number of flat tiles. Above this is the umbrella or spire (*Cūḍāmaṇi*—Burmese, *hti*)—single or with several roofs, usually three, over one another. Like Stūpa, the word Caitya is applied to a monument or *cenotaph,* and in a secondary sense to a temple or shrine containing a *caitya* or *Dhātugarbha.* (In Nepal and Tibet the word *Caitya* is used in the same sense of *Stūpa*).[6] Caityas or Dāgabas are an essential feature of temples or chapels constructed for purposes of worship, there being a passage round the Caitya for circumambulation (*Pradakṣiṇāya*) and from these such temples have received their appellation. The name of Caitya, however, applies not only to sanctuaries, but to sacred trees, holy spots or other religious monuments."[7]

In fact, the *Stūpas,* having the character of sacred monuments are known as the *Caityas,* and the Caitya-hall is really a shrine in which the votive *Caitya* or Stūpa occupies the place of the altar. The word *Caitya* came from *citā* or funeral pyre. Likewise the *Stūpa* with its hemispherical structure certainly emerged out of the earthen funeral mounds. It is likely that originally on the earthen funeral mound a tree was planted and the area was enclosed by fence made of bamboo or wood, which was later replaced by ornamental rails. The custom of rearing *Stūpas* was pre-Buddhist. The Buddha himself asked Ānanda to erect *Stūpas* over the remains of his body in the traditional way.[8] These funeral mounds were associated with primitive religious beliefs and practices, and in course of time they acquired a special Buddhistic affiliation as containing the relic of the Master or his chief disciples.

6. J. Burgess, *Buddhist Cave Temples and their Inscriptions,* London 1883, p. 114.
7. Grünwedel, *op. cit.,* pp. 20-21.
8. *Dīgha Nikāya,* XV. 5. 11; *Sacred Books of the East,* Vol. XI, p. 93.

3. The Pīr Cult

In North India, specially in Bengal and Bihar, among different sections of the Muslim community, there is the cult of Pīr, one of the interesting features of which is the worship of tombs. These tombs of the Pīrs are generally covered with a piece of red cloth, and offerings are made to them. These Pīrs are regarded as holy persons or saints. Their contributions to the cause of religion and their supposed superhuman deeds raised them to the standard of divinities. Besides the celebrated Pīrs of the olden days, there are even living Pīrs, and even Pīr-dynasties. One who is born in such a dynasty is entitled to get the honour of a living Pīr.

The followers of this Pīr tradition do not adhere strictly to all the rules prescribed by official Islam. They have their own esoteric rituals and they base these rituals on their *own* interpretations of the sacred texts. As we have stated above, one of the most important features of this Pīr cult is the worship of the tombs. The Pīr on whose memory the tomb is erected, or the one who is buried therein, is believed to grant his worshipper his desired objects by virtue of his superhuman power. The worshippers of these tombs are not exclusively Muslims. The Hindus also worship these tombs with equal sincerity and devotion.

Now the question is: Who were these Pīrs? Among whom this special cult first developed? By itself the Pīr cult shows that it contains various beliefs and practices which were locally adopted. One thing which must not escape the notice of any observer is that the majority of the surviving tombs of the Pīrs look exactly like the Buddhist *Stūpa*, the same domical structure, big or small, the same ornamental rails, and even the same umbrella. In fact a few of them were really Buddhist *Stūpas,* later converted into the shrines of Pīrs. Small clay figures of horse are usually offered as votive articles to these tombs or *Stūpas.* In every shrine of the Pīrs there is a wish-fulfilling tree (*Kalpavṛkṣa*), and if any one desires to have anything he should tie a brick-bat on any branch of the tree. The brick-bat is a substitute for *fruit,* since he wants to have his desire *fruitful*—a simple instance of imitative magic. As a rule, at every evening candles are to be lighted around the tomb of the Pīr which reminds us of the Buddhist custom of lamp-offering around the *Stūpas.* This point will be stressed in our analysis of the festival of Dīpavālī.

There is reason to believe that in Bengal and Bihar the earlier converts into Islam were the Buddhists. Despite their conversion they did not give up their old religious practices like the cult of the dead saints in the forms of *Stūpa*-worship and others, and this accounts for the emergence of the cult of Pīrs. "A good many Buddhists appear to have been at least nominally converted to Islam after the establishment of Turki-Muslim rule in Bengal....But Bengali Buddhists (and Hindus) who adopted Islam did not and could not adapt their mental make up to the atmosphere of Arabic or Irani or Turki Islam. Saint-worship through their tombs (contemptuously described by the more orthodox or puritanical Bengali Mussalmans as *Pīr-Pirasti* or *Gor-Pirasti* 'worship of saints', 'worship of tombs'), an Islamised verson of the Buddhist worship of *Stūpas* or *Caityas* built over the ashes or relics of great teachers and saints, forms an important cult in the Islam of Bengal and India: and it can legitimately be looked upon as an inheritance, Islamised no doubt, from Buddhistic ritual and practice."[9]

In Bengal, the Muslims are often contemptuously called *neḍe* which might indicate their early Buddhist affiliation. The word *neḍā* means one whose head is clean-shaven, a practice which was a must for every Buddhist monk. The Vaiṣṇavas of Bengal were also contemptuously known as *neḍā* and *neḍī* since they had adopted some of the Buddhist practices like shaving the head, the use of yellow garb and begging bowl, etc. More interesting is to note that the wooden begging bowls, which are used even today by the Muslim *Phakirs* and which they fix on the back of their shoulder, are exactly the same as were used by the Buddhist monks and are still used by them in the Buddhist countries. What is more thrilling is that the term *Pīr* is same as the Buddhist term *Sthavira* or *Thera*. In Persian *Pīr* means an 'old man', 'a venerable one', just as *Sthavira* in Sanskrit or *Thera* in Pali means an 'old man', 'a venerable one'.

4. The Maṭhas

In Bengal during the festival of Holi, which has now become a part of the Dolayātrā festival of Lord Kṛṣṇa, a special type of sweetmeat is offered to the god. This is known as *Maṭha*, a preparation of sugar or molasses. It looks like a straight-edged pyramid, height being greater than the base. Often it looks like a church-steeple

9. S. K. Chatterji in *B. C. Law Volume*, Vol. I, Calcutta 1945, p. 83.

or the common European type of cenotaph, base square or circular and the steeple elongated and conical. Recently, however, there is a tendency to change its traditional form. It is interesting to note that this special type of sweetmeat is used only in connection with the rituals of Holi or Dolayātrā and on no other occasion except in the case of certain East Bengal village cults of Kārtikeya. This is a fact which evokes our interest.

The word *Maṭha* is very suggestive. It denotes a monastery or a shrine. Side by side the word also implies a *structure,* usually straight-edged pyramidal, *erected on a place where a dead body has been burnt.* Such *Maṭhas* erected on the place of burning the corpse are numerous in different parts of Bengal. Specially these are erected on the ashes of reputed persons. May not be the same, but a simliar custom is expected to prevail in other parts of India. However, what interests us greatly is that the sweetmeat called *Maṭha,* served as offering to the god during the festival of Holi, is really an imitative miniature form of the *Maṭha* which is erected on the place of burning the corpse.

5. The Miming of Burning the Dead

Since the festival of Holi is celebrated in all the states of India with local customs and rituals, it is difficult to have a first hand knowledge of them. Therefore I am laying greater stress on the local customs of Bengal, with which I am acquainted, with a request to my Indian readers to compare them with those prevailing in their own states and districts. I think that the similarities will be greater than the differences.

In Bengal, at the evening before the day of Holi, a special rite is performed. It is the miming of the act of burning a deadbody. A human figure is made of different articles and then it is burnt in the same way as a deadbody is generally burnt. This ceremony is variously called *Neḍāpoḍā, Cāncor* and so on, in different places. In the western districts of Bengal it is called *Meḍāpoḍā* the first part of the word being regarded as the corruption of Meṇṭā, an Asura whose supposed body made of different combustible articles serves as the object of burning. A similar custom also prevails in Bihar and parts of Uttar Pradesh, which is known as *Holika-dahan* and *Sammat-jvalan.* The word *neḍāpoḍa* or *meḍāpoḍā* may be a corruption of *maḍāpoḍā* (burning a deadbody), or it may suggest the burning of a *neḍā* i.e., a Buddhist or Vaiṣṇava monk, or a saint in general. A verse is also uttered, the first part of the second line of which varies from place to place. This variation is due to the fact that the first part of the second line tells about *sexual intercourse,* and hence it was changed by the moralists, just as the *pracodayāt* of the *gāyatrī* hymn has been converted into *praṇodayāt* by a few moralists, since the root of the former, indicative of the task of infusion, gradually came to assume the meaning of sexual act. The verse with which we are concerned runs as follows: Today is our *neḍāpoḍā,* tomorrow is our *dol;* indulge in coition (later changed into 'the full-moon is up' or 'it bursts open with a sound of *Phat*', etc.), and proclaim the name of Hari (*Balo Hari-bol*).

The sexual tinge of the original verse is not inconsistent with some of the original rituals of *Holi* which were sexual in character. Long ago William Crooke pointed out that the festival of Holi was the natural outcome of the primitive sexual rites of fertility.[10] Hutton categorically states that in the rituals of Holi sexual features are prominent, and he also explains these features in terms of primitive agriculture rituals in which sexuality had a leading part.[11] In some places the festival is celebrated in honour of the goddess Vāsantī which was previously an occasion on which "the most licentious debauchery and disorder reign throughout every class of society. It is a regular Saturnalia of India. Persons of the greatest responsibility, without regard to rank or age, are not ashamed to take part in the orgies which mark the season of the year."[12] In ancient times the festival was called *Vasantotsava* and the noblest princesses danced in public in honour of the goddess of love.[13] "Most of the observers of the feast," says Natesa Sastri, "imagine that the object of their worship is Cupid and that the mock fun they observe are on account of Kāma, the god of love."[14]

But more interesting is the last part of the aforesaid verse which asks to proclaim the name of Hari (*Balo Haribol*). How much dreadful and uncouth can become the proclamation of the name of the god Hari, you cant understand, unless you are a Bengalee. This particular proclamation takes place *only in the time of taking the dead-*

10. *Folklore,* Vol. XXV, pp. 183 ff. cf. *infra,* pp. 154-55.
11. H. H. Hutton, *Caste in India,* Calcutta 1951, pp. 260-61.
12. Rousselet, *India and its Native Princes,* London 1876, p. 173.
13. J. C. Oman, *The Brahmans, Theists and Musalmans,* London 1907, p. 241 f.
14. S. M. Natesa Sastri, *Hindu Feasts and Ceremonials,* Madras 1903, pp. 44 ff.

body on the burning ground, and that is why everyone dislikes to hear the name of Hari in this special way. The North Indian slogan of carrying the deadbody *Rām nām sath hai* is far better, polite and gentle. In any case, what we mean to say is that in the said verse which is concerned with the rituals of Holi we have not only a reference to the burning of a dead body, but with it is also conspicuously associated a typical slogan which is used only in the time of carrying the corpse.

6. The Symbolism of Red

The most important rite of the festival of Holi is the use of a red-powder (*ābīr* or *phāg* as it is generally called) which is to be smeared on the bodies of friends and relatives and even on the bodies of the strangers. Sometimes water is coloured red with this powder and is sprinkled on human bodies. Now-a-days young men and women also use other colours, but the approved colour is *red*.

In a preceding chapter we have dealt with the religious and ritual significance of this red colour which being a symbol of blood, is treated everywhere in the world as the life giving power. "It is a world-wide custom for menstruating or pregnant women to daub their bodies with red ochre, which serves at once to warn the men away and to enhance their fertility. In many marriage ceremonies the bride's forehead is painted red.... a sign that she is forbidden to all men save her husband and a guarantee that she will bear him children....Among the Valenge, a Bautu tribe, every woman keeps a pot of red ochre, which is sacred to her sex and used to paint her face and body for ceremonial purposes. Of the many occasions for which she needs it, the following may be noted. At the end of her confinement both mother and child are anointed with it: in this way the child will live and the mother is restored to life. At initiation the girl is painted red from head to foot. So she is born again and will be fruitful. At the conclusion of mourning, after stepping over a fire, the widow is painted the same colour: so she returns from the contamination of death."[15]

The bones of the Upper Palaeolithic and Neolithic interments are found painted red. This widespread custom clearly has a ritual significance since *red is the renewal of life.* To paint the bones with the ruddy colouring of life was the "nearest thing to mummification

15. G. Thomson, *Studies in Ancient Greek Society,* I, pp. 209-10. cf. *supra*, pp. 88 ff.

that the palaeolithic peoples knew; it was an attempt to make the body again serviceable for its owner's use".[16] "The symbolism becomes quite clear when we find, as we commonly do, that the skeleton has been laid in the contracted or uterine posture. Smeared with the colour of life, curled up like a babe in the womb—what more could the primitive man do to ensure that the soul of the departed would be born again?"[17]

7. The Original Form of Holi

The present form of the Holi festival therefore contains the relics of some primitive rituals connected with the concepts of fertility, death and renewal of life. The evidences by themselves are fragmentary and regional in nature. Despite these shortcomings a faint picture of its original form comes within the range of our vision, and in that form it was evidently a primitive rite of death and resurrection, a funeral rite, the purpose of which was to secure a new life for the departed one. Gradually this rite developed a wider significance and impersonal character, symbolising the events of the deaths and renovations in nature. The death of the year in winter and its revival in spring with the growth of new leaves on the trees probably served as the basis for the later conceptions culminated in the present form of this festival. In fact, everywhere in the world the natural year begins with the spring. Even the English calendar shows that the months of September, October, November and December were respectively the seventh, eighth, ninth and tenth months of the year. January and February being respectively the eleventh and twelfth months, the year was really to begin from March which is the time of spring. Indian year also begins with spring, and from this point of view it may not be unreasonable to hold that the festival of Holi, even in its present form, symbolises the death of one year and the birth of another.

8. The Full and New Moon

The festival of Holi is celebrated on the full moon day of spring, while that of Dīpāvalī or Dewali on the new-moon night at the

16. R. A. S. Macalister, *Textbook of European Archaeology,* Cambridge 1921, Vol. I, p. 502.
17. G. Thomson, *op. cit.*, p. 210.

beginning of winter. Winter and spring, as we have seen above, symbolise respectively the death and revival of the year, the annual cycle of birth and death in nature. Now we are to see whether these two celebrations, one in the full moon and the other in the new moon are mutually correlated and also whether the moon is functionally connected with these rituals. The basis of such connection, if there be any, should also be investigated.

We have seen how the ideas of natural and human fertility are basically related to those of death and revival, conceptually the latter being the natural development of the former. In this context the function of the moon, as an agent of fertility and reproduction had a positive effect on the primitive mind. In many places of the world the moon is conceived as the governor of the fertilising aspects of nature. In primitive belief, it was the moon who was the controller of water and moisture, of production and fertility. In Vedic myth, the moon is the ruler of all fertilising waters,[18] and this belief is also found among the ancient Chinese, Japanese and Egyptians.[19]

"There is good reason for believing that among many primitive peoples the moon, rather than the sun, the planets or any constellation, first excited the imagination and aroused feelings of superstitious awe or of religious veneration."[20] The licentious character of the moon, as we find in the Purāṇas, has its parallel elsewhere. The *male* moon-god is everywhere in the habit of kidnapping women.[21] The tribes of Central Australia represent the moon as claiming that all women belong to him by right, and that it is by his consent only that they are permitted to marry mortal husbands.[22] In Greenland, it is believed that the moon comes down at night to make sexual intercourse with women, and "young maids are afraid to stare at the moon imagining that they may get a child by the bargain."[23] Corresponding beliefs centering round the moon also prevail in Europe.[24] Can the celebration of the festival of Holi in the full-moon day, in which men and women were not ashamed to

18. A. Macdonell, *Vedic Mythology*, p. 107.
19. Cf. Mayers, *The Chinese Reader's Manual*, p. 288; Griffis, *Japanese Fairy World*, p. 299; Wilkinson, *Manners and Customs of the Ancient Egyptians*, Vol. III, p. 375.
20. Hutton Webster, *Rest Days*, pp. 124 ff.
21. *Journal of American Folklore*, Vol. XX, p. 28.
22. Spencer and Gillen, *Northern Tribes of Central Australia*, pp. 412 ff.
23. Egede, *A Description of Greenland*, p. 209.
24. Aranason, *Icelandic Legends*, Vol. II, p. 635; Dyer, *English Folklore*, p. 41; Logan, *The Scottish Gael*, Vol. II, pp. 332, 360.

take part in the orgies, be therefore traced to such beliefs in the wonder working erotic power of the moon?

In a preceding chapter we have seen that from the time of the *Ṛgveda*[25] there was a mystical belief that the moon was the divine guardian of a girl, and according to the *Gṛhyasaṃgraha*[26] and the *Pāraskara Gṛhyasūtra,*[27] he enjoys a girl when she develops the signs of puberty. In the *Kauṣitakī Upaniṣad* it is stated that "from the wise moon, who orders the seasons, consisting of fifteen parts when he is born, from the moon who is the abode of our ancestors, the *seed* is derived. The *seed,* even myself, the gods gathered up into an active man, and through an active man they brought me to a mother."[28]

In primitive thought the moon is not only regarded as the cause of conception and generation, but also as the regulator of the periodic function of women, the controller of menstruation and the guardian of the embryo and the placenta.[29] Among the Chukchis, the magician "when he desires to make especially powerful incantations, must strip himself naked and go out of his house at night when the moon is shining.[30] In Ghana the same word means both 'moon' and 'magic'.[31] In Ashango, moon is conceived as the source of magical power.[32] The Thonga megicians of South Africa in the time of performing their functions are said to have become *Thwaza* or possessed by the moon.[33]

Since the moon is specially conceived as the source of magical powers and the cause of conception and generation, it is evident that the ideas of regeneration or rebirth and the rituals connected with them have some logical bearing on the functioning of the moon. The conception of rebirth is conspicuously associated with the moon, also because of its eclipses symbolising death and revival. That is why during the eclipse men usually follow the traditional customs which are *connected with the event of a man's death in a famlily.* Old utensils are given up which is followed by a ceremonial bath. The

25. X. 85. 40-41.
26. Quoted in the Com. of *Gobhila Gṛ. Sū.*, III. 4. 6.
27. I. 4. 16; cf. *Saṃvarta Saṃhitā,* 64-67.
28. *Sacred Books of the East*, Vol. I, p. 233 f.
29. Elliot Smith, *The Evolution of the Dragon*, p. 48.
30. Bogorus, *The Chukchee,* pp. 305, 448.
31. Ellis, *The Tsi-speaking Peoples,* p. 19.
32. Chailler, *Journey to Ashango Land*, p. 238.
33. Junod, *op. cit.*, Vol. II, pp. 451, 453.

regular course of moon by itself suggests the death and revival theme. The periodical death and revival of the moon is responsible for the observance of various local rites throughout India which are mainly characterised by ceremonial bath and fasting.

The Hindu religious calendar follows the lunar line according to which dates are fixed for worship and ritual. The bright half (*Śukla-pakṣa*) is regarded better than the dark-half (*Kṛṣna-pakṣa*) for such purposes. The full-noon days are considered suitable for such public festivals or the Rāsa-yātrā, Jhulana yātrā, etc., the cult of the goddess of wealth and fortune, and so on. The birth-days of the celebrated saints are often conspicuously connected with the full-moon days. While the celebrations of the full moon are especially connected with rebirth, a new life, those of the new-moon are with death and funeral aspects. The night dedicated to the god Śiva who with his followers lives in the places of cremation surrounded by ghosts and goblins belongs to the dark half (*Kṛṣṇa-pakṣa*). So is the ritual of Dīpāvalī which is observed on the dark new-moon night. In Bengal this ceremony is associated with the annual worship of the goddess Kālī who has been always identified with death (*mṛtyurūpā*). In other parts of India, Dewali is observed on the new-moon night independently without any connection with the worship of Kālī which proves that this connection is regional and later. This connection is first mentioned in Kaśināthas *Śyāmāsaparyāsavidhi* which was composed in 1768. We are to remember that although Kālī is a very old goddess, her worship became popular in Bengal not before the seventeenth century. But Dewali existed even before that evidently as a death festival, and it was probably due to this that in later times with the popularity of the conception of Kālī as the goddess of death, it was connected with her annual worship.

9. The Fire Festivals of Europe

The main feature of the festival of Dewali, as is known to all, is to light candles. If we seek a similar ritual we can easily find it in the pre-Christian fire festivals of Europe. According to the Teutonic mythology, found in the collection called *Edda*, the god Balder, the beautiful, apprehended a danger and he was afraid. Having seen him moved, his mother requested all the objects of the world not to do any harm to Balder and they complied with her request. But she forgot about mistletoe which she considered to be too small to cause any harm. But a wicked god, called Loke, came to know of this, and with the help of mistletoe he was able to kill Balder.

The event happened thus. When the gods came to know that every object of the world had promised not to cause any harm to Balder, they began to strike him with different objects for amusement. But Balder remained unhurt. When the game was on the move, Loke handed over an arrow, containing mistletoe, to Balder's blind brother. The arrow was shot and at once Balder was killed.

The gods became naturally very much grieved for this mishap. They all prayed to Death for bringing Balder back to life. Then Death assured them that Balder might be brought back to life if everyone of the world would lement for him. Although most of the earthly beings were ready to lament, there were a few who were not, and hence Balder could not be restored to life. Thereupon his deadbody was laid on the funeral pyre which was prepared on a ship. Odin, the king of the gods, whispered something on the ear of dead Balder. Then the ship was put on fire. Thousands of torches were lighted from that fire and they were raised up on the top of every house.

Since then, in every year, in order to commemorate the death of Balder, developed the custom of lighting torches on the roof of each house, and thus the fire festival came to be introduced. Clearly, this European Dewali was originally meant for the commemoration of death at the root of which worked the belief in contagious magic, the belief that one event was likely to influence another. This belief is older than the story of Balder, and as such the ritual of lighting torches on selected places was not only the symbol of the funeral pyre of Balder; in reality it was an older rite connected with death, and to rationalise this primitive rite the myth of Balder was invented.

10. Dewali and Death

Otherwise it is not possible to explain the universal custom of lighting the candle on or around the tomb. Among the Muslims and the Christians this custom is widely in vogue as also among peoples belonging to different sects. The lamp is offered for various purposes. It is the commonest method of appealing to the man buried under the tomb. The flame of light is the symbol of relation with the dead and the departed soul, and since this connection with death is direct, the relation of Dewali with the world of the ghosts is close. This explains why the preceding night of Dewali is called in Bengal *Bhūta-Caturdasī*, the night of the ghosts, which is observed by lighting fourteen candles. On every night after the Dewali, throughout the month of Kārtik (October-November), a lamp is to be raised on a pole made of bamboo, a custom which is known as raising the *Ākāśapradīpa* (the sky-lamp).

In India Dīpāvalī or Dewali is definitely connected with death. Its earliest mention is found in Bhadravāhu's *Kalpasūtra* which is an ancient sacred text of the Jains. It should be remembered that in India Dewali has a special importance among the Jains. The North Indian pompous celebration of Dewali has derived its main features from the Jains of Gujarat and Rajasthan. Mahāvīra, the twentyfourth Tīrthaṅkara of the Jains passed away on the last day of the month of Āśvina in 468 B. C. According to the *Kalpasūtra,* as soon as the news of the death of Mahāvīra came to be known, the Mallas and the Vṛjis observed the lamp festival in the honour of the departed lord.[34] It was arranged to commemorate the demise of Mahāvīra, and since then the Jains have been performing this celebration every year on the day of his *nirvāṇa*. In this case the Jains must have also followed an ancient custom, an ancient faith, according to which there is an intrinsic connection between the dead and the flame of lamp. Since this connection has long been established in human mind, the common custom is that when a man dies and his body is taken to the burning ground, a lamp has to be kept lighted at the place where he breathed his last. Likewise when the image of any god is taken away for immersion, a lamp has to be kept lighted on the altar where the image was installed.

In terms of contagious magic if we associate the flame of funeral pyre with that of the lamp, an idea apparently transpires that those places or peoples became sources of inspiration of the Dewali or similar festivals where or among whom had developed the custom of burning the dead. The custom of burning the dead, although ancient, is not universal. The oldest custom of the disposal of dead is perhaps exposure, to keep the body in a secluded place, relics of which are still found among the Iranian followers of Zarathustra.

34. *Sacred Books of the East,* Vol. XXII, p. 266.

But they also light a candle on the place where the death takes place. The second custom is burial and this is also older than burning. But candles are also lighted on the tombs. Are we then to infer that those peoples among whom the custom of burning did not exist borrowed the idea of lamp offering from those who developed the custom of burning the dead?

I do not think so, although in the case of rituals borrowing is a constant feature. Since the discovery and use of fire was the most important event in human history, its influence was keenly felt in all spheres of life, including even the traditional rituals. Fire being the helper in every human action, the idea also developed that it was able to lead the dead into the desired region. Thus fire got easy access in the funeral rites even among those peoples who did not burn their dead. In the Vedic age the customs of burial and burning existed side by side, and hence we are quoting a verse from the *Ṛgveda* to show precisely what was the role of Agni (fire) in this case. "Again, O Agni, to the Fathers send him who, offered in thee, goes with our oblations. *Wearing new life* let him increase his offspring: let him *rejoin a body,* Jātavedas" (X. 16. 5).[35]

Therefore, burning or reducing into ashes is not the sole function of Agni. He can animate anything by his heat, and as such he can cause rebirth. As we have repeatedly said, to the ancients death did not mean end of everything. With death was inseparably associated the idea of resurrection. The flame of lamp or that of fire is the symbol of this rebirth or resurrection, and that is why its ritual use is found in everything connected with death. We have seen that the mystery of plant-life is inextricably blended with the primitive concept of rebirth, and if Dewali is a ritual of death and rebirth, it is likely that it should maintain a relation with plant life. Is it the reason behind the Bengalee custom of eating fourteen kinds of vegetables on the day before the commencement of the Dewali festival? Perhaps this ritual eating has now become a mechanical affair and many of the accompanying rituals have now sunk into oblivion, but it is not at all difficult to understand that once all these carried a special significance. From full-moon to new-moon, birth and death of a period consisting of fourteen days, each symbolised by a kind of plant, the Dīpāvalī on the new moon night which is an embodiment of death, the faint phase of moon on the next night as

35. R. T. H. Griffith, *Hymns of the Ṛgveda,* Vol. II, Delhi 1963, p. 402.

the herald of new birth—if these fragments are collocated side by side, can we not visualise a dim and veiled picture of the philosophy of life which our primitive forefathers had acquired through experience, those seemingly fundamental ideas justifiable at the time when they were propounded, but with fuller experience had proved to be inadequate?

VIII

HOOK SWINGING

A Study in the Proletarian Cults and Rituals of Bengal

1. Prologue

In parts of Eastern India, especially in Bengal, a few interesting rituals and festivals are performed in the month of *Caitra* (the last month of the Hindu calendar corresponding to the period from the middle of the March to that of April) mainly by the lower strata of the Hindus, those who earn their livelihood by manual labour and also by agriculture, craft and other technical occupations. These rituals and festivals which also reveal, along with other features, the professional characteristics of the simpler peoples, are dedicated to a variety of local deities and also to Śiva and, significantly enough, they do not find mention in the Purāṇas and also in the medieval religious manuals simply because of their connection with the toiling masses, the lower castes who had very little to do with the Smārta-Pauranic ideals of Brahmanism. There are reasons to believe that these festivals and rituals are continuation of a very primitive tradition which existed side by side with the sophisticated ones of the higher peoples, and despite the professed indifference and even bitter antagonism of the literate class to the beliefs and practices of the toiling masses, their survival and continuation throughout the ages could not be stopped. Rather, during the age that marked the decadence of Buddhism and the advent of Islam, some of the cults and rituals of the simpler peoples were adopted by the higher. In order to save their skin and property from the hands of the Muslim plunderers, the higher peoples had at least to make a *show* of cultural identity with the lower on whose physical strength they had to depend. As a result, there were occasional *proletarian revivals* in the field of religion, as we shall presently see.

2. The Rituals of Year-Ending

Throughout the month of *Caitra* a sort of religious and ritualistic movement, marked by the sound of drum-beating and the procession of the drummers, can be observed in different parts of the country. It is believed that the god Śiva remains unusually heated during these days, and since he requires to be cooled down, men and women are found in the Śiva shrines carrying pots of holy water to be poured upon the phallic form (*liṅga*) of the god. Those who are specially devoted, take the vow of asceticism (*sannyāsa*), wearing ochre-robe, eating only once a day by cooking what is got through alms, sleeping on the ground, abstaining from sexual intercourse and observing a number of taboos in relation to different aspects of life. This vow of asceticism may also be observed by women, and in fact, female ascetics, clad in ochre robe, are found in large number going side by side with the males, collecting alms and performing rites. If they menstruate during this period, the blood is regarded very sacred, and pieces of the cloth that contains the blood are used as amulets against diseases and other physical disabilities. The month of *Caitra* is also regarded as that of Śiva's marriage with Nīlāvatī who in her previous birth was no other than Satī, the daughter of Dakṣa who committed suicide at the insult caused by her father to her husband. Married women as a rule take part in the rites of *Nīla* which is a part of *Caḍaka* rituals. The rites of *Nīla*, dedicated to the goddesses Nīlā, Nīlāvatī, Nīlacaṇḍikā, Nīlaparameśvarī and often to the male god Nīladevatā, which are mainly sexual in character vary from place to place. In eastern Bengal, throughout the month of Caitra the ritual (*del*) of Pāṭ-ṭhākur takes place. It is a disguised ritual of female organ. The form of the object of this cult is a wooden plank on the right side of which is planted a *trident (triśūla)*, and the left side is fashioned in the shape of a female organ. All these have now-a-days been conspicuously associated with Śiva but there are reasons to believe that previously other local gods had to do something with these rituals. The religious elements of the *Caḍaka* festival show that they contain the cults of a variety of deities, and also a good number of sectarian features, some of which may be traced even to Buddhism. The *Gājana* rituals are dedicated not only to Śiva, but to Dharma, Nīla and other deities as well. One of the popular features of all these rituals is the test of endurance, the physical pain that the staunch devotees are to suffer through self-torture, sometimes amounting even to death. Lying on the bed of sharp nails, jumping upon open daggers, perforation of the tongue by an iron rod, etc. are a few of such horrible features of the *Gājana* festivals.

Formerly in the hook-swinging of the *Caḍaka,* the iron-hook was to be fixed on the back of the swinger through his muscles. This cruel custom had been abolished by the British Government in the nineteenth century.

3. The Focus of Attention

The focus of our attention in this chapter will not, however, be the particulars of these rituals. We are mainly concerned with the *proletarian revivals* which had characterised the social and religious life of eastern India from the twelfth century onwards. When Buddhism ceased to exist as Buddhism, many of its elements were absorbed by the existing religions like Śaivism and Vaiṣṇavism. Some of its features like the cult of the dead were even absorbed by a group of newly converted Muslims, as we have seen in the preceding chapter. But there was an independent group of cults and rituals, a good deal of which have survived to our day as the suppressed religion of the masses, that had played a leading role in the stupendous social and religious transformation which was taking place after the decline of Buddhism and with the advent of Islam. The following observation of Prof. S. K. Chatterji[1] on these cults and rituals is worth-quoting. "The original or national cults of the pre-Aryan peoples are found in the worship of many caste or tribal deities, or village gods, who have no place in the official Hindu pantheon of pan-Indian acceptance; at times they have just succeeded in finding place in some Sanskrit Purāṇa, but in other cases they have advanced only as far as the threshold or the ante-chamber of the hall of official Hinduism by having their legends rendered in the vernacular only. Thus there are village godlings of the type of Gabhur Dalan and Mochrā Siṅgha worshipped in the South Bengal Delta, who are unknown to any Purāṇa, and unsung even in the vernacular; there are Dakṣin Rāy and Kālu Gāzi godlings who control the tigers in the Sundarbans of the forest lands of the southern Delta whose exploits are narrated only in Bengali, and whose fame has not yet travelled beyond Bengal; and finally, there are deities of the type of Śītalā, the goddess of small-pox, and Manasā, the goddess of serpents, who have received admission into the pantheon of Puranic gods and goddesses,

1. *B. C. Law Volume,* 1945, ed. D. R. Bhandarkar and others, p. 76.

honoured, although they are newcomers, beside Śiva and Devī, Viṣṇu and Lakṣmī. The nature of pre-Aryan religion and ritual, in its mythology and its ideas and practices, among the various pre-Aryan groups of peoples, it has not been possible to establish as yet: most of it now survives in the rites and cults obtaining in remote villages, which are now always under the aegis of official Brahmanical Hinduism." According to Chatterji, these cults and rituals of pre-Aryan origin are obtained among the Dravidian, Austric, Tibeto-Burman and other peoples of Bengal, recent and prehistoric, who formed the original inhabitants of Bengal, upon whom the Upper Gangetic Aryan speech and culture were imposed. We are not, however, concerned with the linguistic and racial questions involved in these cults and rituals. We shall therefore take them simply as things *proletarian* and try to analyse their features in terms of their functional role in the religious and social life of this country.

4. Buddhism versus Śaivism

The last two kings of the Buddhist dynasty of the Candras of South East Bengal gave up Buddhist faith, Laḍahacandra becoming a Vaiṣṇava and Govindacandra a Śaiva.[2] The Pāla kings, who ruled Bengal and Bihar from the eighth century onwards, although claimed to have been staunch followers of the Buddhist faith (*Paramasaugata*) were also eager to suppress the social evil styled *Varṇasaṅkara* like typically zealous Brahmanical kings.[3] Many of the Pāla kings even repudiated Buddhism. The well known Bhagalpur plates represents Nārāyaṇapāla (854-908 A.D.) as a devotee of Śiva, recording the king's gift of a village in favour of the temple of Śiva-bhaṭṭāraka and the *Pāśupatācārya-pariṣad* in a locality called Kalasapota and also referring to his boasts of having built one thousand-roomed temple for the said god in the same locality.[4] D. C. Sircar refers to a newly discovered inscription[5] which speaks of a great Śaiva religious establishment in North Bengal, the pontifs of which were Vidyāśiva, his disciple Dharmaśiva, his disciple Indraśiva, his disciple, Śarvaśiva and his disciple Mūrtiśiva. King Mahīpāla I (c. 990-

2. D. C. Sircar, *Religious Life in Ancient and Medieval India,* Delhi 1971, pp. 253-57.
3. *Gauḍalekhamālā* (Monghyer Plate of Devapāla, v. 36), p. 36.
4. *Indian Antiquary,* Vol. XV, pp. 304 ff.
5. Paper read on 18-2-1974 at the Centre of Advanced Study in Ancient Indian History and Culture, Calcutta University.

1040 A.D.) is stated to have dedicated a temple to Indraśiva. Śarvaśiva is described as the *guru* of Mahīpāla's son Nayapāla (1040-1055 A.D.). The inscription also says that in his old age Śarvaśiva retired, having placed Mūrtiśiva in the position of the *guru* of the Gauḍa king.

These Śaiva teachers belonged to the Mattamayūra sect of Central India. The teachers of this sect bore, as a rule, the epithet *Śiva* or *Śambhu* at the end of their names. That those Śivācāryas of the aforesaid Pāla inscription were associated with the Mattamayūras belonging to a region outside Bengal is indicated by the fact that Dharmaśiva built a Śiva temple at Vārāṇasī while the Paramāra king Bhoja is mentioned in connection with Rūpaśiva who was a friend of Mūrtiśiva and caused the latter's *praśasti* to be composed and image to be made and is said to have revived the lost philosophy of the god Śiva. So far as the religious practices and rituals of the Mattamayūras are concerned, it has come down to us that there were dances, music, mimicry and physical tortures in honour of Śiva. They indeed behaved like intoxicated (*matta*) peacocks (*mayūras*) and many of their rituals were saturated with sexual elements. H. Goetz even ascribes the sexual bas-reliefs of Khājuraho to Mattamayūra inspiration.[6]

It was possible for Śaivism to take the lead, to fill up, to a considerable extent, the vacuum in the field of religion that followed the decline of Buddhism by absorbing numerous cults and rituals of the lower peoples within its fold. But in doing so, Śaivism in this part of the country had to change its original character. Although Śiva has an ancient and glamorous history, in the folklore of Bengal he is represented as an agriculturist working in the field and at the same time making love with black and healthy women of the lower peoples. Officially and non-officially, Śiva was made to preside over numerous popular cults and rituals, as a result of which Śaivism as an *organised* religion rapidly became defunct and survived only as a part of the medieval Śākta religilon.[7]

6. For the Mattamayūras see *Indian Historical Quarterly*, Vol. XXV, pp. 15 ff.; J. N. Banerjea, *Paurānic and Tāntric Religion*, Calcutta 1965, pp. 106-08; V. V. Mirashi's Intro. to *Corp. Ins. Ind.*, Vol. IV; R. D. Banerji, *Haihayas of Tripurī*, MASI, XXIII; H. Goetz in *Arts Asiatiques*, Tome V, 1958, Fasc. I, pp. 35 ff.
7. For this transformation see my *History of the Śākta Religion*, New Delhi 1974.

5. Buddhism and Vaiṣṇavism

While Śaivism was absorbing numerous popular cults and rituals which were previously under the guardianship of Mahāyāna Buddhism, Vaiṣṇavism of Bengal was not lagging behind to absorb within its fold a few significant Buddhist elements. The Sena kings of Bengal, who succeeded the Pālas, were although devout Śaiva in their religious conviction, were not reluctant to patronise Vaiṣṇavism. From the evidence of the *Gītagovinda* of Jayadeva, which was a production of the Sena court, it is clear that the followers of the Viṣṇu cult in the twelfth century did not hesitate to declare the Buddha as an incarnation (*Avatāra*) of Viṣṇu and to introduce Buddhist Sahajayāna ideas in so far as the sexual matters were concerned. From the twelfth century onwards until the advent of Śrī Caitanya, Vaiṣṇavism was overcharged by sexual elements at the root of which lay the conception of the union of male and female principles symbolised by Kṛṣṇa and Rādhā, previously symbolised in Buddhism by the concepts of Śūnyatā and Karuṇā, and it is against this background that the significance of Jayadeva's *Gītagovinda* should be understood which emphasises only upon the erotic aspects in the relation between Rādhā and Kṛṣṇa. Nāvājīdāsa in his *Bhaktamāla* rightly calls it *Kokakāvya-navarasa-śṛṅgāra-kau-āgāra*. It is indeed a metrical amplification of things described in Kokkoka's *Ratirahasya*. Jayadeva himself has often been described as belonging to the Sahajiyā tradition. This also holds good in the case of Śrī Caitanya and many of his distinguished followers.

What is Sahajayāna? As is known to all, Mahāyāna Buddhism in its later phases became a composite religious system of heterogeneous faiths and practices saturated with the elements of esorterism, sex rites, gods, demi-gods, demons, ghosts, magic, charms, sorcery, what not. Sahajiyā Buddhism or Sahajayāna was an offshoot of this composite religious system. Other offshoots of later Mahāyāna Buddhism gave rise to what was known as Tāntric Buddhism and its ramifications. There was an obvious link between Sahajayāna and various forms of Tāntric Buddhism, but while the latter maintained more or less a technical character, confined among esoteric circles and secret societies, the former had wider acceptance among the masses. Of the leading features of Sahajayāna the following may be noted: (1) sharp criticism and rejection of all external formalities in regard to religious practices (II) protest against and rejection of priestly and scriptural authority, celebacy, penances, austerities and the like, (III) recognition of the human body as the seat and habitat of all religious and spiritual experience, (IV) recognition of the *guru* as essential for any spiritual quest, and (V) recognition of the experience of the ultimate reality as one of inexpressible happiness (*mahāsukha*). The Tantric Buddhist identification of ūnyātā Świth the male and Karuṇā with the female principle occupied a significant place in Sahajayāna and with the consideration of the human body itself as the seat of all human experience including that of *sahaja-mahāsukha,* the image and practice of *mithuna* (sexual commerce) became the most important element in the religious practice of Sahajiyā Buddhism in which women came to occupy the most important position.[8]

This Sahajiyā tradition was quickly absorbed by Bengal Vaiṣṇavism, numerous traces of which are preserved in Vaiṣṇava literature. The Vaiṣṇava theory and practice of unconventional love (*parakīyā*) is a direct adaptation of Sahajiyā Buddhist way of life. Dasgupta has shown that the Vaiṣṇava poets and apostles like Jayadeva, Vidyāpati, Caṇḍīdāsa, Rūpa, Sanātana, Jīva Gosvamin and others were believed to be exponents of Sahajiyā practice.[9] Even Śri Caitanya himself has been held as having practised Sahaja Sādhanā with female companions and attained perfection through it. He is said to have practised Sahaja Sādhanā in company of Sāṭhi, daughter of Sārvabhauma.[10] It is said in the *Vivartavilāsa* of Akiñcana Dāsa that all the great Vaiṣṇava apostles practised Sahaja-Sādhanā with female companions: Śrī Rūpa with Mīrā, Bhaṭṭa Raghunātha with Karṇ-bāi, Sanātana with Lakṣmī Hīrā, Lokanātha with a Caṇḍāla girl, Kṛṣṇadāsa with the milkmaid Piṅgalā, Śrī Jīva with a barber woman called Śyāmā, Raghunātha with Mīrā-baī, Gopāla Bhaṭṭa with Gaura-prīyā, and so on.

Historically speaking, however, the Buddhist Sahajiyā ideas, which had influenced many later cults and rituals, despite their Buddhist tone and colour, had their origin in the primitive sex rites surviving in India throughout the ages as an important religious undercurrent of esoteric practices. We have already occasion to discuss the nature of these esotric, and sometimes open, sexual practices and the material basis of the ideas involved in all these. The *real*

8. S. B. Dasgupta, *Obscure Religious Cults,* Calcutta, 1969, pp. 51 ff.
9. *ibid.*, pp. 113 ff.
10. cf. *Caitanyacaritāmṛta,* Madhyalīlā, Ch. XV.

origin of other later cults containing marks of Buddhist influence is also to be sought in the aforesaid primitive tradition, as we shall presently see.

6. The Nātha Cult

Prof. Niharranjan Ray observes: "Judging by the north Indian regional literatures on the Nāthasiddha *yogis* and the variety of myths and legends connected with them, it would seem that the Nātha movement was at least a pan-north Indian one, and if Matsyendranātha is regarded as one of the originators of the cult, its antiquity must be at least as old as that of the Sahajayāna. Apart from a general predilection towards occult practices and acquisitions of supernatural powers, the Nāthasiddhas owed their religious affiliation to the Śiva-Śakti cult, but their religious discipline was that of *Haṭhayoga,* which was almost an article of faith with them. Yogic practices, somewhat of the nature and character of those of the Nātha *yogīs,* were common to the Sahajayāna Buddhist and other esoteric sects, but with the Nātha-*yogīs* these were the most important means of achieving their goal while with the others these constituted only one of the disciplines. With the former it was altogether physiological while with the latter it was also a psychological discipline."[11]

The followers of Nāthism did not accept the term *Sahaja* but many of their ideas and practices were derived from the Sahajiyā Buddhist tradition. The Nātha objective is to attain *jīvanmukti* or immortality in life and they believe that by making the vital fluid flow upwards (*ultā-sādhanā*) and by disciplining of the body and mind (*kāya-sādhanā*), the imperfect physical body can be transformed into a ripe (*pakkva*) and then into a divine (*divya*) body. The sun and moon identified respectively with Śakti and Śiva, female and male principles, are believed to reside in the right and left nerve channels. The latter as a male principle is supposed to stand for nectar-essence (*somarasa, amṛta, mahārasa*) which the former as a female principle representing fire or heat (*agni*) always wants to consume, and therefore the Nātha-yogic aim is to save this *amṛta,* which is the source of immortality, from being consumed. That is why the Nātha yogis try to keep themselves away from women as far

11. N. R. Ray, *The Sikh Gurus and the Sikh Society,* Patiala 1970, p. 127.

as possible.[12]

Nāthism, its origin and historical development, its theories and practices, etc. have all been thoroughly studied, analysed and described in details by competent scholars.[13] Previously it was held that Nāthism was originally an esoteric Buddhist cult and that in course of time having seceded from Buddhism it assumed a Saivite colour. Recent researches, however, do not encourage this view. Although on the basis of the Tibetan sources it is not difficult to show that the *historical* origin of Nāthism was somehow connected with the later phases of Buddhism, its *real* origin lay more outside Buddhism than inside it, which must be traced to the primitive cults, beliefs and practices. The Buddhist tone and colour were due to the fact that many of the primitive and proletarian elements which characterised Nāthism and other forms of contemporary religious systems were given for a time being shelter and nourishment by Mahāyāna Buddhism, as is known to all students of religious history.

7. The Proletarian Elements

The Nātha yogis are known in Bengal as *Jugi* which is a term of contempt. The lay followers of this cult are formed into a distinct *jugi* caste. Their main occupation is, till very recently, weaving coarse cloth. Of the five Ādi Siddhas of the Nāthas, Mīnanātha belonged to the group of the fishermen. In Nepal and Tibet he was known by the synonym Matsyendranātha and was identified with the Buddhist deity Avalokiteśvara. Among a class of Bengali Muslims, Matsyendra turned into a Pīr called Machandali or Mocharā. The next teacher Gorakṣanātha too was a fisherman. In non-Bengali tradition he is called Keoṭyā i.e. Kaivarta. The derivative meaning of Jālandharī, which was another name of the third Siddha Hāḍī-pā, is net-holder. Jālandharī was called Hāḍī-pā not only because he did the work of a Hāḍī (the sweeper caste in Bengal) but also because he belonged to the same easte. He served as a stable-sweep at the palace of queen Mayanāmatī of Pāṭikā.[14]

12. *ibid.*, pp. 128-29.
13. S. B. Dasgupta, *op. cit.*, pp. 191-255; H. V. Guenther, *Yuganaddha*, Banares 1952, Kalyani Mallick, *Nāthasampradāyer Itihas* (Bengali), Calcutta 1950, H. P. Dwivedi, *Nātha Sampradāya* (Hindi), Allahabad 1955.
14. See Sukumar Sen in *Cultural Heritage of India*, Vol. IV, Calcutta 1956, pp. 280-290.

In some places of Eastern India Gorakṣanātha is taken to be the god of the cow and songs are sung of him in an annual festival. Briggs in his *Gorakhnath and the Kānphaṭa Yogis*, pp. 182 ff. says that the etymological meaning of the word *gorakṣa* seems to be responsible for the tradition that he was the son of Śiva by a cow. There are the Punjabi and Nepalese traditions of Gorakṣanātha's being born in cowdung or upon a dunghill. According to the Tibetan tradition, Gorakṣa was a cowherd. In the legends of queen Mayanāmatī we find that king Gopicandra was unwilling to accept Hāḍi-pa as his *guru* because the latter belonged to a despised caste. When he ultimately accepted Hāḍi-pā as his preceptor, the latter took him to a prostitute called Hīrā and compelled him to remain there as her servant doing all sorts of humblest menial works. If these legends have any suggestivity, they only point out how these cults were closely associated with lower castes and despised professions.

In the Yogic Sādhanā of the Sahajiyās the female principle is variously called as Caṇḍālī, Ḍombī, Śavarī, etc. The coinage of such names amply indicates the connection of the Sahajiyās with the lower strata of society. Not only the Nātha teachers, but many of the Buddhist Siddhācāryas as well came from the lower castes and despised professions. Of the traditional eightyfour Siddhācāryas mentioned in the Tibetan texts, Lui-pa, Kaṅkāli-pa, Khaḍga-pa, Kaṇha-pa, Thagana-pa, Kṣatra-pa, Tanti-pa, Kūsūli-pa, Mahila-pa, Rāhula-pa, Celuk-pa, Nirguṇa-pa, Bhikhana-pa, Kalakala-pa, Dhahuri-pa, Kamala-pa, Sarvabhakṣa-pa, Putuli-pa, and Anaṅga-pa were Sūdras, Ajogi-pa, Meko-pa, Bhali-pa and Udhari-pa came from the trading class, Mīna-pa and Gorakṣa-pa were fishermen, Camāri-pa was a leather-worker, Dhombhi-pa was a washerman, Acinti-pa was a wood-cutter, Kampari-pa was a blacksmith, Jogi-pa or Ajogi-pa was a Ḍoma, Gundari-pa or Gorur-pa was a fowler, Carpai-pa was aṭ *kāhār,* Kanthāli-pa was a tailor, and Panaha-pa was a shoe-maker. Yoginī Maṇibhadra was a Gṛhadāsī or maid-servant.[14a]

The upholders of *Sant* tradition, who preached the doctrine of *bhakti,* i.e. devotion to a personal god without any religious or ritualistic formality, also came mostly from the non-privileged social strata. They preached their ideas among the toiling masses and in doing so they were actively opposed by the upholders of the orthodox

14a. B. N. Sharma, *Social Life in Northern India,* Delhi 1966, pp. 351-52.

Brahmanical tradition. The existing religious systems approved and upheld by the Purāṇas and the severity of the social laws enumerated in the Smṛti texts had no appeal to the toiling masses. This accounts for the rise of new cults and disciplines outlined by their own men, the proletarian religious leaders. The main features of this new wave were the revival of primitive beliefs and practices, of course not in their original forms, a simpler and less formal approach to the personal deity, orientation of the life by the instructions of the *guru* or preceptor, a liberal and respectful attitude towards women and denial of the caste system. To what extent these aims were achieved is a question of historical enquiry. The earlier reformers like the Buddha or Mahāvīra, who were not proletarians, also stood for many of these principles, but their success was partial. The Buddha could abolish the caste system within his Saṅgha but not among the people at large. Rather, in course of the history of Buddhism, the Brāhmaṇa members of the Saṅgha, by virtue of their literacy got hold of the leadership and introduced even within the Saṅgha a form of caste system. The success or failure of any reform movement depends on the class character of its leadership. In the medieval reform movements the same thing happened in many cases. Those who denounced the caste system and established sects of their own in which admission was open to all, themselves became victims of caste system in course of time. But where the leadership did not lose its proletarian character, the castification of sects did not take place, but the secr as a whole came to be looked upon as a lower caste, as has happened in the case of the Nāthas.[15] (See section 12).

15. Recently, however, the Nāthas are getting influenced by the caste prejudices. Sri Gosthabihari Devnath, a Nātha teacher and scholar, in his Bengali work on Nāthism has asserted that the Nāthas were originally Rudraja Brāhmaṇas, i.e. Brāhmaṇas born of Rudra, and his views have received a wide acceptance among a section of the Nāthas who are now adopting Brahmanical sacraments. It is also interesting to note that some of the modern religious teachers have been able to secure a large number of followers from the lower strata of society by declaring them as descendants of the higher castes like the Brāhmaṇas or the Kṣatriyas. As for example, the Namaḥ-śūdras have been given the position of Pārasava Vipras, the Aguris of the Ugra-Kṣatriyas and so on. A considerable number of the Marwaris of Calcutta are calling themselves Vedic Vaiśyas who are disciples of such teachers. The popularity of this mentality is due to the sense of inferiority current among the so-called lower castes and the desire of their getting higher social status in the existing caste system.

8. The Dharma Cult

For the basis of our understanding of a few apparently meaningless proletarian rituals, the significance of which is not expected to be clear from the fragmentary nature of the rituals themselves, we have spoken a lot of words in the preceding sections from which it is possible to form an idea—neither transparent nor opaque, but rather translucent—of a period of transformation in religious life, of the growth of various sects, of the thought-processes involved therein and of the revival of a kind of proletarian spirit which served as a driving force behind such movements. Now we shall deal with a very interesting proletarian cult in which a lot of popular ceremonies and rituals are involved. This is the cult of Dharma which is widely current in different parts of West Bengal. It is an admixture of some relics of decaying Buddhism, popular Hindu ideas and practices, a large number of indigenous beliefs and ceremonies, and ingredients derived also from Islam.

Regarding the antiquity of this cult we may refer to a tortoise-shell inscription of about the eleventh century A.D. It was found in the village of Vajrayogini in the Dacca district and was first published by N. K. Bhattasali[16] whose reading of the inscription was not, however, correct. Subsequently D. C. Sircar edited the inscription[17] from which it appears that a person named Manaṃraśarman caused a *Dharma* to be made on his behalf. The material on which the inscription is incised is also conspicuously associated with the cult of Dharma. Tortoise-shells or earthen images of tortoise covered by these shells were worshipped as Dharma Ṭhākur whose worship in the shape a tortoise is still prevalent in the Burdwan and Presidency divisions of West Bengal. K. P. Chattopadhyay whose work on Dharma worship[18] is of great anthropological interest, examined numerous images in the districts of Birbhum, Midnapure and 24 Parganas which were shaped like tortoises.[19] Sukumar Sen also points out that "the emblem of Dharma—rather his *pāda-pīṭha* on which was placed or engraved the *pādukā* (boots or sandals) of Dharma—is a tortoise. In most cases, it is a natural bit of stone shaped like a tortoise; in other cases it is

16. *Annual Report of the Dacca Museum for 1939-40*, pp. 7-8.
17. *Journal of the Royal Asiatic Society of Bengal, Letters*, Vol. XV, pp. 101 ff.
18. *ibid.*, Vol. VIII, 1942, pp. 99-135.
19. *ibid.*, pp. 104-105.

a chiselled stone image of the same."[20] In the introduction to *Rūparāmer Dharmamaṅgal,* edited by Sukumar Sen and Panchanan Mandal, the god Dharma is clearly associated with *kūrma* or tortoise. Sen and Mandal further point out that, although the worship of Dharma is now prevalent only in West Bengal, it was in former times also current in other parts of Bengal.[21] They trace it in the present day ceremony of *Del* or worship of Pāṭ Ṭhākur in East and North Bengal and point to the existence of Dharma Ṭhākur's *Gādi* in the Bogra district. They further connect the Dharma cult with the Chaṭ Parva or Ṣaṣṭhī-parva prevalent in Bihar.[22]

The Dharma cult was responsible for the creation of a type of literature in Bengali language.[23] From the literary works bearing on the cult of Dharma it is abundantly clear that this cult was current among the low class peoples like the Hāḍis, Ḍoms, Bāgdis, fishermen, carpenters, etc. Archaeological investigations have revealed that images and temples of Dharma Ṭhākur as well as ideas and practices related to this cult are also to be found in some parts of Orissa, particularly in Mayurbhanja and its vicinities.

9. The Dharma Cult and Buddhism

S. B. Dasgupta has rightly observed: "The Dharma cult is a result of a popular comingling of a host of heterogeneous beliefs and practices; it will therefore be incorrect to style it purely Buddhistic or Hindu or indigenous either in origin or in nature,—it is as much a hotchpotch in its origin as it is in its developed form and nature."[24]

It was MM. Haraprasad Sastri who played the pioneer's part in bringing to the notice of the public the existence of such a religious cult and the literature on it. According to Sastri, the Dharma cult is the *Living Buddhism in Bengal.* He pointed out that Dharma's *dhyāna* represents the deity Śūnyamūrti and Nirañjana, which connect

20. *B. C. Law Volume,* p. 672.
21. Sen and Mandal, *loc. cit.*, p. 1.
22. Cf. D. C. Sircar, *Religious Life in Ancient and Medieval India,* Delhi 1971, pp. 189-196.
23. For general informations about the Dharma literature of Bengal see S. B. Dasgupta, *op. cit.*, pp. 308-412.
24. *ibid.*, p. 260.

the cult with the theory of the *Void,* so popular with the later Buddhists, and show the latter's influence on the former.[25] As a popular religious cult, the worship of Dharma owes many of its elements to that form of later Buddhism which is known as Vajrayāna. The texts of the Dharma cult like the *Śūnya Purāṇa* or the *Dharma Pūjā Vidhāna* remind us of the liturgical texts of the Vajrayāna. Dr. P. C. Bagchi also thinks that the Dharma cult should be regarded as a survival of Buddhism in Bengal.[26] K. P. Chattopadhyaya speaks of the 'Wheel of Dharma' in connection with the Dharma Ṭhākur Cult.[27] It is interesting to note that the followers of the Dharma cult still observe the *Buddhapūrṇimā* (the days of the birth, enlightenment and death of the Buddha) and the *Āṣaḍhī-pūrṇimā* (the day on which *Dharmacakra* was first preached by the Buddha) as highly auspicious festive days.[28]

But side by side it must be admitted that the epithets *Nirañjana* and *Śūnyamūrti* on which Sastri relied so much in emphasising the Buddhist elements may also denote different things. Since 'white disease' or leucoderma is resulted from the curse of Dharma and since he is described as all white in form and garment, the epithets *Nirañjana* and *Śūnya* may denote as well his spotless form. This is what has been suggested by Sukumar Sen. Sastri has also confused the tortoise shape of Dharma with the form of a Buddhist Caitya and ignored the fact that Buddhist literature does not represent Dharma in the shape of a tortoise. Buddhist scriptures represent Ādi Dharma as a *goddess* who revealed herself from the centre of a triangle and produced the Buddha, Dharma and Saṅgha from its three sides. Dharma that was produced from its second side is the wife of the Buddha produced from the first side, and is the mother of other Buddhas.[29] But these conceptions have little to do with the tortoise form of Dharma Ṭhākur whose name, however, connects him with the Buddhist *Ratna.* In the Kailan inscription of Srīdhāraṇarāta (seventh century) and the Sundarban inscription of Ḍommanapāla (twelfth century) the expression *Ratnatraya* is used to indicate a Buddhist establishment. The three *Ratnas* of the Buddhists—

25. *Proceedings of the Asiatic Society of Bengal,* 1894, p. 135; *Journal of the Asiatic Society of Bengal,* 1894, pp. 55-61, 65-68.
26. P. C. Bagchi in *Dacca History of Bengal,* Vol. I, p. 425.
27. K. P. Chattopadhyay, *loc. cit.*, pp. 112, 115, figs. 2-3.
28. Dasgupta, *op. cit.*, p. 272.
29. A. Getty, *Gods of Northern Buddhism,* p. 28.

Buddha, Dharma and Saṅgha—came to be worshipped later in Buddhist monasteries and they were represented in human forms. The Buddhist image of Dharma was that of a four-armed god showing the *añjali* posture against the breast by one pair of hands and carrying the rosary and double lotus in the other.[30] Difficult to say whether this deified form of the abstract concept of Buddhist *Dharma* contributed anything to the growth of the Dharma cult of later times.

10. Dharma and the Brahmanical Deities

Therefore, admitting the fact of a relation between the liturgical works of the Dharma cult with those of later Buddhism, what we can say is that it bears only a faint relation to Buddhism and that the cult as a whole belongs to religious systems other than Buddhism. These religious systems also served as *accretions* on a *kernel* which was basically primitive and proletarian, as we shall presently see.

In Vedic literature the word *dharma* is used denoting various personified forms.[31] In Brahmanical mythology, Dharma is sometimes a separate deity (virtue personified as a bull, dog or dove and identified with Viṣṇu or Prajāpati) and sometimes another name of Yama and of Yudhiṣṭhira. No representation of an independent deity called Dharma is known.[32] Yudhiṣṭhira is worshipped in Madras region as Dharmarāja whose cult cannot, however, be related to the Dharma cult of Bengal.[33] In the liturgical texts of the Dharma cult, however, the tradition of Dharma's identity with Yama seems to be very popular.

Dharma's association with the tortoise reminds us of the tortoise incarnation of Viṣṇu. Dharma is often called Svarūpanārāyaṇa. In the *Dharmamaṅgalas* we come across not only Dharma in the form of Viṣṇu of dark blue colour with four hands each containing the conch-shell, disc, mace and lotus, but also descriptions of the ten incarnations of Viṣṇu in the forms of the ten incarnations of Dharma. Vaiṣṇavite myths and legends, found in the epics and Purāṇas, are sometimes attributed to the god Dharma. The identification of

30. D. C. Sircar, *op. cit.*, p. 197.
31. cf. *Śat. Br.*, XIII. 4.3.
32. Sircar, *op. cit.*, p. 197; Dasgupta, *op. cit.*, pp. 268 ff.
33. For the Dharmarāja cult of South India, see K. P. Chattopadhyay, *loc. cit.*, pp. 129-30.

Dharma with Rāma in the *Dharmamaṅgalas* has been brought about mainly through the mediacy of Hanumān. But the tradition of Dharma's identity with Viṣṇu or Rāma appears to be less popular than the tradition of his identity with Yama, Sūrya and Śiva. The Brahmanical gods whose ingredients have mostly been absorbed by Dharma are these deities as we shall see later while dealing with the cult of Kālārkarudra in connection with the *Caḍaka* rituals.

11. Dharma and Sun

Panchanan Mandal and Sukumar Sen[34] suggest that the cult of the Vedic and Iranian Sun-God, Vedic Varuṇa, the war-god of such peoples as the Ḍoms and Caṇḍālas, and several other deities, mostly non-Vedic, contributed to the origin and development of the Dharma cult. K. P. Chattopadhyay[35] lays greater stress on Dharma's relation with Vedic Varuṇa and the latter's association with the Sun. He also brings the Dharma Pennu of the Khonds and Dharma of the Santals in relation to the Dharma cult. As to the Solar origin of Dharma Ṭhākur, Sukumar Sen observes: "Those who have studied this cult in letter and in practice will find out readily that Dharma is the sun-god. The tortoise (*Kūrma, Kaśyapa*) as the symbol or emblem of the (rising ?) sun is probably a non-Aryan concept. But the identification of the tortoise with the sun appears early in Indo-Aryan religion, at least as early as the *Śatapatha Brāhmaṇa* (VII. 5. 15). As an Aryan god the sun moves in a chariot. So does Dharma. As a matter of fact the ceremony of *Rathayātrā* was originally connected with Dharma. Like the sun-god, Dharma cures incurable diseases like leucoderma. The sun-god has a bird as his *vāhana* and the god of death (Yama) is his son. Dharma's direct creation Ulūka (owl) combines the two personalities. The monkey cult was originally associated with the sun worship. In the cult of the Dharma, Hanumān is his factotum. Dharma is also the Iranian sun-god. He wears *boots,* dresses like a warrior and rides a horse."[36]

So far as Sen's observation is concerned, the Aryan non-Aryan question appears to be redundant. As regards the *Rathayātrā* festival

34. *Rūparāmer Dharmamaṅgal,* intro.
35. *loc. cit.*
36. *B. C. Law Volume,* p. 672.

D. C. Sircar[37] observes that it is popular in the religious life of South India and it seems to have been brought to Eastern India by the South Indians. The Gaṅga kings appear to have popularised the Rathayātrā at the Puri temple and the practice seems to have spread to other Vaiṣṇava temples in these parts. But the Rathayātrā festival is more primitive and it was connected in different parts of the world with rain magic as Frazer has rightly shown in his *magnum opus, The Golden Bough.* The relation between the Rathayātrā and rain magic is amply indicated in the Nepalese Buddhist tradition which has a close bearing on the Nātha cult. S. Levi in his *Le Nepal* has recorded the tradition that once Gorakṣa came to Nepal in search of his *guru* Matsyendra who was no other than Avalokiteśvara Padmapāni, but as the mountain was difficult to access he tied nine serpents with a *tortoise* (the symbol of Dharma) and sat on them, as a result of which there was drought in the valley for long twelve years. Then Matsyendranātha was cleverly brought by the king in Nepal and his presence caused rain in abundance. According to another version Gorakṣa, being offended in Nepal, imprisoned the clouds and put them under his seat for twelve years, as a result of which there was drought and famine. By chance Matsyendra was then passing through Nepal and having seen his *guru* when Gorakṣa stood up the clouds were let loose and there was rain in abundance. Thus Matsyendra, in the form of Avalokiteśvara Padmapāni, came to be regarded with universal respect in Nepal as the bestower of rain, and his deed is celebrated, still to the present time, by the famous *Rathayātrā.*[38] Dharma Ṭhākur's connection with agriculture and rain is also very well known. Sen has pointed out that Dharma is a god of water as well and that barren women are bestowed with the gift of progeny by him when worshipped with austerities.

12. The Proletarian Substratum of the Dharma Cult

Referring to the Dharma cult of Bengal Prof. Suniti Kumar Chatterji observes: "He is also a god of agriculture, and in Bengal we have a strange conception of Śiva as a farmer, a conception not found elsewhere in India, which appears to be an extension of this aspect of the divinity Dharma to Siva when the latter came to be

37. *op. cit.*, p. 199n.
38. S. B. Dasgupta, *op. cit.*, p. 385.

identified with the former. I have to note one very special thing about Dharma: his great annual festival is everywhere accompanied by ritual dances, and sometimes by mimicry and drama: without these dances by his worshippers (who usually take up a vow and observe strictly some regulations in living for a month), this annual festival (*gājan,* from *garjana,* as it is called) cannot be held. These dances are accompanied by songs, and are performed by troups of devotees."[39] According to Prof. Chatterji these features have very little to do with the so called Aryan or Sanskrit culture, the way of life of the higher caste Hindus. He also suggests that we should look upon the very respectable Sanskrit name *dharma* with suspicion and may ask ourselves whether the name is a Sanskritisation for some original non-Sanskrit name which had a similar sound with the Sanskrit word. An easy Sanskritisation of the Kol name *durom, duram* or *daram* into Dharma is quite possible.[40]

According to Sukumar Sen, "Śaiva Nātha cult was not entirely unconnected with Dharma worship. The four early Nātha *Siddhas* are mentioned in the cosmogony of the Dharma cult as directly created from the ashes of the body of Dharma. Durlabha Mallika's version is the earliest available form of the Maināmatī-Govindacandra legend. Therein we find the cosmogony peculiar to the cult of Dharma fully implied. Another point of contact between the two cults is the wearing of the symbolic footprint or foot gear (*pādukā*) of Dharma by the Nātha Siddhas as well as by the Dharma priests (*paṇḍita*)."[41] The proletarian character of Nāthism has been referred to in section 7 of this chapter.

Sen also observes: "Dharma is predominantly a war-god of fighting tribes like the Ḍom and others. According to the tradition recorded in the ritualistic treatises, Sadā the Ḍom was the first to worship Dharma. Next man was Āsoyā the Gāral (*Caṇḍāla*). The latter is said to have offered to Dharma 'tanks of wine' and 'hillocks of rice cakes': *madyer puṣkarṇī dilā piṣṭer jāṅgāl.* Sacrifice of animals such as goat, duck or pig is made even now in the annual *gājana* ceremony of Dharma. Wine and rice cakes are also offered. At some places the image is bathed in wine just before the commencement of the ceremony. The genuine priests of Dharma generally belong to the Ḍom or Gāral caste and comparatively rarely from

39. *B. C. Law Volume,* p. 78.
40. *ibid.,* pp. 79-80.
41. *ibid.,* p. 670.

other castes such as Bāuri, Dhopā, Śuri, etc.....Dharma was the god that was pleased only with the most cruel austerities. One had to burn incense over head, to walk over live coals, to pierce the most delicate parts of the body with iron spikes, even through the chest before the deity relented and offered the desired gift of son. The hardest penance was self-immolation (*hākanda*), when the devotee cuts off his own head....The cult of Dharma is the quintessence of the native culture, both spiritual (religious) and material. All minor native deities such as Bāsali, Jāṅguli (i.e. Manasā), various Kṣetrapālas, Ḍākinis and Śākinis gathered round Dharma as his courtiers (*āvaraṇā-devatā*) and thus obtained general recognition and worship. The legend about the origin of the cultivation of rice has insinuated itself into the grand ceremony (i.e. *gājana*). Other native industries also, such as production of molasses, smelting of copper and iron, etc. have not been overlooked. Thus in the elaborate *gājana* ceremony we witness the slow emergence of early Bengali culture in its main aspects."[42]

13. The Gājana of Dharma and Śiva

Some of the characteristics of the *gājana* rituals have been discussed in the preceding sections. These rituals are performed mainly, if not exclusively, by the proletarian peoples, and we have seen that, besides the most cruel austerities inherited from primitive religious beliefs,[43] and collective dancing, singing and drumming, which are also legacies of primitive magical practices, the *gājana* rituals contain the professional characteristics of the simpler peoples. According to the followers of the Dharma cult there are five ages—*Setai* or golden, *Nilāī* or silver, *Kaṃsāi* or copper, *Rāmai* or iron and *Goṃsai* or age to come. This metallic classification is significant. In the liturgical texts of the Dharma cult as well as in the verses recited during the *gājana* of Śiva and Dharma, we have accounts of the origin of corn, *beta*, double drum (*ḍhāka*), conch (*śaṅkha*), thread, copper, iron, earthen pots and vessels for incense and so on. The word *gājana* appears to have been derived from *garjana*, meaning *roar*, which reminds us of storm and thunder, and as such the ritual in its original character might have stood for rain-magic, the most

42. *ibid.*, pp. 673-74.
43. *Encyclopaedia of Religion and Ethics*, Vol. II, p. 206.

important technique of food production. Since in ancient and medieval India the villages were mainly the centres of production, and not the cities of the well-to-do persons living on the surplus supplied by the villages, these cults and rituals reveal the material culture and social institutions of the rural proletariat. Long ago, Ram Comul Sen remarked that the word *gājana* was an abbreviation of *grāmajana*, meaning the *villagers*, things rural or rustic.

According to Prof. Niharranjan Ray,[44] Dharma Ṭhākur is basically a primitive tribal god and his present form is due to the intermixture of countless heterogeneous elements. The god Dharma has no fixed form. Sometimes he is worshipped in the form of a crude stone. Often unused phallic form of Śiva is worshipped in the name of Dharma. The Dharma stone bears the characteristics of the sun-stone and the phallus serving the purpose of rain and fertility charms. These functions are also shared by Śiva whose agricultural character was mainly responsible for bringing the two deities under the same roof and for treating them as identical. That is why the Śaktis of Śiva like Bāśuli, Caṇḍī, Durgā, Pārvatī, etc. have been associated with Dharma who is frequently styled as Maheśvara, Mahādeva, Devadeva and the like which are commonly used epithets of Śiva.

The Gājana of Dharma and that of Śiva have become identical. "In the book *Ādyer Gambhirā* by Mr. Haridas Palit we have an elaborate account of the *gājana* of Dharma. Even a cursory glance on the verses that were sung with dancing and beating of double drums will show how confusedly Śiva and Dharma have been mixed together in these ceremonies and the verses themselves are really fragments found in the liturgical works of the Dharma cult and the *Śivāyanas* of Bengal. It is very interesting to note that this ceremony of *gājana* is also found in some districts of East Bengal in the form of Nīla Pūjā (i.e. worship of the deity Nīla), and this elaborate religious ceremony, which takes place in the last week of the Bengali year and takes about a week's time to be completed, is never suspected by the people in these districts to be anything but a Hindu religious function primarily concerned with the Hindu deity lord Śiva.[45] The fragmentary verses that are generally recited in connection with the various ceremonies of this function have striking affinity

44. *Bāṅgālīr Itihās* (Beng.), Vol. I, p. 586.
45. See D. C. Sen, *Vaṅga Sāhitya Paricaya*, Calcutta University Pub., Part I, pp. 159-161.

with the verses found in the liturgical works of the Dharma cult and also in the *gājana* of Dharma of West Bengal not only in matter and spirit, but sometimes in language also with slight deviations."[46]

In the beginning of the nineteenth century, W. Ward saw the *gājana* and *caḍaka* of Dharma in the villages of Pusuri and Raikali. Since Ward had no idea about the existence of a distinct Dharma cult and the rituals of Dharma did not appear very different to him from those of Śiva, he considered Dharma Ṭhākur to be another form of Śiva. According to him, "a black stone of any shape becomes the representative of this god. The worshippers paint the part designated as the forehead and place it under a tree; others place the stone in the house and give it silver eyes, and anoint it with oil and worship it. Almost every village has one of these idols. A festival in honour of this god is observed by the lower orders . . . The ceremonies are like those of the swinging festival with the addition of bloody sacrifices, the greater number of which are goats. At this time devotees swing on hooks, perforate their sides with cords, pierce their tongues with spits, walk upon the fire and take it up in their hands, walk upon thorns and throw themselves upon spikes, keeping a severe fast. The people who assemble to see these feats of self torture are entertained with singing, music and dancing, etc."[47]

14. Gājana and Caḍaka: The Participating Deities

All the items mentioned by Ward are still in vogue and they are shared by the *gājana* and *caḍaka* rituals dedicated now-a-days mainly to Śiva. These two sets of rituals stand in reciprocal relation and the one cannot be distinguished from the other. We may rather say that the *caḍaka* and kindred ceremonies are offshoots of the traditional *gājana,* and some of the constituents of the latter like hook-swinging, etc. were absorbed and specialised by the grown offshoots. We can thus define the *gājana* as a very primitive ritual-complex surviving throughout the ages among the lower orders of society as well as among the tribal peoples which has always found expression with the growth of the proletarian cults in different parts of the country at different ages.

46. Dasgupta, *op. cit.*, pp. 279-280.
47. W. Ward, *A View of the History, Literature and Religion of the Hindoos,* Vol. II, p. 184.

Of the tribal cults and rituals of eastern India, supposed to have some bearing on this primitive ritual complex, reference may be made to the Māndā, Saharul, Ba-parav, Bate-ili, Phāgu, Phāguā, Soherāi, Akhān-Sendrā, Karam, Jitiya, Deothān, Jādurā, Khaḍḍi-parav, Pauṣ-parav, Māgh-parav and Cait-parav of the Muṇḍas, Sāhare, Sakrāt, Bāhā, Māghsin, Eroksim, Mākmore, Bātāuli and Yamnanā of the Santals, Saharul, Grāmapūja, Grām-bāndā, Goerā, Soharaï and Karam of the Oraons, Karam, Goera, Tusu, Sarul, Māghi, Māghsim, Akhām, Bāhā and Sakrāt of the Mahālis, Saharul, Des-sikār, Dalma-pūjā, Karam, Bāndhnā, Buru, Māghpūjā, Tusu, Makar-saṃkrānti, Pañcavahīnī, Bardelā, Deośāli, Grām-devatā, Kudrā and Viṣāicaṇḍi of the Bhūmijs, Pati-Aṣaḍi, Garbhu, Caḍak, Rakam, Māghi, Jituā, Vasumatī and Mahādeo of the Malpāhāris, Pauṣ-parav, Māgh-parav, Khāria-pūjā, Saharul, Bāhā, Gosāpunya, Bātāuli, Gram-parav, Bāndhna, Gohāl-pūjā and Jemmamā of the Hos, Sosābanga, Nav-jom, Karam, Jitiā, Desāi, Sohrāi and Grām-ṭhākur of the Birhors, Śiva, Dāk, Goerā, Tusu and Māghi of the Korās, Barām, Bāndhnā, Jāthel and Tusu of the Lodhās, and so on.[48] The exact relation of these tribal cults and rituals with the primitive ritual complex we have described as *gājana* has not yet been established. About 40 years ago, K. P. Chattopadhyay[49] in one of his valuable articles had established the common basis of *Māndā, Caḍaka* and Dharma cult.[49a] Others require to be worked out.

48. A. Mitra, *Rāḍher Saṃskriti O Dharma Ṭhākur* (Bengali), Calcutta 1972, pp. 255-56.
49. *Journal and Proceedings of the Asiatic Society of Bengal,* New Series, Vol. XXX, 1934, pp. 151-161.
49a. The Manda festival which has a wide currency among the Mundas, Oraons and other tribes and castes of Bihar, to which reference has been made above, is a form of *Caḍaka.* Like the Sannyāsis of Gājana the participants of the Manda, who are called Bhoktās and supposed to be possessed by Śiva, have to follow certain rules and regulations and observe a number of taboos. For about a month before the commencement of the festival they beg from door to door carrying a nailed log which is regarded as the image of Pārvatī. On the second day of the festival a rite called *Kāndhāiyā* 'or carrying on the shoulder' is performed. The Bhoktās sit on a line and the high priest, usually a Gosain, steps on their shoulders to reach the place of Śiva. Then takes place at night the rite of *phulkudnā* or 'stepping on flowers'. Before the shrine of the god, who is generally Śiva, a trench, about fifteen feet in length and three or four feet in width, is dug and filled with live charcoal. When the fire is perfectly ready, the Bhoktās walk across it. Sometimes they jump on the fire until it is

Of the deities associated with this primitive ritual complex, we can divide them on the basis of their class character. Connected with Dharma are Bāṇa and Bāṇeśvarī, the god and goddess symbolizing the hoe, and the sisters of the latter—Nandiśvarī, Śankheśvarī, Dudheśvarī, Ghāgeśvarī, Khageṣvarī, etc.,—all local deities. Of the *kāminyās* or consorts of Dharma, we have Ṣaṣṭhi, the goddess of childbirth, Śītalā, the goddess of small-pox, Manasā, the goddess of snakes, Dhavaladevī, the goddess of leprosy, Caṇḍī, Durgā, Kālī, etc. who were previously the consorts of Śiva, and so on. In the *Dharmapūjāvidhāna* the following deities are mentioned as *āvaraṇadevatās* who are connected with the *gājana* and other rituals of Dharma. They are Gaṇeśa, Sūrya, Śiva, Viṣṇu, Durgā, Lakṣmi, Viṣahari, Bhairava, Bāśuli, Sarasvatī, Kuvera, Ṣaṣṭhī, Bhagavatī, Vasumatī, Viśālākṣī, Vaṭukanātha, Kṣetrapālas, Brahmāṇī, Māheśvarī, Vaiṣṇavī, Vārāhī, Nārasiṃhī, Indrāṇī, Cāmuṇḍā, Brahmā, Garuḍa, Viśvakarmā, Dvārapālas, Nandī, Kāmadeva, Baṇeśvara, Paṇḍāsura, Dikpālas, Śvetapaṇḍita, Nīlapaṇḍita, Kaṃsāripaṇḍita, Ramāipaṇḍita, Nine Agnis, Magarapaṇḍita, Kālughoṣa, Bhaṭṭadharādhara, Bhāskara-nṛpati, Sādhupura Datta, Tāmbuli, Uttararāḍha, Dakṣiṇarāḍha, Āśoyā-Caṇḍāla, Ādinātha, Dīnanātha, Cauraṅgīnātha, Gorakṣanātha, Pañcagauḍa, Gauḍeśvara, etc. The reason behind the inclusion of Brahmanical deities has been explained in the tenth section of this chapter. Besides the major gods of the Five Cults (*Pañcopasanā*), the list contains the Bhairavas, the Mātṛkās, the Dikpālas, the Kṣetrapālas, the Dvārapālas, the Nātha teachers, the Paṇḍitas of the Dharma cult and deified human beings. From other sources we come across a new set of deities like Kālārkarudra, Kālāgnirudra, Gambhīra, Carakī, Hājarā, Nīlacaṇḍikā, etc. These deities are especially worshipped in connection with the *Caḍaka* rituals and liturgical texts were also composed in their honour, as we shall see in a subsequent section.

15. The Death and Resurrection Theme in Gājana Rituals

That the *gājana* and *caḍaka* dedicated to Dharma, Śiva and other deities have a close bearing on the primitive conceptions of death and

extinguished. Females also take part in these performances. They are called Sokthāins. The function over, dance competitions, sometimes mask dances, are held. On the last day, the hook-swinging, with the Bhoktas its participants, takes place. See section 19.

resurrection[50] is amply indicated by a few of the surviving rituals which may be classified into five distinct groups on the basis of their contents.

To the first group belong the simple vegetation and fertility rites which as we have seen in different chapters of this work, have given birth to the myths of the dying gods and mourning goddesses all over the world, the annual death and revival of the god symbolizing the annual death and revival of plant life. In many parts of Bengal the dead spirit of vegetation—Dharma, Śiva or anything, even the *caḍaka-tree*—is kept under water for the whole year in a pond, and during the *gājana* the image is recovered in which the power of life is ceremonially infused, as if the dead is brought back to life again. The throwing of images into water and the mourning for them recall the European custom of throwing the dead spirit of vegetation under the name of Death, Yarlis, Kostroma and so on into the water and lamenting over it. Keeping the vegetation-deity submerged under water is a well known and widely current form of rain magic, and we have many instances in which certain stones are conceived as the rain-making god, and in the time of drought they are carried in procession and dipped in a stream.[51] A banana-leaf serves as the only garment of the priest performing the bathing rite of Dharma and this reminds us of the ceremonial nudity connected with rain and fertility charms.[52]

In the third chapter we have dealt with the ritual use of wine as the source of fecundity and rebirth. It is the fluid power that gives a new life to everything. Even in the Vedic hymns wine is regarded as the drug of immortality. Its life-giving power has given to it the name *mṛtasañjivanī*, that which enlivens even the dead. The magical use of wine, so common in fertility and funeral rites, also finds expression in the *gājana* of Dharma and other deities. A gigantic vessel of wine called *bhāṇḍāl* is brought in front of the deity. Smaller vessels are also brought. Dances are held around the principal vessel and the participants become quite senseless which is caused sometimes by mere pretention, sometimes by the actual intoxicating effect of the liquor and sometimes by inhaling the smoke of powerful incense. In many places mock or actual fights are held among the participants for the possession of the vessel. In some villages of

50. See chapter seven.

51. Frazer, *The Golden Bough,* p. 75.

52. *Supra.*

the Birbhum district the Dharma-stone is carried in procession to the house of a *Śuṇḍī* (belonging to the wine-making caste) who anoints it with oil and wine. At places again the actual task of brewing is performed before the god. Where Brahmanical influence is greater, milk is used instead of wine. Such wine rituals are also current in different parts of South India.[53]

Fire festivals connected with the ideas of death and resurrection form an integral part of the *gājana* ceremony. These festivals consist of dancing around the fire, procession with burning torches, fire gymnastics, walking on the fire, jumping upon burning woods and so on and can be connected with primitive fire cults, relics of which are found in the parallel European customs like May Fire, Bon Fire, Midsummer Fire, etc. We have seen that the Holi and Dewali festivals are connected with primitive conceptions of death and resurrection which were based upon the observation of death and revival in plant life. In different parts of India, especially in many districts of Uttar Pradesh, Bihar and Orissa, fire festivals are held during the celebration of Holi, and the ashes thus produced from the kindling of the fire are sprinkled on the ground for the multiplication of crops and fruits. Prof. N. K. Bose connects the origin of the fire-rites of Holi with such tribal rites as the Meria-killing of the Khonds. It was a human sacrifice for increasing the productivity of the fields. They believe that Mother Earth bestows power of life through harvest and that power of life can be returned to her by offering a life, i. e. by a human sacrifice. Accordingly, the body of the victim was burnt and the ashes were sprinkled on the earth. This rite was also characterised by heavy consumption of wine and indiscriminate sexual intercourse, and this explains the relation between Holi and the sex rituals mentioned in the preceding chapter, relics of which are still found in the sexual gestures and obscene types of mock-fights, dances, songs and jokes forming essential features of the festival in different parts of the country. Human sacrifice for enhancing the fertility of the fields, which survived till lately among the wild tribes like the Khonds, was, once widely current among the peoples of India, but with the spread of relatively advanced ideas, which were evolved under different historical conditions, it went practically out of vogue. But its relics are not completely stamped out which still survive in the forms of stepping

53. Whitehead, *Village Gods of South India* (YMCA), pp. 49 ff. See *Supra*, pp. 53-55.

on the fire, burning of animals, burning of artificial human bodies, imitation of the act of killing, and so on (N. K. Bose, *Hindu Samājer Gaḍan*, Beng., Visvabharati, pp. 71-77)

The death and resurrection theme also finds expression in the ritual of an actual deadbody which is connected with the *gājana* and *caḍaka* of Dharma. In this ritual a game is played with the head of a dead person. The *Bāṇavrata* of Śiva is also a ritual connected with corpse in which a human skull is anointed with vermilion and oil which becomes the occasion of a collective dance in which the priests and devotees are the participants. The phallus of Śiva which is kept for a whole year under the water of a pond is then recovered and worshipped. The head priest gives a show of the supernatural power he has acquired through such rituals by perforating his tongue and by other feats of physical endurance.[54]

It is generally believed that the *gājana* is the festival of Siva's marriage with Devī or of Dharma's marriage with Mukti and the participants called *Bhaktyās* or *Bhaktiyas* who take the vows of asceticism are the members of the bridegroom's party. But why should the jubilant marriage party follow the custom of maintaining the traditional state of impurity by using mourning dress made of unwashed raw cotton, by hanging around the neck a key which is the specific mark of death in the family, by eating sun-dried rice self-cooked in a secluded spot which is done by the kinsmen of the dead, by abstaining from sexual intercourse, sleeping on the ground, allowing the hair, beard and nails to grow and so on which are exclusively funeral observances ? The common Hindu rule is that when a death takes place, the kinsmen of the dead must consider themselves as impure until the *śrāddha* rite is performed. This is called *Aśauca-pālana* or maintaining the state of impurity. The whole thing therefore appears to be a miming of a very primitive ritual-mourning, centering round the myth of annual death and resurrection of a vegetation deity, an Indian parallel of Adonis, Attis or Osiris who symbolized the spirit of corn, dying every year and again rising from the dead.[55]

16. The Caḍaka of Dharma

Dr. Amalendu Mitra has collected important data from the

54. H. K. Mukherjee, *Bīrbhūm Bibaraṇī* (Bengali), Vol. II, pp. 5-9.
55. For the rituals see A. Mitra, *op. cit.*, pp. 50-115.

Birbhum district of West Bengal regarding the *Caḍaka* of Dharma Ṭhākur.[56] The main features of this *Caḍaka,* as recorded by Dr. Mitra, are hook-swinging, perforation of the tongue, fire-festivals, wine-ritual, cult of Bāṇa Gosain or Bāṇeśvara, collective dancing, and offering of small images of horse. The significance of some of these features have been discussed above.

Of the remaining features, cult of Bāṇeśvara deserves special mention. This cult in some places is also connected with the *gājana* and *caḍaka* of Śiva. Although worshipped as a god, basically Bāṇeśvara represents a weapon, an arrow (*bāṇa*). The primitive custom of piercing the body with sharp weapons, of perforating the tongue, etc., commonly called *Bānfoḍā,* has been rationalised through the conception of this deity. During the worship of Dharma, the image of Bāṇeśvara becomes the occasion of a ceremony of circumambulation. We have also a female form of this deity. As we have remarked above, this god was probably a primitive agricultural deity connected with hoe-cultivation, and in course of time he had developed a relationship with other agricultural deities like Dharma or Śiva. An arrow or a spear-like instrument is considered to be the symbol of this god upon which fruits and vegetables are thrown so that they get pierced. This rite may have some bearing on the aforesaid *bānfoḍā* which is so common a feature of the *caḍaka* and *gājana* of Dharma.

Small terracotta images of horse are offered to the Dharma shrines and wooden horses also play a significant part in the *Gājana* and *Caḍaka* of Dharma, but not in those of Śiva. Small clay figurines of horse are also offered to the Pīr shrines. In popular belief horse is the vehicle of Dharma, but this does not explain the custom, although in Vedic mythology horse is the vehicle of the Sun god, some of whose characteristics have been absorbed by Dharma Ṭhākur, as we have seen above. The horse is connected with many a primitive belief, especially with those that were associated with ideas of fertility, as we have seen in the first chapter while dealing with the rituals of the Aśvamedha or the horse sacrifice. Sir James Frazer in his *Golden Bough* has given many examples of primitive agricultural beliefs and practices connected with horse and come to the conclusion that the horse represents the fructifying spirit both of the tree and of the corn, and hence the cause of the use

56. *ibid.*, pp. 146 ff.

of terracotta and wooden horses in the Dharma cult should be traced to such primitive fertility beliefs.

The same motive also explains the use of cane in the *gājana* of Dharma. The cane is not only kept in the shrine, but during the festival the participants pat the ground with canes in the name of Dharma. Imitations of beating the imaginary enemies with the sticks are also made. These enemies are surely malignant spirits who cause harm to the community in various ways. Referring to similar customs observed elsewhere Frazer remarks: "It comes to be thought desirable to have a general riddance of evil spirits at fixed times usually once a year in order that the people may make a fresh start in life freed from all the malignant influences which have been long accumulating about them."[57] In the cults of the South Indian village gods sticks and swords are used to drive away the evil spirits.[58] The use of stick has some specific functions also, especially in the cases of natural and human productivity. Among different tribes of Southern India patting the ground by a stick is done in connection with childbirth and puberty rites.[59] The Oraon farmers before transplanting the rice-seedlings pat the ground with a stick evidently to infuse productive power into the earth.[60]

17. Kālārkarudra: The Brāhmanised Form of Dharma

Prof. Chintaharan Chakravarti[61] refers to a god named Kālārkarudra as one of the principal deities honoured in the rituals of *caḍaka.* This god is described in a few recent manuals[62] as being like 10 million rising suns in splendour, having the sun, the moon and fire as his eyes, having the digit of the moon in the locks of his matted hair brightened by the glow of lightning and carrying in two of his hands a bell and a sword, and with the other two forming the *mudrās* of dispelling fear and granting boons. Terrible to look at and laughing as thunder, this god is the dispeller of the fear of those that bow

57. Frazer, *op. cit.*, p. 722.
58. Whitehead, *op. cit.*, p. 49.
59. E. Thurston, *Castes and Tribes of Southern India,* Madras 1909, Vol. V, p. 344.
60. S. C. Roy, *The Oraons of Chota Nāgpur*, Ranchi 1915, pp. 142 ff.
61. *Journal of the Asiatic Society of Bengal, Letters,* Vol. I, 1935, pp. 429 ff.
62. Harimohan Chakravarti, *Kālārkarudrapūjāpaddhati,* Calcutta 1319 B. S.; Nrisimha Vidyabhushan, *Caḍakapūjāpaddhati,* Calcutta 1336 B. S., and a MS of of *Kālārkarudrapūjā* in the possession of Pandit Baman Chandra Gautama of Kotalipara in the Faridpur district which Prof. Chakravarti could use.

down to him.

As his name implies, this god is the combination of three deities—*Kāla* or Yama, *Arka* or the Sun and *Rudra* who came to be known as Śiva. One of the manuals which Prof. Chakravarti has used actually describes this god as the combination of Kāla, Arka and Rudra. Of these, Kāla, the god of death, is described as the destroyer of all animals, the giver of the desired boon to the devotee, the fearful, the knower of all religion, the Vaiṣṇava, the son of the Sun having a terrible face, four hands, huge feet, a black complexion, red and deep-set eyes, a big body, a bright lotus like face, having a great buffalo as his carrier, having in his hands an iron mace, a net, wine and a staff. Arka (the sun) is described as the sea of endless qualities, the lord of all the worlds, having the red lotus as his seat, a jewel on the head, a reddish hue of the body, carrying two lotuses in two of his hands, and forming with the other two the gestures of dispelling fear and granting boons. Rudra is described as the lord of the universe, seated on the bull, the giver of boons, the dispeller of fear, three-eyed, five-faced, with his body besmeared with ashes, with a small drum and trident in his hands, with the head marked by the moon, and having a serpent on his neck.

This Kālārkarudra is evidently a recent Brahmanical adaptation of Dharma under a new name supposed to connote the surviving principal deities forming the substrata of the earlier conception of Dharma Ṭhākur as a composite popular deity. It has sufficiently been demonstrated in the preceding sections how the cult of Death (Yama or Kāla), Sun (Arka) and Śiva (Rudra) contributed to the growth of Dharma cult, and there is no need of repeating the arguments once again.

18. Nīlacaṇḍikā and Others

The consort of Kālārkarudra is Nīlacaṇḍikā or Nīlaparameśvarī, also known as Nīlā or Nīlāvatī. She is identified with Śakti or the supreme goddess. In the *Kālārkarudrapūjā-paddhati* referred to by Chakravarti, we have the name Nīlaparameśvarī who has been identified with Kālī. This goddess should be worshipped on an image drawn, with blue powder, of a half-bodied being riding on a horse. The worship of Nīlā or Nīlacaṇḍikā appears to have been at the root of the name Nīlapūjā given to the function, in general, in Eastern Bengal. We have already the occasion to refer to the *gājana* of Nīla. In the *Caḍakapūjāpaddhati,* also mentioned by Chakravarti, we have the worship of a male god who is known as Nīla whose image is drawn on an earthen platform with 'five powders'. The god is described, as half-bodied, two-armed, three-eyed, having a blue body and terrible appearance. His vehicle is horse.

Another god worshipped in connection of *caḍaka* is Kṣetrapāla to whom worship is offered at midnight. There is also a Śaivite deity of this name.[63] This god is naked, has his tawny hairs dishevelled, has the sun and the moon as his eyes, carries a fearful staff in his right hand and a skull full of wine in the left. Animal sacrifices are offered to this deity by the left hand. Needless to say that basically he was the protector of agriculture impersonating one of the functional aspects of Dharma. From the *Kālārkarudrapūjā* Chakravarti refers to a deity called Gambhira who is also worshipped in connection with *Caḍaka* outside the temple. This god is described as having purely white complexion, a camphor-like white body, which helps us to identify him with any local form of Dharma getting the status of an independent god. Two other deities, to be worshipped outside the village, are Kedāra and Hājarā. Of the former we get no iconographic description, while the latter is described as white-coloured, four-armed, naked and possessing matted hair. This deity appears to be different from a god called Gopāla Hājarā who is worshipped in connection with the cult of Jayadurgā in different parts of East Bengal.[64]

19. The Rituals of Caḍaka

In modern times the popular festival of *Caḍaka* has been conspicuously associated with the worship of Śiva and in some cases with that of Dharma, as we have seen above. This festival is widely current in Bengal and in some parts of Orissa.[65] The main cult characterising the festival is that of Śiva whose worship is performed daily during the month of *Caitra* with an image, a water vase or a *liṅga* or a *Dharmaśilā* (stone representing the god Dharma) as the

63. C. Chakravarti in *Indian Historical Quarterly,* Vol. IX, pp. 237 ff.
64. Idem in *Man in India,* Vol. XI, p. 47; *Journal of the Anthropological Society of Bombay,* Vol. XIV, pp. 69 ff.
65. For Orissa see S. N. Roy in *Journal of the Anthropological Society of Bombay,* Vol. XIV, pp. 188 ff.

symbol of the deity. The main function takes places during the last three days of the month.

Of its special religious features mention should be made of *Mudrābhañjana* or the initial worship which is connected with some local deity. The rituals are not same in all the places. In eastern Bengal, about a week before the day of the principal worship the phallic image of Śiva is taken out and kept dipped in a pot (*gambhirapātra*) full of water, the magical significance of which have been mentioned above. Then we have the Adhivāsa or preliminary purification, popularly known as *gṛhasannyāsa* or *girisannyāsa* which is performed in the dwelling house while the principal worship is performed in any temporarily erected hut. This is followed by the worship of the Dvārapālas (deities that guard the doors) and gods like Kṣetrapāla. Lastly the deities are bathed with different sorts of water (e.g. water of the Ganges, water of the sea, rain-water, etc.) and with other liquids like milk, curd, honey, ghee, etc.[66] A specially noteworthy feature of the whole function is that non-Brahmins including members of the lowest castes are allowed to take prominent part in it. It is these peoples that serve as *Bālās* or *Sāṅgas* (popularly known as Sāiñ). Salutation by the *Sāṅgas* is an imposing ceremony. Each of them is required to bow down before the deity for a specific number of times with specific postures and in some cases to the accompaniment of specific tunes of music. The term *Sāṅga* reminds us of the Buddhist term *Saṅgha* meaning community of brethren, and the Bengali word *Sāṅgāt* means a companion. In any case, the denotative names of the *Sāṅgas* indicate the function they have to discharge. Thus the Jalasābhaṭa is to bring in water, the Sthānapatra is to sweep, and so on. They also take part in all festivities and undergo physical tortures.[67]

K. P. Chattopadhyay has given a vivid description of a modern *Caḍaka* ceremony.[68] Except in places where there are brick-built temples, the first thing that is done is to construct a temporary thatched hut for the deity who is generally Śiva. An earthen figure of a crocodile is made of earth. A square mound of earth is built up with a circular projection in the front. At the centre of the mound is kept an earthen pot full of Ganges water. A small phallic image of Śiva is brought on an earth dish and put on the pot. All the

66. C. Chakravarti, *loc cit.*
67. *ibid.*, pp. 429-32.
68. *Journal of the Royal Asiatic Society of Bengal, Letters,* Vol. I, 1935, pp. 397-406.

preparations are made by the chief devotee, called *Mūla Sannyāsī* in Central Bengal at *Pat Bhakta* in West Bengal. In some places each of the devotees are furnished with a cane stick. The devotees fast during the day time on the 25th Caitra, put vermilion marks and rice paste on the waterpot, and the deity is then installed by the priest. Certain details of worship have to be gone through every day. Then comes the special ceremonials of each date which are

1. The swing over the fire.
2. The jump on thorns.
3. The jump on knives.
4. The piercing with arrows.
5. The marriage of Śiva and fire dance.
6. The swinging on the *caḍaka* tree.
7. The propitiation of the resuscitated ghosts.

In most places the swinging over the fire is done on the 26th and in a few places on the 25th and 27th. The frame erected for swinging consists of two tall bamboo poles set apart about ten feet from each other and with a cross bar of bamboo being fixed at the height of six feet from the ground. The fire is lit of the wood of the *Kul* tree. The fire is allowed to burn out to some extent so that there is plenty of live charcoal. The devotee gets up on the cross bar and hangs his head downwards, supporting himself by twisting his leg over the cross bar. The function over, the devotee and his assistants dance on the live charcoal until the embers are put out. Often a handful of embers is carried quickly to the altar of the god and offered to him like flowers.

On the next day (27th Caitra) the jump on thorns takes place. The date palms and thorny branches of the *beyunch* tree are heaped for this purpose. After the usual preliminary worship, the devotees come to the heap of thorns and drop flat on it and roll on it shouting, 'worship to the old Śiva'. The jump on knives usually takes place on the 28th. The knives are fixed on a plantain stem. The devotees get up on the frame of bamboo already described. Two men carrying a sack of straw stand in front. Another lays on it the plantain stem with knives and holds it firmly. The devotees then jump one by one on the knives, calling on Śiva. The height between the sack and the cross bar varies from four to twelve feet in different places. In some places the jump on knives is preceded by what is termed *maṇibhāṅgā* or jewel-breaking. A date-palm tree is selected and worshipped, and the devotees climb it to pluck with the teeth the thorny blade at the tip of the top leaf. The blade is carried in the mouth, held between the teeth all the way back to the place of worship, and kept until another ceremony, *phalchoḍā* or throwing the fruits, is over.

The next day (29th Caitra) is known everywhere as the date of the *Nīla*, Siva's marriage with Nīlāvatī, which is marked by the imitation of marriage rituals especially performed by women. The afternoon rituals are performed by the males with a scarf over the head indicating that they are doing women's part. The details are in fact exactly similar to the marriage rites of peoples of the rank of pure artisans and similar castes in Bengal. The nine *grahas* or planets are worshipped in connection with this marriage by drawing up a circle made by powdered rice. Formerly, on this date the ceremony of piercing with arrows used to be performed. At present the actual piercing still survives in some outlying villages, although it has been made illegal for many years. Iron-rods or thin shafts are pushed through the skin into the ribs. A pair is used by each devotee. It was also formerly the practice to perform certain other penances, involving piercing of the skin of the body in various other places. The most important of these was that known as the *kālikāpātāri*. The devotee had the skin pierced in many places by thin short arrows with the red *jabā* flower stuck at each end. Generally he went off into a trance after a time and was thought to return to life only on hearing the *Hākanda Purāṇa* or the description of the Dharma worship.

The next day (30th Caitra) is the day of *Caḍaka* or swinging on the *caḍaka* tree which consists of (1) a thick pole of palm or some wood fixed upright on the ground, (2) a rotator fixed on it, and (3) a strong bundle of bamboos fixed horizontally on the rotator which would carry the human load at one end and a balancing load at the other. After a conventional worship of the *caḍaka* tree, the lighter end is pulled down by a guide rope and the devotee gets up to swing round. Formerly the devotee used to be suspended by iron hooks attached to the bamboo frame, and fixed in the muscles of the back. Now-a-days he is simply tied by a rope.

On the next day, i.e. on the first day of the Bengali year, is performed the last function, the resuscitation of the dead (*dānobārāno*). The chief devotee cooks a *sol* fish, roasting it in ember. Some parboiled and husked rice is also cooked and rice wine is poured on the fish and the rice, which are placed in an earthen pot. These are taken at midday to a tree standing in some lonely meadow, and the food is poured on a plantain leaf and left for the ghosts to devour. This offering is sometimes made in the meadow where the village dead are cremated. Some devotees smear their faces with mud to personate demons or ghosts. They dance and shout and finally eat the fish and rice. A dark coloured mask is sometimes used. These supposed ghosts are collectively called *Saṅ*. Recently, however, the procession of *Saṅ* has changed its character. Instead of being the ceremony of resuscitation of ghostly beings, it has now become that of miming the social vices of the well-to-do class, which reveal the proletarian attitude towards the corrupt practices of class society.

20. Conclusion

K. P. Chattopadhyay appears to be quite correct when he says that all these rites and cults are closely connected with each other and that they are all based on a belief in resurrection, or coming to life after death and are intended to celebrate annually the return to the life of the diseased members of the community.[69] The circle of birth and death might have found a ritual expression in the hook-swinging. Long ago Ram Comul Sen pointed out that the term *caraka* (*caḍaka*) may be a transformation of *cakra* meaning a circle, and such interchange of letters is a common grammatical feature of the regional languages, which is known as *viprakarṣa* (cf. Ratna-Ratan).[70] The festival of hook-swinging has its parallel elsewhere.[71] The swinging festival of Siam appears to have some resemblance with that of the *caḍaka*. Physical tortures similar to those practised on this occasion are stated to be practised in connection with the worship of Kārtikeya in Kataragama in Ceylon.[72] But our point of interest is the basic proletarian character of these cults and rituals for which they were treated without enthusiasm and with contempt. Not even a passing reference to these cults and rituals is made by the famous Smṛti writers of Bengal—Govindānanda and Raghunandana

69. *ibid.*, p. 406.
70. *Journal of the Asiatic Society,* 1833, No. 24, p. 609.
71. Cf. J. N. Powell, 'Hook-Swinging: Mysore' in *Folklore,* Vol. XXV, 1914.
72. *Kalyāṇakalpataru,* Gorakhpur, Vol. II, p. 755.

—whose works, the *Varṣakriyākaumudī* and the *Tithitattva,* contain what may be said to be a comprehensive survey of religious practices of Bengal during the 15th-16th centuries.[73] The reason of such suppression or hushing up of the facts of proletarian life by the advocates of the Smārta-Purānic ideals can easily be understood.

73. C. Chakravarti, *loc. cit.*

BIBLIOGRAPHY

ATKINSON, E. T. *Himalayan Districts of the North-Western Provinces of India*, Allahabad, 1884.

BAGCHI, P. C. *Pre-Dravidian and Pre-Aryan in India*, Calcutta, 1929.

BANCROFT, H. H. *Native Races of the Pacific States*, London, 1885.

BARBOSA, D. *Description of the Coasts of East Africa and Malabar*, trans. H. E. Stanley, Hakluyt Society, London, 1866.

BATES, H. W. *The Naturalist on the Amazons*, London, 1873.

BHANDARKAR, R. G. *Collected Works*, Poona, 1936.

BHATTACHARYYA, B. T. *Indian Buddhist Iconography*, Calcutta, 1958.

BHATTACHARYYA, N. N. *Indian Puberty Rites*, Calcutta, 1968.

Indian Mother Goddess, Calcutta, 1970.

History of Indian Cosmogonical Ideas, New Delhi, 1971.

History of the Śākta Religion, New Delhi 1974.

History of Indian Erotic Literature, (in press).

BILLINGTON, M. *Women in India*, London, 1895.

BOAS, F. Chinook Texts, Washington, 1896.

BOSE, S. C. *The Hindus as They Are*, London, 1881.

BRĀHMAṆAS. *Aitareya*, trans. A. B. Keith, Harvard Oriental Series, XXV, Cambridge, Mass., 1920.

Taittirīya, ed. R. Mitra, Calcutta, 1855-70.

Śatapatha, trans. J. Eggelling in

SBE XII, XXVI, XLI, XLIII.
Pañcaviṃśa, ed. A. Vedantavagisa, Calcutta, 1869-74.
Kauṣītaki, ed. E. B. Cowell, Calcutta 1861, trans. A. B. Keith, Harvard Oriental Series, XXV, Cambridge, Mass., 1920.

BRIFFAULT, R. *The Mothers,* London, 1927, sec. ed. 1952.

BRIGGS, G. W. *Gorakhnāth and the Kānphaṭa Yogīs,* Calcutta, 1938.

BUDDHIST TEXTS. *Dīgha Nikāya,* trans. *Dialogue of the Buddha* by T. W. Rhys Davids, London, 1899, 1910, 1921; selections from in *SBE.*
Majjhima Nikāya, trans. *Further Dialogues* by Lord Chalmers, London, 1926-27; selections from in *SBE* by T. W. Rhys Davids.
Saṃyutta Nikāya, trans. *Book of the Kindred Sayings* by Mrs. C. W. F. Rhys Davids and F. L. Woodward, PTS, London, 1917-30.
Aṅguttara Nikāya, trans. *Book of Gradual Sayings* by F. L. Woodward and E. M. Hare, PTS, London, 1932-36.
Vinaya Piṭaka, trans. by H. Oldenberg and T. W. Rhys Davids in *SBE,* Oxford, 1881-85.
Jātakas, ed. V. Fausböll, 7 Vols. London, 1877-97; trans. under the ed. E. B. Cowell, London, 1895-1913.
Mahāvagga, see under Vinaya.
Suttavibhaṅga, see under Vinaya.
Dīpavaṃsa, ed. and trans. by H. Oldenberg, London, 1879.

BURGESS, J. *Buddhist Cave Temples and their Inscriptions,* London, 1883.

CASATIS, E. *The Basutos,* London, 1861.

CHAKRAVARTI, H. M. *Kālārkarudrapūjāpaddhati,* Calcutta, 1319 B. S.

CHALMIRS, J. and GILLEN, W. *Works and Adventures in New Guinea,* London, 1885.

CHANDA, R. P. *Indo-Aryan Races,* Rajsahi, 1916,rep. with an *intro* by N. N. Bhattacharyya, Calcutta, 1969.

CHATTOPADHYAYA, D. P. *Lokāyata,* New Delhi, 1959, sec. ed. 1968.

Bhāratīya Darśan, in Bengali, Calcutta, 1961.

CHILDE, V. G. *New Light on the Most Ancient East,* London, 1954.

What Happened in History, London, 1957.

CHURCH, G. E. *Aborigines of South America,* London, 1912.

CRAWLEY, A. E. *The Mystic Rose,* London, 1902.

CROOKE, W. *Popular Religion and Folklore in North India,* Westminister, 1896.

Tribes and Castes in the North-Western Provinces and Oudh, Calcutta, 1896.

Religion and Folklore in Northern India, Oxford, 1926.

DALTON, E. T. *Descriptive Ethnology of Bengal,* Calcutta, 1872.

DASGUPTA, S. B. *Obscure Religious Cults,* Calcutta, 1969.

DEGLE, L. *Three Years in Savage Africa,* London, 1898.

DENNET, R. E. *At the Back of Black Man's Mind,* London, 1906.

DHARMAŚĀSTRAS. *Manu,* trans. G. Bühler, *SBE,* Oxford, 1886.

Bṛhaspati, trans. J. Jolly *SBE,* XXXIII, Oxford, 1889.

Kātyāyana, ed. and trans. by P. V. Kane, Bombay, 1933.

Nārada, trans. J. Jolly, *SBE*, XXXIII, Oxford, 1889.
Viṣṇu, trans. J. Jolly, *SBE*, VII, Oxford, 1880.
Yājñavalkya, *Parāśara*, *Dālabhya*, *Yama*, *Laghuyama*, texts with Bengali trans. Aryasastra Series, Calcutta: other legal texts, Vaṅgavāsī Press, Calcutta, ed. P. Tarkaratna.

DHARMASŪTRAS. *Āpastamba*, ed. G. Buhler, Bombay 1892-94, trans. in *SBE*.
Baudhāyana, ed. E. Hultsch, Leipzig, 1884; trans. in *SBE*.
Gautama, trans. in *SBE*.
Vasiṣṭha, trans. in *SBE*.

DVIVEDI, H. P. *Nātha Sampradāya*, in Hindi, Varanasi, 1966.

EGGELLING, J. See under Brāhmaṇas, *Śatapatha*.

EGEDE, H. *A Description of Greenland*, original Danish from Copenhagen, first Eng. trans. London, 1745, latest ed. London, 1923.

EHRENFELS, O. R. *Mother-right in India*, Hyderabad, 1941.

ELLIS, A. B. *The Tsi-speaking Peoples*, London, 1887.

ENGELS, F. *Origin of the Family, Private Property and the State*, Moscow, 1952.

FARNELL, L. R. *Cults of the Greek States*, Edinburgh, 1896-1904.

FERGUSSON, J. *History of Indian and Eastern Architecture*, London, 1876.

FRAZER, J. G. *The Golden Bough*, 12 Vols. London, 1913, rep. London, 1966.
The Golden Bough (abridged ed.), London, 1951.
Totemism and Exogamy, London, 1910.
The Dying God (from *GB*, III of

1907 ed.).
Adonis Attis Osiris (from *GB*, IV of 1907 ed.).
Balder the Beautiful (from *GB*, VII-VIII of 1913 ed.).
Spirit of the Corn and the Wild (from *GB* XI of 1913 ed.).

GAIT, E. A. — *Census of India: Report 1901, Bengal*, Calcutta, 1902.

GENERAL REFERENCE WORKS — *The Cambridge History of India*, ed. E. J. Rapson, Vol. I, Cambridge, 1922.
History and Culture of the Indian People: (1) The Vedic Age (2) Age of Imperial Unity (3) The Classical Age (4) Age of Imperial Kanauj (5) Struggle for Empire, Ed. R. C. Majumdar, Bharatiya Vidya Bhawan, Bombay, 1951-57.
Encyclopaedia of Religion and Ethics, ed. J. Hastings, Edinburgh, 1908-18.
Sacred Books of the East, ed. F. Max Müller, Oxford.
Pinkerton, *Voyages and Travels*.
History of Bengal, Vol. I, ed. R. C. Majumdar, Dacca University, 1943.
Das Kapital Centenary Volume, ed. Mohit Sen and M. B. Rao, New Delhi, 1968.
Annual Report of the Dacca Museum.
Archaeological Survey of India: Reports. *B. C. Law Volume*, ed. D. R. Bhandarkar et al, Calcutta, 1945.
Social Life in Ancient India, ed. D.C. Sircar, Calcutta, 1971.
Religions Life in Ancient India, ed. D. C. Sircar, Calcutta, 1971.
Sanskrit-English Dictionary, by M.

Monier Williams, Oxford, 1899.

Census of India: Reports.

GETTY, A. *Gods of Northern Buddhism*, Oxford, 1928.

GHOSAL, U. N. *A History of Hindu Political Theories*, London, 1923, sec. ed. 1927.

GONDA, J. *Ancient Indian Kingship from the Religious Point of View*, Leiden 1966.

GOULDSBURY, G. and SHEANE, H. *The Great Plateau of Northern Nigeria*, London, 1911.

GṚHASŪTRAS *Āpastamba*, trans. in *SBE*, XXX

Āśvalāyana, ed. A. G. Stenzler, Leipzig, 1861, trans. in *SBE*, XXIX.

Baudhāyana, ed. R. Shamasastri, Mysore, 1920.

Khadira, ed. A. M. Sastri and L. Srinivasacharya, Mysore, 1913; trans. *SBE*, XXIX.

Pāraskara, ed. G. S Nene, Banares, 1926, trans. in *SBE* XXIX.

Gobhila, trans. in *SBE*, XXX.

Hiraṇyakeśī, trans. in *SBE*, XXX.

Śāṅkhyāyana, trans. in *SBE*, XXIX.

GRIFFITH, R. T. H. *Hymns of the Ṛgveda*, Delhi, 1963.

GRÜNWEDEL, A. *Buddhist Art in India*, London, 1901.

GUPTE, B. A. *Hindu Holidays and Ceremonials.*

HARDY, S. *Eastern Monachism*, London, 1860.

HARRISON, J. E. *Prolegomena to the Study of Greek Religion*, Cambridge, 1908.

Ancient Art and Ritual, London, 1935.

HARTLAND, E. S. *Primitive Paternity*, London, 1909.

HODGSON, B. H. *Religion and Literature of the Nepalese Buddhists*, London, 1874.

HOOK, S. H. *Myth and Ritual*, Oxford, 1933.

HOWITT, A. W. *Native Tribes of South-East Australia*, London, 1904.

HUME, R. A. *Thirteen Principal Upaniṣads*, Oxford,

1921.

HUTTON, H. H. *Caste in India*, Calcutta, 1951.

IYER, L. K. A. K. *The Cochin Tribes and Castes*, Madras 1909.

JAIMINI, SŪTRAS trans. by J. G. Jha Allahabad, 1910, of *Śabarabhāṣya* by *idem*, Baroda, 1933-36 (*GOS*).

JAIN, SŪTRAS trans. by H. Jacobi in *SBE*, XXII, XLV.

JEVONS, F. *Introduction to the History of Religion*, London, 1896.

JHA, G. *Pūrvamīmāṃsā and its Sources*, Banares, 1942.

JOHNSTON, H. H. *British Central Africa*, London, 1917.

JOURNALS See under *Periodicals*.

JUNOD, H. *Life of a South African Tribe*, London, 1927.

KANE, P. V. *History of Dharmaśāstra*, Poona 1930, 1941, 1946.

KARTSEN, R. *The Civilization of South American Indians*, London, 1926.

KEIFER, O. *Sexual Life in Ancient Rome*, London, 1963.

KEITH, A. B. *Religion and Philosophy of the Veda and the Upaniṣads* (Harvard Oriental Series, Nos. XXXI, XXXII), Cambridge, Mass., 1925.

Ṛgveda Brāhmaṇas, (Harvard Oriental Series XXV), Cambridge, Mass., 1920.

Vedas of the Black Yajus School (Harvard Oriental Series, Nos. XVIII, XIX) Cambridge, Mass., 1914.

KERN, H. *Manual of Indian Buddhism*, Strassburg, 1898.

KIDD, D. *The Essential Kaffir*, London, 1904.

KOSAMBI, D. D. *Myth and Reality*, Bombay, 1962.

MACALISTER, R. A. S. *Textbook of European Archaeology*, Cambridge, 1921.

MACDONELL, A. *Vedic Mythology,* Strassburg, 1898. *History of Sanskrit Literature,* London, 1905.

MACDONELL, A. and KEITH, A. B. *Vedic Index,* London, 1912.

MACKAY, E. J. H. *Further Excavations at Mohenjodaro,* Delhi, 1938.

MĀDHAVĀCĀRYA *Sarvadar ṡanasaṃgraha,* trans, E. B. Cowell London, 1914.

MAHĀBHĀRATA trans. by K. M. Ganguli, pub. P. C. Ray, Calcutta, 1926.

MAJUMDAR, N. G. *Exploration in Sind* (Memoirs of the Archaeological Survey of India, No. 48), Delhi, 1934.

MAJUMDAR, R. C. *Corporate Life in Ancient India,* Calcutta, 1919.

MALLIK, K. *Nāth Sampradāyer Itihās,* in Bengali, Calcutta, 1950.

MARSHALL, J. *Mohenjodaro and the Indus Civilization,* London, 1931.

MATEER, S. *Native Life of Travancore,* London, 1883.

MITRA, A. *Rāḍher Saṃskṛti,* in Bengali, Calcutta, 1971.

MONIER, WILLIAMS M. *Sanskrit English Dictionary,* Oxford, 1899.

MOOKERJI, R. K. *Fundamental Unity of India.*

MOORE, L. *Malabar Law and Custom,* Madras, 1909.

MORGAN, L. H. *Ancient Society,* New York, 1877.

MOURA, J. *Le Royaume du Cambodge,* Paris, 1883.

MUKHERJEE, H. K. *Bīrbhūm Vivaraṇī,* in Bengali.

NEGAM AIYA, V. *Travancore State Manual,* Trivandrum, 1906.

NANJUNDAYYA, H. V. and IYER, L. K. A. K. *Mysore Tribes and Castes,* Mysore, 1928-35.

NATESE SASTRI, S. M. *Hindu Feasts and Ceremonials,* Madras, 1903.

OMAN, J. C. *The Brahmins, Theists and Musal-*

mans, London, 1907.

PADFIELD, J. E. *The Hindu at Home*, Madras, 1896.

PANIKKAR, G. *Malabar and its Folk*, Madras, 1909.

PERIODICALS *Journal of the American Oriental Society.*
Journal of the Asiatic Society of Bengal.
Journal of the Royal Asiatic Society.
Journal of the Anthropological Institute.
Journal of the Royal Anthropological Institute.
Journal of the Anthropological Society of Bombay.
Journal and Proceedings of the Royal Asiatic Society of Bengal.
Journal of American Folklore.
Journal of the Oriental Institute.
Bombay Gazetteer.
Folklore.
Indian Antiquary.
Epigraphia Indica.
North Indian Notes and Queries.
Archaeological Survey of India: Annual Reports and Memoirs.
Annual Report of the Dacca Museum.
The Modern Review.

PIGGOTT, S. *Prehistoric India.*

PILLAI, N. K *Census of India: Travancore*, 1931, Trivandrum, 1932.

PLAYFAIR, A. *The Garos*, London, 1909.

POWERS, S. *Tribes of California*, Washington, 1877.

PURĀṆAS *Agni*, trans. M. N. Dutt., Calcutta, 1901.
Brahma, Vaṅgavāsī Press ed., Beng. trans. P. Tarkaratna.
Brahmāṇḍa, Vaṅgavāsī Press ed., trans. in Bengali, P. Tarkaratna.

Garuḍa, trans. M. N. Dutt, Calcutta 1908.
Kūrma, Vaṅgavāsī Press ed., Beng. trans. P. Tarkaratna.
Mārkaṇḍeya, trans. F. E. Pargiter, Calcutta, 1904.
Matsya, Vaṅgavāsī Press ed., Beng. trans. P. Tarkaratna.
Varāha, Vaṅgavāsī Press ed., Beng. trans. P. Tarkaratna.
Vāyu, Vaṅgavāsī Press ed., Beng. trans. P. Tarkaratna.
Viṣṇu, trans. H. H. Wilson, London, 1864-70.

RADHAKRISHNAN, S. *Indian Philosophy*, London, 1927.

RAY, N. R. *Bāṅgālīr Itihās*, in Bengali, Calcutta, 1949.
The Sikh Gurus and the Sikh Society, Patiala, 1970.

RAYCHAUDHURI, H. C. *Potitical History of Ancient India*, Calcutta, 1953.

RISLEY, H. *Tribes and Castes of Bengal*, Calcutta, 1891.
Census of India, I. B. (1901) *Ethnographic Appendices*, Calcutta, 1902.
Peoples of India, Calcutta, 1915.

ROBERTSON SMITH, W. *Religion of the Semites*, London, 1889, sec. ed. 1927.

ROSCOE, J. *The Baganda*, London, 1911.

ROTH, H. L. *Natives of Sarawak and British North Barneo*, London, 1896.

ROUSSELET, E. *India and its Native Princes*, London, 1876.

ROY, S. C. *Oraons of Chotanagpur*, Ranchi, 1915.

RUSSELL R. V. *Ethnological Survey of the Central Provinces*, Allahabad, 1911.

RUSSELL, R. V. and HIRA LAL *Tribes and Castes of the Central Provinces of India*, London, 1916.

SAṂHITĀS *Ṛgveda*, ed. F. Max Müller 1890-

92; trans. R. T. H. Griffith, Benaras 1896-97; in parts Max Müller in *SBE*, XXXII, Oxford, 1891 and H. Oldenberg in *SBE*, XLVI, Oxford, 1897.

Sāmaveda, ed. with trans. Th. Benfey, Leipzig, 1848; ed. with Beng. trans. S. Samasrami, Calcutta, 1873.

Yajurveda: *Kāṭhaka Saṃhitā*, ed. Von Schroeder, Leipzig, 1900-11; *Maitrāyaṇī Saṃhitā*, ed. *idem*, Leipzig, 1881-86;

Vājasaneyi. Saṃhttā, ed. A. Weber, London, 1852;

Taittirīya Saṃhitā, ed. *idem*, Berlin, 1871-72; for translation see under Keith.

Atharvaveda, ed. R. Roth, Berlin, 1856; trans. in part by M. Bloomfield in *SBE*, XLII, Oxford, 1897; by W. D. Whitney, Cambridge, Mass., 1905.

SANDERS, N. K. — *Epic of Gilgamesh*, Pelican.

SELIGMANN, C. — *Expedition to Torres Straits*, Cambridge, 1904.

SEN, D. C. — *Vaṅga Sāhitya Paricaya*, in Bengali, Calcutta, University.

SEN, S. and MANDAL, P. — *Rūparāmer Dharmamaṅgal*, in Bengali, Calcutta.

SIRCAR, D. C. — *Successors of the Sātavāhanas*, Calcutta, 1939.

Religious Life in Ancient and Medieval India, Delhi, 1971.

SPENCER, B. and GILLEN, F. — *Northern Tribes of Central Australia*, London, 1904.

ŚRAUTASŪTRAS — *Āpastamba*, ed. R. Garbe, Calcutta, 1882-1903.

Āśvalāyana, ed. in Bibliotheca Indica Series, Calcutta,

Kātyāyana, ed. V. Sharma, Benares 1933-37.

Lāṭyāyana, ed. in Bib. Ind. Calcutta.

Śāṅkhyāyana, ed. A. Hillebrandt, Bib. Ind., Calcutta 1886-89.

Baudhāyana, ed. W. Caland in Bib. Ind., Calcutta, 1904-23.

STEVENSON, S. *Heart of Jainism*, London, 1915, rep. New Delhi, 1970.

SŪYAGAḌA See under Jain Sūtras.

SWANTON, J. R. *Ethnology of the Hadia*, London, 1905.

THOMSON, G. *Aeschylus and Athens*, London, 1941, 1950.

Studies in Ancient Greek Society, Vol. I, London, 1949.

Religion, London, 1950.

THURSTON, E. *Omens and Superstitions of South India*, London, 1912.

THURSTON, E. and RANGACHARI, K. *Castes and Tribes of Southern India*, Madras, 1909.

TOD, J. *Annals and Antiquities of Rajasthan* (ed. W. Crooke), London, 1920.

UNDERHILL, M. M. *Hindu Religious Year*, Calcutta, 1921.

Upaniṣads See under Hume.

Uttarādhyayana Sūtra See under Jain Sūtras.

VATS, M. S. *Excavations at Harappa*, Delhi 1950.

VIDYABHUSAN, N. *Caḍakapūjāpaddhati*, Calcutta, 1336 B. S.

WARD, W. *A View of the History, Literature and Religion of the Hindus.*

WEBSTER, H. *Primitive Secret Societies*, New York, 1932.

WHITEHEAD, BISHOP H. *Village Gods of South India*, YMCA, Calcutta, 1916.

WINṬERNITZ, M. *History of Indian Literature*, Calcutta, 1927; rep. New Delhi 1972.

INDEX

Adhvaryu, his functions in the Aśvamedha 4, 7.
Āditya 5.
Adonis 18, in death and revival myths 102, 115, gardens of 106-10.
Ahiṃsā, economic basis of the concept 15-16.
Agni, as sacrificial fire 3, 10, as distributor of wealth 42, 44, 63, as the divine guardian 95, as regenerating principle 127-28.
Agricultural societies, kingship in 16-17; rituals in 12-14, 54-55, 93-113; see under *Fertility* and *Sex*.
Aindra Mahābhiṣeka 1.
Ambuvācī 105.
Ancient equality, relics of 41-45.
Anitis 100.
Aphrodite 100, 102.
Aśvamedha, antiquity of 2, original purpose forgotten 1-3, in earlier texts 3-6, primitive form 6-7, anointing of the horse 3, 4, 6, queen's role in 3-5, 7-10, sexual rites in 7-10, ritual background of 10-12, fertility beliefs involved in 12-14, in terms of socio-political changes 14-16, in women's ritual cycle 16-18, the dying god theme expressed in 18-22, relation with the Puruṣamedha 23-24, rituals foreshadowing dramatic literature 24.
Attis 103, 115.
Āvaraṇa-devatās, of Dharma 148,152.

Balder, myths of 125-26.
Bāṇeśvara 155-56.
Brahmā, priest 4.
Brahman, meaning food 43, 62, 63.
Bṛhaspati, *sūtras* of 2.
Bṛhaspatisava, ritual of 49-50.
Buddhism, rise of 15-16, rites of initiation in 76-78, tribal character of 79-80, *stūpas* associated with 116-17, later phases of 133-37, relation with Pīr cult 117-18, with Śaivism 133-34, with Vaiṣṇavism 135-37, with Nātha cult 138-40, with the cult of Dharma 142-44, with caste system 140, Tāntric and Sehajiyā forms of 135-37.

Caḍaka, as ritual of year-ending 130-32, proletarian character of 130, 132, 133, 138-40, 146-48, 154-57, 160, 163-64, socio-religious background of 133-48, of Dharma and Śiva 148-50, 155-57, participating deities 150-52, relation with

Manda and other festivals 151-52, death and resurrection theme in 152-55, 162-63, description of the rituals of 159-63.

Casting the lot 42-44.

Caste system 6, 16, 26, 49-50, 67-68, 71-72, 92-93, festivals and rituals of the lower castes 130-33, teachers belonging to the lower order 138-39, castification of sects 140, despised castes in priestly functions 147-48, 160.

Cattle, social importance of 27-28, role in accumulation of wealth 15-16, lifting of 14, 27-29; in *Ṛgveda* 14, 28, flesh tabooed 15.

Caturthīkarma 94, 96.

Chandas, ritual use of 61-64.

Chariot race, for distribution of wealth 55-56.

Class society 11-12, growth of 27-29, ugliness of 41-47, accumulation of wealth in 15-16, purposes of the rituals change in 12, 23, 29, 65-68.

Collectivity, in rituals 11-12, 62-67, in drinking 53-55, in distribution of wealth 15, 38-44.

Commonwealth 15, as relic of primitive communism 38-44, individual appropriation of 45-46.

Cybele 102, 115.

Dakṣiṇ Rāy 132.

Dāśarājña 31.

Dasyu 28.

Death, conception of 114, of the gods and their revival 18, 21-22, 114-115, and fertility 56, and Holi 118-22, and Dewali 126-27, theme in Gājana rituals 152-55, Bāṇavrata and the idea of 155, cult of the dead 115-16, the Buddhist Stūpas 116-17, miming of burning 119-21, games relating to 56, 155, resuscitation of the dead 162-63, funeral drinking 54, 55, death and Mother Goddess 56, 111.

Defloration 93-95.

Demeter, myths of 108-10.

Dewali, as the rite of new moon 122-25, relation with Mother Goddess cult 125, with fire festivals of Europe 125-26, original character of 126-29, among the Jains 127.

Dharma cult 141-42, relation with Nāthism 146-47, 152, with Buddhism 142-44, with Brāhmaṇical deities 144-45, with Sun cult 145-46, proletarian substratum of 146-48, Gājana of 148-50, 155-57, Caḍaka of 150-52, Brāhmanised form of 157-58, deities connected with 152, tribal affiliation of 151.

Dialogues, obscene and abusive 2, 4, 7-9, contribution to the growth of drama 24.

Dicing, King's taking part in the ritual of 26, the dice and Ṛta 36-38, for equal distribu-

tion of wealth 42-44, dicer as distributor 44-45.
Distribution, of wealth 15, 38-44, of food and booty 43-44, Greek system of 43, by the dicer 45, by chariot race 55-56, principles of equality in 15, 38-44, growing inequalities in 12-16, 27-29, 45-46.
Division, see *Distribution*.
Drama, origin of 22-24.
Durgā 99, 101, 107, 108.
Dying gods 18-22, 102, see under *Death*.

Ear-piercing 82, 83.
Earth Goddesses 51, 52, 56, 58, 101, 102, 110-111, menstruation of 88, of Harappa culture 111-113, see under *Mother Goddess*.
Eating rituals 5.

Father-right 45, 83-85.
Fertility rites, in connection with the Aśvamedha 7-10, 12-14, 17-20, with Tāntric cults 54, with primitive beliefs regarding women's functions 96-98, with Liṅga and yoni cults 99-100, with sacred prostitution 100-101, myths generated from 101-102, cults developed from 102-106, 108-11, survivals of 106-108, behind the concept of divinities 108-11, behind the ideas of death and resurrection 114-15, beliefs behind the symbolism of red 121-22, and moon 123-25, in Holi 122, 154, in Dewali 128-29, in Gājana 153.
Fire festivals 125-26, in Gājana 154-55, phulkudnā in Manda 151, swing over the fire 161.
Food, desire for 57-58, division of 43-44, means of obtaining 60-62, role of songs 63, the Mahāvrata rite 64-65.
Funeral rites, see under *Death*.

Gabhur Dalan 132.
Gājana, ritual of year-ending 130-31, of Dharma and Śiva 148-50, of Nīla 149, 158-59, participating deities 150-52, allied tribal rites 151, death and resurrection theme in 152-55, Bhaktyās of 155, different ceremonies 158-63.

Hair-shaving 82.
Hiraṇyagarbha Mahādāna 71-72.
Holi, original form of 122, as a death rite 118-21, significance of the red powder used in 121-22, sexual and fertility aspects 120, 122-25, 154-55, the Holi ashes 154.
Hotṛ 2, 4, 6.
Hunting age, rituals of 5.

Indra, as cattle-lifter and tribal chief 27-29.
Initiation, concept of rebirth in 70-72, Upanayana 72-74, at puberty 76, Buddhist and

Jain 76-78, tribal character of religious initiation 79-80, tribal rites of 70-72, 80-84, into womanhood 85, 89-95.

Ishtar 18, 101, 102.

Isis 18, 102, 115.

Iṣṭi 3.

Itu 104-05.

Jainism, rise of 16-17, monastic rules of 79, rules of initiation 76-77, Dewali festival connected with 127.

Kālārkarudra 157-58.

Kālu Gazi 132.

Kārtikeya, of the prostitutes 102-06, of Kataragama in Ceylon 163, rituals of 104-05.

Kīkaṭas 28.

Killing, of the priest 6, 13, of the king 17-19, ritual of 19-22, of Purūravas 19-20, human sacrifice 23-24, Meria-killing 154.

Kings, performing rites of royal inauguration 1-6, 25-27, 49-53, killing of 17-19, election of 31-33, qualifications of 32, in popular assemblies 33-36.

Kingship, growth of 27-29, in pastoral societies 27-29, in agricultural societies 16-17, and Aśvamedha 8, Rājasūya 25-26, Vājapeya 49-53, class society 31-36.

Kṣetrapāla 159.

Lakṣmī 108.

Liṅga cult 99-100.

Literature, birth of 22-24.

Mādhava 2.

Māgh Porai 13.

Magic, principles of 11-12, as an illusory technique 29, among tribes 11, 13, and rituals 48-49, and melody 58-60, and Vedic sacrifices 10-12, 62-65, agricultural 12-14, 54-55, 93-113, fertility 17-20, 96-115, 121-25, 154, rain 111-12, 145-46.

Mahāvīra 127.

Mahāvrata 11-12.

Māhīdhara 8.

Mahiṣī 3.

Manda festival 151-52.

Maruts 56, 63.

Maṭhas 118-19.

Mattamayūra 134.

May-pole 114.

Menstruation, in primitive rituals 21, the universal dread 85-87, the colour of life 121-22, sanctifying significance of 87-88, as life-giving power 88-89, menstrual rites 89-93.

Meria-killing 154.

Mitra 41.

Mochra Khan 132.

Moira 43.

Moon, as the deity of fertility 18, as the guardian of the girls 95, licentious character of 123, cause of conception and generation 124, source of magical powers 124-25.

Mother Goddess, as Mother Earth 51, 52, 56, 58, 101, 102,

110, 111, menstruation of 88, Earth Goddess of Harappa culture 111-13, goddess of speech 51, Aditi, the great Mother 51, 58, Durgā 99, 101, 107, 108, Lakṣmī 108, Kālī 125, Sītā 108-10, Tārā 109, goddess of death 56, prostitution connected with the cult 100-01, 105, Greek Egyptian and Western Asian goddesses 18, 100-02, 108-10, 115, Corn Mothers 101-02, fertility rites in relation to 106-08, agricultural basis of 111-13.

Mylitta 100.

Nāthism, 137-38, Haṭhayoga and Kāyasādhana 137, Buddhist influence on 138, proletarian elements in 138-40, Siddhas of 139, caste question involved in 140, relation with Dharma cult 147, and Nepalese tradition 146.

Navapatrikā 99.

Nīla 131, Nīlāvatī, Śiva's marriage with 162, Nīla-caṇḍikā 131, 158-59, Nīla-parameśvarī 131, Nīla-Devatā 131, 159, Gājana of 149, 158-59.

Non-violent religions, growth of 15.

Obscene rituals and dialogues 2, 4-10, 64-65 , 93-95, 119-20.

Osiris 18, 115.

Pālāgalī 3.

Paṇi 4, 6.

Pāriplava Ākhyāna 4, 6, 24.

Pariṣad 32, 33.

Parivṛkti 3.

Pastoral society 5, cattle lifting in 14, 27-29, accumulation of wealth in 15-16, rise of kingship in 27-29, and class society 11-12, 41-47.

Pāṭ-ṭhākhr 131.

Persephone 108-10.

Physical torture 131, 148, 160-62.

Pīr cult 117-18.

Popular assemblies 31-36.

Prajāpati, ritual significance of his legends 20-22, identity with sacrifice 60-64, King's identity with 68-69.

Pravrajyā 77-80.

Primitive communism 15, 38-44, 62-66, relics of 38-44, ancient equality 41-45, relics in distribution of wealth 36-45, 55-56, in food 43-44, growth of social inequalities 12-16, 27-29, 45-46.

Proletariat, their cults and rituals in general 130-64, specific proletarian elements in cults and rituals 133-34, 138-40, teachers belonging to 139-40, role in Dharma cult 146-48, participation in Gājana 148-50, and Caḍaka 150-52, festivals connected with 159-63.

Prostitution, primitive basis of 4-10, 64-65, 93-95, 119-20,

relation with agricultural rituals 100-01, cults of 102-106.
Pṛthu 22.
Puberty rites, ideas of rebirth involved in 70-72, upanayana as a relic of 72-76, 80-90, in Buddhist and Jain initiation 76-80, among the tribes 81-82, 84, 89-93 of women 89-95.
Purūravas 22-24, ritual killing of 19-20.
Puruṣamedha 13, 22-23.
Puṣen 3, 21-22.

Queen, role in Aśvamedha rituals 2-9, sexual cycle of 17-18, in Vājapeya 52-53.

Rājā, original and changed meaning of the term 29-31, see under *King*.
Rājasūya 2, 25-47, important features of 25-27, relation with Vājapeya 49-50, mimic cow raid in 27-29, as a means to understand the growth of kingship 29-33, popular elements in 33-36, significance of the ritual of dicing 26, 36-38, 42-44, 45, in terms of the principles of Ṛta 38-40, relics of ancient equality 41-42, casting the lot 42-45, significance of the recital of Śunaḥśepa legend in 45-47.
Rathayātrā, magical significance of 146.
Rebirth, concept of 70-72.
Red, symbolism of 88-89, 121-22.
Revolving legend 2, 4.
Rohita 46.
Ṛta, conception of 36-38, symbol of tribal equality and justice 39-41, relation with Varuṇa 38-41, annihilation of 45-47.
Ṛtusaṅgamana 94.
Rudra 20-22.

Sabhā, functions of 32-38, distribution of wealth in 35-36, casting the lot in 36-38, the dicer in 44-45, decline of the power of 32-33.
Sabhāsthānu 44-45.
Sacrifice 9-12, and magic 10-12, 60-65, as productive technique 60-62, see under *Yajña*.
Sahajayāna 135-37, 139.
Śaivism 133-34, 148-52.
Sāmans, magical use of 58-60.
Samiti 32-38, as assembly of tribal chiefs 34, as tribal war council 35, election of the 'kings' in 34.
Saṉ 163.
Sarasvatī, of the prostitutes 104.
Satī legends 131.
Sattra 2, 12, 64, 65, as communistic sacrifice 67.
Savitṛ 3.
Sexual rites 7-10, 12-14, 17-20, 54, 96, 111, 122-25, 153-54, sexual union in the Aśvamedha 6-8, in the Sattras 64-65, identified with sacrifice 9-10, in agricultural rites

12-14, sexual cycle of the queen 17-18, incestuous union 20-22, dialogue of Agastya and Lopāmudrā 24, sexual taboos 75-76, 86-87, cults 97-100, character of Holi 120, of Sahajiyā cults 136.
Sītā 108-10.
Śiva 159-60, 62, Bāṇavrata of 155, marriage 131, 148, 149, 155.
Śunaḥśepa legend 26, 45-47.

Tammuj 18, 102, 115.
Tāntric cults 54.
Tārā, of various colours 109.
Tribal society, modern misunderstanding of 30, 34-35, nature of 27-29, Ṛta and tribal society 36-41, councils 32-36, destruction of 45-47, rites of 12-14, 54-55, 93-113, tribal initiation 70-72, 75-76, 79-80, food-gatherers 6, pastorals 5, 14-16, 27-29, festivals 151.
Trita 5.

Upanayana, rituals of 72-73, primitive basis of 73-74, relation with puberty rites 75-76, see under *Initiation* and *Puberty rites*.
Upasampadā 77-80.
Udgātṛ 7-9.
Urvaśī 19, 20, 22-24.
Uvaṭa 8, 9, 12.

Vaiṣṇāvism 135-37.
Vājapeya 2, 10, 12, 48-69, relation with Rājasūya 49-50, essentials of 50-52, popular character of 53, collective drinking in 53-55, chariot race in 55-56, as ritual of food and drink 57-58, the use of Sāmans in 58-60, as a means to understand the original character of Yajña 60-65, collectivity in 62-64, in class society 65-69.
Vāmadeya Sāman 9, 51, 60.
Varuṇa, as the guardian of Ṛta 36-44, symbol of ancient social justice 40-42, subsequent degradation of 45-47.
Vāstoṣpati 22.
Vāvātā 3, 7-9.
Veṇa 22.
Venus 18, 100, 101.

Wine, ritual use in Vājapeya 53-55, different kinds of 54, in the Somayāgas 54, as one of the Tāntric *pañca makāras* 54, magical power of 54, in fertility and funeral rites 55, 153-54.
Women, identification with earth 97-113, their ritual cycle 16-18, part in the Aśvamedha 3-10, primitive beliefs regarding their functions 96-98, prostitution 100-06, initiation into womanhood 85, 89-95, defloration of 93-95, see under *Fertility, Moon, Mensturation, Mother Goddess, Queen, Prostitution, Puberty rites, Red, Sexual rites.*

Yajamāna 65-68.
Yajña, identified with sexual union 9-10, relation with magic 10-12, 62-65, as a productive technique 60-62, legends of its leaving the gods 62-68, see under *Sacrifice*.
Yama 5.
Year-ending, rituals of 130-31.
Yoni, cult of 99-100.